WOMEN POLITICIANS

AND

THE MEDIA

WOMEN
POLITICIANS
AND
THE MEDIA

Maria Braden

❖ ❖

THE UNIVERSITY PRESS OF KENTUCKY

Published by The University Press of Kentucky

Scholarly publisher for the Commonwealth,
serving Bellarmine College, Berea College, Centre
College of Kentucky, Eastern Kentucky University,
The Filson Club, Georgetown College, Kentucky
Historical Society, Kentucky State University,
Morehead State University, Murray State University,
Northern Kentucky University, Transylvania University,
University of Kentucky, University of Louisville,
and Western Kentucky University.

Editorial and Sales Offices: The University Press of Kentucky
663 South Limestone Street, Lexington, Kentucky 40508-4008

Library of Congress Cataloging-in-Publication Data

Braden, Maria, 1946-
    Women politicians and the media / Maria Braden.
        p.   cm.
    Includes bibliographical references (p.   ) and index.
    ISBN 0-8131-1970-7 (cloth : acid-free recycled paper). —
ISBN 0-8131-0869-1 (paperback : acid-free recycled paper)
    1. Women in politics—United States. 2. Women in mass
media—United States. I. Title.
HQ1236.5.U6B73   1996
320'.082—dc20   95-47152

This book is printed on acid-free recycled paper meeting
the requirements of the American National Standard
for Permanence of Paper for Printed Library Materials.

Manufactured in the United States of America

For Lachy and Bill

❖ CONTENTS ❖

❖ ILLUSTRATIONS ❖

❖ Acknowledgments ❖

Many people have helped make this book a reality. In particular, I want to thank Kelley Popham and Kathy Larkin for their persistence in ferreting out evidence. I am grateful to the Freedom Forum for giving me a grant with no strings attached, and to Buck Ryan for supporting my request for unencumbered time to work on this. I also want to thank those who helped arrange interviews with the people in this book, especially Elaine Ryan and Eleanor Lewis, and those who agreed to be interviewed. I am indebted to Pat Matthews and Scoobie Ryan and others who read parts of the manuscript in draft form and made suggestions. I thank also Jane Rossi, Marcia Weinstein at the Kentucky Commission on Women, and the Center for the American Woman and Politics for providing information. I deeply appreciate my family's patience and support, especially my daughter Mia's reminder about what really matters. Finally, without Carmen Manning-Miller's faith that it would happen, this book would not be.

❖ *Chapter 1* ❖

GOING FORWARD,
WALKING BACKWARD

"The press was as kind as it knew how to be. It meant well and did all for us it knew how to do. We couldn't ask it to do more than it knew how." [Laughter] — Susan B. Anthony, 1893

SUSAN B. ANTHONY DIDN'T THINK MUCH OF THE PRESS. BUT SHE WAS SAVVY ENOUGH to lace her speech with gentle irony instead of insulting reporters directly. Journalists had heaped ridicule on the women's suffrage movement for years, but Anthony knew that news coverage was a key to getting the women's message to the public—and that biased coverage was better than no coverage at all. More than a century later, women politicians are still discovering what Anthony had learned—that journalists often ask women politicians questions they don't ask men. That reporters describe women politicians in ways and with words that emphasize women's traditional roles and focus on their appearance and behavior. That they perpetuate stereotypes of women politicians as weak, indecisive, and emotional. That they hold women politicians accountable for the actions of their children and husbands, though they rarely hold men to the same standards.

News coverage of women politicians is not always blatantly sexist, but subtle discrimination persists. In some ways this bias is harder to pin down and eradicate. Perhaps it was to be expected that reporters in 1916 would ask Jeannette Rankin, the first woman elected to Congress, how she liked having an office across from an eligible bachelor. But it's harder to understand why journalists continue to ask inane questions that trivialize and stereotype women politicians.

In 1993, for example, reporters asked Representative Marjorie Margolies-Mezvinsky (D-Pennsylvania) over and over what it was like to be a woman in

Congress. "It began to feel as though they thought this was the only thing I knew about," she says. In 1994 reporters kept asking New Jersey governor Christine Todd Whitman, "What's it like to be a woman governor?" Whitman would ask her press secretary through clenched teeth, "How am I supposed to answer that?" In 1995 a female reporter for the *Village Voice* labeled Congresswoman Susan Molinari (R-New York) "perky," and a male *Washington Post* reporter described veteran Senator Nancy Kassebaum (R-Kansas) as "demure"—words that would never be used to describe a man. Molinari shrugs off such adjectives, saying she doesn't have time to worry about labels. But words add up. If they are repeated often enough in the media, their cumulative effect is to diminish a woman's stature as an effective legislator.

When the news media imply that women are anomalies in high public office, the public is likely to regard them as bench warmers rather than as an integral part of government. In Senator Barbara Boxer's phrase, they are frequently depicted as "strangers in the Senate"—and in the House and the governor's mansion. More women than ever hold high-level government positions, yet they are still portrayed by the media as novelties. Being perceived as different can be an advantage, however. In fact, some of the more persistent media stereotypes sometimes work to the benefit of women politicians. The media have often portrayed women as political outsiders, whether they are or not—and that's an asset when the country's mood is strongly anti-incumbent. Barbara Boxer (D-California) was depicted as an "outsider" in her 1992 Senate race, for example, even though she had served five terms in the House and had gotten caught up in the House banking scandal. And Carol Moseley-Braun (D-Illinois) was portrayed as an outsider in her Senate race the same year, although as recorder of deeds for Cook County, she was a cog in the Democratic political machine.

It's better to be portrayed as a novelty than not to be mentioned at all, and the news media play an important role in whether a candidate gets noticed in the first place. One of the worst things that can happen to a politician is to receive little or no media coverage. Yet academic studies show that's what often happens to women candidates, especially if they're newcomers. "Bias is easy to spot," former *Washington Post* editor Ben Bradlee has said, "except for the bias of omission."

Reporters and editors don't conspire to stereotype, trivialize, or ignore women as a way of keeping them from running for public office. Nor do they plot to denigrate women when they succeed. In fact, for most of this century journalists have prized the notion of objectivity—that a news story should be free of bias and personal opinion. But news, after all, is whatever journalists say it is. It is said that the news media mirror society, but that is not exactly the case. The news media reflect certain aspects of the social and political culture. Journalists may be idealistic and conscientious individuals, but no matter how hard a journalist tries to adhere to the creed of objectivity, news stories reflect the values of both the individual and his or her news organization. Rather than mirroring the whole of society, the media have tended to reflect the values of those who assign, report, and produce the news, a majority of whom have been white males.

When Jeannette Rankin ran for Congress eighty years ago, for example, women were not expected to work outside the home but rather to be accomplished at what were considered the "womanly" arts of cooking, sewing, and singing. Newspapers of the day reflected that cultural expectation. Women, for the most part, didn't make news. Men were in the public arenas of government and business, while women's domain was private. Women's work was represented in newspapers by "hearth and home" columns that dealt with gardening, cooking, sewing, and social matters. The few women employed by newspapers worked on the women's pages, primarily writing society news. The rest of the paper was male turf, written by men for men.

The media operate much like a camera with a telephoto lens, zooming in on certain issues, events, and people and bringing them into sharp relief. But only so much will fit in the frame. Other things must be left out, and still others will be in the background of a picture, out of focus and considered unimportant. Just as there's a finite amount of film in the camera, there's limited space in a newspaper and limited time on a broadcast, so only a certain number of events or people can be represented. Walter Lippmann was one of the first to note, more than seventy years ago, that journalists "do not try to keep an eye on all mankind. . . . The news is not a mirror of social conditions, but the report of an aspect that has obtruded itself." Journalists act as "gatekeepers," deciding what will pass through to the public. Reality is filtered through their brains and packaged according to traditional news values, and the result is called news. As sociologist Michael Schudson wrote in *Discovering the News*, "The daily persuasions of journalists reflect and become our own." Voters' attitudes are shaped both by the kind of information delivered by the news media and by the way it is delivered. So, for example, reporters who tagged Kentucky governor Martha Layne Collins as a former beauty queen and referred to her male primary opponent as a physician were not inaccurate—Collins had won a minor pageant twenty-five years earlier. But in labeling her a beauty queen they chose to devalue her more substantive experience as a teacher and elected official.

News is based on fact, so it's true, but it isn't necessarily the whole truth. Facts are tested for newsworthiness against a set of traditional news values, which include prominence, unusualness, timeliness, conflict, and controversy. Those values are still taught in journalism schools across the country as a guide to framing stories for maximum reader interest, even though studies by Carol Gilligan and others have shown that women tend to be more interested in such values as compromise and collaboration and less interested in controversy and conflict. But it is harder for journalists to nail down a story based on consensus than it is to report on the friction between opposing viewpoints.

As Edward Jay Epstein has said in *News From Nowhere*, television news in particular tends to focus on conflict. "It is generally assumed that high ranking figures of authority involved in heated conflicts or challenges to their authority are more likely to produce news than news makers who are explicating developments or policies in a complex world. The more heated the dispute or challenge, the more certain the news story." Newspapers reflect this emphasis too. Political stories that contain conflict and controversy are likely to get more space and better play than stories about compromise and consensus. Many political stories, particularly election campaign coverage, are framed in terms of conflict, with more emphasis given to the "horse race"—who is winning and who is losing—than to substantive coverage of issues. Some politicians seem dismayed by that emphasis.

Nancy Kassebaum, respected for her skillful moderation of opposing views in the Senate committee she chairs, says a continuing problem for women politicians is that they may not be geared to power politics, and consensus-building doesn't play well in the press. But she says that's changing. Former Senate majority leader George Mitchell has said the media's equation of controversy with news has undermined the public's belief in their elected representatives. "If it's not controversial, it's not news," he said. "If it lends itself to sensationalism, it achieves a high level of attention."

Being the first or being unusual also rates media attention and tends to bump less obvious but equally important attributes. In the traditional "man bites dog" mode, it makes good copy to portray women as outsiders, to represent them as doing something new and unusual—something that deviates from a traditional role. "Women are at their most newsworthy when they are doing something 'unladylike,' especially arguing with each other," observed Kathleen Newland in *The Sisterhood of Man*. Representative Bella Abzug (D-New York), for instance, introduced significant legislation, but the media often got caught up in describing her floppy hat or assertive, "unladylike" manner. As long as the news media take that approach, women are less likely to see national political office as an attractive opportunity.

Image is a primary concern for office holders and office seekers in our media-saturated society, and it continues to be one of the biggest problems women face in running for high public office. A double standard has long existed in the press, with details about the way women look frequently inserted in news stories about women politicians but not in stories about men. Sometimes that's as a result of references made by opponents during election campaigns, but sometimes description reminiscent of society-page writing creeps into political reporting about women for no apparent reason.

Perhaps it was to be expected back in the 1920s and 1930s when women stood out against the congressional backdrop of dark suits and cravats. Someone like Kentucky Democrat Katherine Langley was bound to make a splash in the press when she appeared on the House floor in the late 1920s "gowned in midnight blue trimmed in brilliant red." But the press attention to dress went a little further than simply noting her unusual garb. One Capitol Hill reporter claimed that Langley's dress actually interfered with floor business. "She offends the squeamish by her unstinted display of gypsy colors on the floor and the conspicuousness with which she dresses her bushy blue-black hair."

Even more conventionally dressed congresswomen who blended in with their male counterparts have been described in detail. In terms of media coverage, it may be worse for a woman to be attractive than homely. That's what Illinois Republican Charlotte Reid discovered when she was sworn into Congress in 1963. The *Chicago Tribune* reported that "the gallants of the House observed primarily that she was beautiful." And in 1969, despite many legislative successes, Reid made headlines when she wore a black wool, bell-bottomed pantsuit on the House floor. Yet, she complained to an interviewer, "No one paid much attention to my speech on behalf of the Equal Rights Amendment."

In the 1960s, during her first campaign for public office, Republican Massachusetts congresswoman Margaret Heckler found she could neutralize the public response to her gender by wearing a gray flannel suit at every campaign stop. She says that allowed her to blend into "the gray Massachusetts sky and the gray male political arena" so the voters would be forced unconsciously to identify her with the issues and forget about the fact that she was a woman. The strategy apparently worked because after her victory her opponent said he had belatedly discovered some devastating material about her background that he would have used against her during the campaign: "You're a mother," he said accusingly, "you have children."

Media attention to the physical appearance of women continued through the 1970s and 1980s, and examples still crop up. The coverage of First Lady Hillary Clinton's changing hairstyle is a continuation of the practice of focusing on women's physical appearance rather than their capabilities. Senator Barbara Mikulski (D-Maryland), first elected to the House in 1976, said her physical appearance was always cited in the Baltimore press. She joked that a typical story might say, "Barbara Mikulski, who is short and round, in her uphill fight against the political machine, said today, 'No more expressway in southeast Baltimore.'" But the press never described her opponents as "middle-aged, pot-bellied incumbents who are facing a downhill race against Barbara Mikulski." Mikulski said one of the major problems in her unsuccessful 1974 campaign for a Senate seat was that she didn't fit the image of a U.S. senator:

"You know, an Ivy League-looking male, over fifty and over six feet tall." At just over five feet tall, Mikulski couldn't change her gender or her height. So she used humor in her successful congressional campaign two years later. She went on a seven-day fast and a vegetarian diet. "I told people it showed I could keep my mouth shut for a week," she said. "But it also showed them that when I make up my mind to do something, I can follow a goal."

In 1982, the respected *Des Moines Register* covered prosecutor Roxanne Conlin's unsuccessful campaign for governor of Iowa. During the campaign the paper featured six photos showing different hairstyles Conlin had worn over the previous eleven years. Her

Senator Barbara Mikulski (D-Maryland) began her congressional career in 1976 when she was elected to the U.S. House of Representatives.

opponent, needless to say, was not shown in progressive stages of baldness. Former Texas governor Ann Richards, whose hair has been described variously by reporters as a helmet, a symbol of traditional values, and a "patented corona of frozen white hair [radiating] light," says she has learned that a woman in public life can't change her hairstyle. "How you look is how you are. Once you look a certain way and are in the public eye, you do not ever change it," she says, because the public will believe you are capricious and can't make up your mind. "If you're in public life, you better get you a hair style you like as long as you remain in the public eye." Richards doesn't consider her spectacular coif a symbol of anything, media speculation notwithstanding. "It's how I started fixing my hair twenty years ago. If I had thought of it, I would have done something much simpler," she says. "I didn't know I would be doing this for the rest of my life." Finally, some parity: A half page photo in the Sunday *New York Times* soon after the 1994 elections depicted House Speaker Newt Gingrich having his hair done at the Capitol beauty salon. Male politicians are being subjected to the same trivial coverage as women.

Not only are women politicians locked in by images, they are also trivialized by the gender-specific words journalists commonly use to describe them. Former congresswoman Mary Rose Oakar (D-Ohio) was referred to by the *Cleveland Plain Dealer* in 1985 as "the plucky former amateur actress."

Democratic vice presidential candidate Geraldine Ferraro was frequently called "spunky" and "feisty" when she campaigned in 1984. Sociologist Deborah Tannen, a specialist in language use, says journalists probably meant no harm by their description of Ferraro, "but their words bent back and trivialized the vice presidential candidate. . . . Most damaging of all, through language, our images and attitudes are buttressed and shaped."

Ferraro was also followed by the label "bitch." The media didn't always spell out the word, nor did they originate the term. In one notorious instance, they were echoing Barbara Bush's quip to reporters aboard a campaign plane that the woman campaigning against her husband was "a_____, rhymes with rich." Barbara Bush was lashing out at Ferraro in defense of her husband, Vice President George Bush—a traditional wifely protective role that journalists could understand. But journalists have had a harder time shaking off the assumption that women politicians are primarily responsible for the behavior of their families. References to husbands and children have cropped up repeatedly in news stories about women politicians in contexts where family would not be mentioned if the politician were a man. In the 1992 Colorado Senate race, Josie Heath, a strong environmentalist, was criticized for her husband's former employment at a firm that sells asbestos insulation. In Pennsylvania, Lynn Yeakel faced charges of racism in 1992 after it was revealed that her husband belonged to a country club with no black members. And Dianne Feinstein was set back in her 1990 and 1992 California races by conflict-of-interest charges stemming from her husband's career as an investment banker.

Some women try to guard their private lives, to keep family matters separate from political affairs, while others make it a point to show that their lives have many dimensions. Congresswoman Pat Schroeder (D-Colorado) brought her young daughter with her to the floor of the House in the 1970s and to demonstrations over cuts in day care funding. But women are damned if they do and damned if they don't. During her 1993 campaign, Virginia gubernatorial candidate Mary Sue Terry was attacked for being single with no children. Oliver North, who campaigned on behalf of Terry's opponent, George Allen, repeatedly criticized her and said Allen was better qualified because he was a father. Allen's ads reinforced North's message by showing the candidate with his wife and children. Barbara Mikulski says women have always been penalized for their marital status. "It was never right. If you were married, you were neglecting him. If you were widowed, you killed him. If you were divorced, you couldn't keep him. And if you were single, you couldn't get a husband anyway."

Men have image problems too but generally have had more latitude in how they are expected to dress and behave because both history and personal experience have conditioned people toward accepting male leaders. Although women's physical appearance still draws more media attention than that of men, journalism students today are taught to apply an informal fairness standard: Don't describe a woman's appearance in a story unless it's the kind of story in which you would also describe a man's appearance—in a personality profile, for example. And don't describe a woman in terms you would not use for a man.

Another major problem facing women politicians has been the media's skepticism about women's capability for holding public office and making tough decisions. "Is there something in our national mores that makes us think women are unable to direct the ship of state?" asked former U.S. senator Maurine Neuberger in the late 1960s. "We trust them to manage a home, rear children and live within a budget, but not to make the laws that vitally affect the family." In the 1980s, vice presidential nominee Geraldine Ferraro was asked if she would be able to "push the button" to detonate a nuclear explosion. That question may have reflected some public concerns about a woman nominee, but the media must share a good portion of the blame for such perceptions. Prejudice is fueled by bias in language and lack of representation of women politicians in news stories and photos. Sometimes it's a subtle prejudice, as Peggy Lamson observed in 1968: "There is no organized resistance in today's society which keeps women out of the mainstream of public affairs. Perhaps it would be better if there were. The suffragettes of fifty years ago had solid doors to batter down; they joined together and became the militants. Today such barriers as exist are invisible and elusive."

Much had changed by 1992, but even as the media were proclaiming the "Year of the Woman," studies showed that females remained rarities in the news. A study of the August 1992 issues of the nation's top three news magazines, for example, found women referenced only 14 percent of the time, compared with 86 percent for men. August was the month of the Democratic National Convention, run by two women politicians, and the nation's news media were focusing heavily on politics. Yet similar results were reported for newspapers and network nightly news. Media consultant Nancy Woodhull, a founding editor of *USA Today*, said women are still largely invisible in the media. "Unless the media reports your contributions, your opinions—your existence—then for all perceptive purposes you do not exist." It's one reason so many women have stopped reading newspapers. She compared it to "walking into a room and no one noticing that you are there. Eventually you don't go into that room any more. It's a problem for women and a problem for media."

One reason women in Congress have not been as visible as men is that few have racked up years of seniority or attained leadership positions. There are literally thousands of news sources on the Hill—535 of them holding elective office and many hundreds more on congressional staffs and assigned to congressional committees and subcommittees. In general, Congress is covered with a shotgun approach—a wide spray of pellets and little depth. Reporters know that the best official sources will be party leaders or committee heads, those who are part of a daily news event such as running a hearing or introducing a bill or filibustering or demonstrating in some way. Since the congressional leadership—and the president—set the agenda, they're going to get most of the media coverage.

Length of service is the most important factor in succeeding in Congress. For one thing, it takes a while to learn congressional rules and parliamentary procedure. But seniority also brings with it the chance to chair a committee. That's real power—and virtually guaranteed access to the media. Members can introduce any number of bills on any subject, but that doesn't mean the legislation will ever come up for discussion or come to the floor for a vote. It's up to the committee chair whether or when to schedule a hearing on a bill. House Judiciary Committee Chairman Emanuel Celler (D-New York), for example, bottled up the proposed Equal Rights Amendment for two decades until Representative Martha Griffiths (D-Michigan) succeeded in extracting it and masterminding its passage in 1970.

If a woman stays in office long enough she will become the ranking minority or majority member of her committee, in line for the chairmanship. The first women to stay in Congress long enough to be able to run the show were Massachusetts Republican Edith Nourse Rogers, who chaired the House Veterans' Committee, and New Jersey Democrat Mary Norton, who chaired three legislative committees during her twenty-six years in the House. In contemporary politics, Nancy Kassebaum became chair of the Senate Labor and Human Resources Committee after the Republicans gained control of Congress in 1995 and immediately became a popular source because of her committee's confirmation hearings for Surgeon General nominee Henry Foster. First elected to the Senate in 1978, Kassebaum had been widely respected as a thoughtful and effective colleague. But because she was a minority party member, she was not in leadership, and so was rarely quoted.

Covering Congress is a complex proposition. As ABC Capitol Hill correspondent Ann Compton has said, "Congress isn't a thing, it's a process—and it never ends." Stephen Hess, borrowing Theodore Roosevelt's phrase, says covering Congress would be as difficult as "trying to nail currant jelly to the wall" if it were not simplified and made manageable by agreements about what is newsworthy. Gathering news in Washington means interviewing sources, and the media show a tendency to interview the same people over and over about the same stories. As David Broder has written, covering Congress means talking to the most powerful legislators and their legislative aides. In the past, most of them have been men. Reporters also glean information from each other, particularly in places like Capitol Hill, where many journalists are not in competition with each other and are therefore more likely to share bits of information they won't be using. Humor columnist Russell Baker once observed that lunch at the press table in the Senate dining room could be "the equivalent of a full day's leg work in the darkest recesses of Capitol Hill."

Journalists, like everyone else, understand the world through a largely unconscious frame or pattern that helps structure new experiences and ideas. One classic American paradigm has been "Women are the weaker sex." A paradigm of another generation was "Men are the breadwinners; women stay at home and look after the children." Those kinds of cultural belief affect how people perceive the world and consequently how they act—though people aren't always aware of the underlying assumptions that guide their actions. Similarly, journalists may not be aware of the way their perspectives can unconsciously work to shape their conceptions of the news. The journalist who referred to former Vermont governor Madeleine Kunin's arguments as "hysterical" may not have realized that the word he used reflected a view that women are emotional and irrational. "We have come far from the days when a respectable woman's name appeared in the press only on the day she was married and the day she died," Boston University journalism professor Caryl Rivers has written, "but old myths about female unreliability and weakness still drift through the modern media like smoke. Many journalists—women among them—are so accustomed to these myths as to be only barely aware of their existence."

A study published in 1986 confirmed that leading journalists' unconscious attitudes influenced their perception of elements of social controversies. Pure journalistic objectivity is unattainable, according to the authors of *The Media Elite*, since even journalists who make a conscious effort to remain objective do so within a framework of preconceptions: "Many journalists who fancy themselves tough-minded pragmatists are instead captives of conventional wisdom, carriers of intellectual currents whose validity is taken for granted." Jeane Kirkpatrick makes a similar point in *Political Woman*: "Perceptions of reality are a function of expectations as well as events. . . . The expectations and demands an individual brings to a situation greatly influence the accuracy with which events are perceived and the direction in which they are distorted."

Women got the vote nationwide in 1920, but the advent of women's suffrage didn't signal dramatic change in the number of women elected to high office. In 1921 the Senate reluctantly allowed a woman to be sworn in, but only with the understanding that she would promptly relinquish her seat to a man. By 1928, two women had been elected governors and seven had been elected to Congress. Both governors and five of the seven congresswomen were elected either to fill their husbands' unexpired terms or to carry out their policies.

During the same period, a new standard of professionalism for journalism was being discussed. Codes of ethics setting out the rights and responsibilities of journalists were drawn up by journalism organizations. Once a self-taught craft, journalism was being added to college curricula across the country. Objectivity, which prized fair, balanced treatment of subjects, became desirable professional conduct for reporters. The "new" journalism required reporters to select what appeared to them to be newsworthy angles, feature them in a lead, and give readers the rest of the story. Journalists began using shared news values such as prominence, proximity, and timeliness to guide them in selecting and writing the news, but even so their judgments were subjective and inevitably reflected a male-dominated culture. The power of journalists to shape reality had not yet been recognized. "In those days, few sensed that the real power of journalism was the power to define, the power to cover or not to cover," said David Halberstam. "News was not yet viewed as subjective; all events were perceived as of predetermined importance, the presence of a reporter added no particular dimension."

Newspapers and political parties—closely linked around the turn of the century—began to grow apart. Two thirds of newspapers were partisan organs in 1899, but fewer than half had party ties by 1930. New papers such as the *Kansas City Star* urged young voters "not to surrender their consciences and their judgments to the keeping of party bosses, but to maintain their independence and exercise the suffrage according to their own convictions."

Even as the nation's press swung round to the ideal of objective reporting in the 1930s, however, journalists continued their traditional practice of telling stories. Objectivity is an ideal of presenting "pure" information to an audience. But while journalists may have believed in objectivity, they usually constructed a narrative, framing the facts in a way that their readers could relate to. Since reporters and editors and their readers were mostly men, the facts of many stories, including those about women, were filtered through a male lens for a male audience. It was considered high praise, for example, to say that a woman had a "masculine mind" or "behaved like a man." As anthropologist Margaret Mead explained in 1935, a woman still had only two choices. She could be "a woman and therefore less an achieving individual—or an achieving individual and therefore less a woman."

Former *New York Times* columnist James Reston has called this period, from about 1920 to the mid-1950s, the "Era of the Journalist." He described it as "a period of vast convulsions at home and abroad. Just as the slower Victorian age was the era of the novelist, so this later period of wars and depressions, of dying and rising empires, of new and old ideas in conflict, of rogues, statesmen, demagogues, and dictators, was the era of the journalist. This era demanded wider and deeper coverage of the news. For a nation and world in transition, there was not only more to be reported but much more to be explained."

Radio emerged as a popular new medium in the late 1920s and was responsible for getting many women interested in politics. As the *Woman's Journal* noted in 1928, "Everywhere the radio, bringing the candidates into almost direct personal contact with their audience, gave the campaign the intensity of a burning local issue. Throughout the country, women organized listening-in parties, with radio hostesses pledged to invite their friends." The League of Women Voters also sponsored weekly radio debates with speakers from both parties, broadcast nationally by NBC. The *New York Times* noted that radio had led to increased political interest among women. "Women who would never cross their thresholds to go to a political meeting now have politics brought to them firsthand—politics in the raw with all the heat of emotion and personality about it."

Radio news began to develop in the 1930s as the number of receiving sets increased from fourteen million in 1930 to more than forty million by 1940. As radio grew in popularity, newspapers tried to devise a new role for themselves. Radio quickly usurped newspapers' lock on delivering late-breaking news, and the brevity of radio stories also prompted newspapers to tighten up leads and make stories shorter. Until World War II there were few women broadcasters, primarily because radio was not considered a good medium for softer, higher women's voices.

The male face of the media changed with America's entry into the war. As men were drafted for military service, women took over as city editors, reporters, copyeditors, radio broadcasters, and audio technicians. But most returned to the women's pages when men came back from the war. Although women's sections have been characterized as ghettos for soft or trivial news, many serious women's issues such as the fledgling liberation movement, the lack of child care for working mothers, teen pregnancy, drug addiction, birth control, and women's sexuality were explored on women's pages during the 1950s and 1960s, along with more traditional topics.

Nevertheless, mainstream news media have been slow to catch up with the changes in women's lives and have tended to reinforce the status quo. Just as they did in Susan B. Anthony's day, many journalists joked about the women's movement and its leaders in the late 1960s and early 1970s. Women who supported equal rights were commonly referred to as "women's libbers." Some of the ridicule was reflected in news stories—and not all were by men. "It didn't occur to me at the time that I should insist upon its being taken seriously," said the *New York Post's* Leslie Van Gelder, who had covered the 1968 Atlantic City demonstrations against the Miss America Pageant. ". . . . I featured overmuch the burning of bras, girdles and curlers. I tried to be light and witty so it would get in. I was afraid that if I reported it straight, it wouldn't get in at all." As Jean Gaddy Wilson, executive director of New Directions for News, put it: "The most significant development affecting the media is that women massively changed long ago, but those powerful changes were displayed simply as the odd, the unruly, the shrill, not reality. Media still don't see it."

General-interest magazines took note of the phenomenon of women in politics but didn't necessarily promote political opportunities for women. A case in point was the 1956 *Life* magazine update on women in politics. After thirty-six years of suffrage, said the magazine, "U.S. women are a force from grass roots to Senate," this despite the fact that Margaret Chase Smith was the only woman in the upper chamber. Although it depicted women involved in politics, *Life* also took pains to reassure its readers that women politicians hadn't forgotten where they belonged. Three-quarters of a profile headlined "A Lawmaking Homemaker" focused on the legislator's housekeeping ability.

The large mainstream women's magazines have done a little better. In 1958 *McCall's* carried an article by then-senator John F. Kennedy titled "Three Women of Courage," one of whom was Jeannette Rankin. Kennedy wrote that progress had been slow for women in public life and that society's view of women's capabilities had "regrettably, advanced all too little" in three centuries. He quoted from John Winthrop's seventeenth-century journals, in which the mental breakdown of a governor's wife was attributed to her "giving herself wholly to reading and writing. For if she had attended to her household affairs, and such things as belong to women, and not going out of her way and calling to meddle in such things as are proper for men, whose minds are stronger, she would have kept her wits."

Thirty-six years later, *McCall's* was the first women's magazine to obtain an exclusive round-table interview, moderated by National Public Radio's Cokie Roberts, with the seven women senators serving in the 103rd Congress. Yet the way the magazine played this coup indicates the mixed signals such magazines continue to send their readers. No teaser for the article appeared on the cover, and the feature was buried in the back of the book, following the recipe section. Still, women's magazines have emphasized the successes of women politicians, in some cases playing up the qualifications of various women for the presidency and in others hammering away at readers about the need to vote. *Glamour,* for instance, which targets young women mainly with articles about sex, fashion, and relationships, ran articles just prior to the 1994 general election headlined "Three Soundbites to Scare You into Voting," and "Vote! We Won in the Year of the Woman, Let's Not Lose Now." *Vogue* has weighed in with stories about the gender gap in voting patterns and touted various women politicians for president or vice president over the years.

Women's magazines have also provided forums enabling women politicians to connect with other women. After she got to Congress, for example, Jeannette Rankin discovered she couldn't count on the press to focus on the things she felt were important. So she learned to use women's magazines and newspapers to ensure direct and unfiltered communication with her constituents. She wrote a weekly "letter" for the Chicago *Herald* and several articles explaining her ideas to readers of the *Ladies Home Journal.* Other women politicians have followed Rankin's example, writing articles for women's magazines to connect directly with women readers.

Television was introduced in the late 1940s, and its popularity spread rapidly across the country in the 1950s. Until television sets became widely available, the only moving news pictures many people saw were those on movie newsreels, where women frequently were pictured as decorative accessories. The networks dominated television news delivery until the 1980s, when the addition of cable and satellite transmissions made news available around the clock. New technologies have enabled news to be delivered more quickly and to far vaster areas than were ever imagined forty years ago. Cable News Network (CNN), which offers news twenty-four hours a day, is supplemented by hard-news shows such as ABC's *Nightline.* Magazine format shows like *20/20* or *Eye to Eye* abound and docudrama "news" shows such as *A Current Affair* and *Hard Copy* have become staples of primetime television.

Talk shows allowing viewers to chew over news events and personalities crowd today's television schedule. Public radio provides four hours of news programming each weekday, and on public television the *MacNeil/Lehrer NewsHour* is aired five nights a week. Women politicians have benefited from this proliferation of television options because it has increased their visibility. The MacNeil-Lehrer show, for example, needs at least a dozen spokespeople each night to discuss issues. CNN and programs such as *Nightline* also need knowledgeable speakers. There's a CNN political talk show, *CNN & Co.*, that features female columnists and policy makers. Lawmakers even get exposure occasionally on the Comedy Channel, participating in programs such as *Politically Incorrect.*

Women politicians are also more visible than in the past now that legislative action is broadcast from the floor of Congress via C-SPAN (Cable-Satellite Public Affairs Network). House proceedings have been televised since 1979, but the Senate waited until 1986 to follow suit. The Senate, always considered the more deliberative body, feared that the introduction of television cameras would disrupt the legislative process. Some thought members would grandstand for the cameras, something that has happened from time to time, but television finally has been accepted as a part of daily business. More than twenty million Americans watch C-SPAN each month.

Nearly all American households own at least one television set, and since the early 1960s a number of public opinion studies have shown that almost two-thirds of Americans say television is their main source of news. Americans not only rely on the media for information but say that the media are generally believable, with television believed to be twice as accurate as newspapers. One reason for this stated trust in the credibility of television is that it relies on pictures—and people have been taught that pictures don't lie. A televised image validates the reality of a situation or person. But as Neil Postman has written, the interpretation of a picture is often determined by the commentary about it: "Since there are very few images that are self-explanatory, the viewer's attitude toward an image will be formed by words."

Sometimes the words trivialize women, as they did Geraldine Ferraro when she stood triumphant before cheering delegates to the 1984 Democratic National Convention. Tom Brokaw commented, "Geraldine Ferraro. . . . The first woman to be nominated for Vice President. . . . Size six!" But on the whole, women politicians have benefited from being on television. Although they may have been ignored as sources by newspapers, they are legitimized when viewers see them included in television's overall pictures of Congress or as articulate members of congressional committees or giving speeches.

Television also can create a national audience for women politicians who may have had only a regional or local reputation through the print media. Texas representative Barbara Jordan became a national figure after her televised keynote address to the Democratic National Convention in 1976, for example, and so did Christine Todd Whitman after she gave the GOP response to President Clinton's State of the Union message in 1995—even though Clinton's speech ran long and pushed Whitman's response out of prime time.

The fact that television makes its impact through images was difficult for women initially because the conventional image of a politician was the man in the suit. Ten years ago women were advised in handbooks on political life to try to create an authoritative image. "Always try to be filmed with book-lined shelves behind you as this always makes you look weighty and authoritative," recommended Sue Slipman in the 1986 book *Helping Ourselves to Power: A Handbook for Women on the Skills of Public Life*. But after sizable numbers of women were elected to Congress and other positions of power, it became easier for women to be themselves rather than trying to imitate a male version of authoritative behavior.

Nancy Kassebaum, for one, is aware of the importance of knowing how to behave on camera, but more than anything, she tries to be herself. "Aggressive courting of television is not my style," she says. "It's problematic because television creates an image. They want clever quips." It's also harder for women than men to project the "right" image on television, she says. In terms of appearance, it's easy for a man simply to put on a suit, while a woman's garb may be criticized for appearing too feminine or too masculine. Kassebaum has heard criticism of her hair, which she keeps cropped short. People say, "Can't you do something about your hair?" She responds "I wish I could" and goes on with it.

Television has been called "the most important change since World War II in just about every aspect of American life and certainly in the environment in which government functions." There's no doubt that television journalism, no matter how shallow or fleeting, has enormous influence. Stephan Lesher put it this way: "Journalism is an inherently imprecise, wholly subjective, seat-of-the-pants business, relying entirely on personal judgment and opinion in identifying, gathering, and presenting news. Yet because of the stupefying reach, immediacy and impact of electronic journalism, reportage—however incomplete and misleading it may be—influences crucial decisions, and worse, be-

Senator Nancy Kassebaum (R-Kansas) was the only woman in the Senate when she was first elected in 1978.

comes the foundation for what we remember as fact years later. That misconception then forms the basis on which we often make subsequent decisions."

Because it is built around brief soundbites, television news tends to oversimplify issues and overemphasize conflict, some women politicians say. "You cannot get a message out on television—it costs too much if you're paying for it, and if you're not and they use you, they don't want you for more than three or four seconds," says Representative Louise Slaughter (D-New York). "The 30-second sound bite does tend to simplify things that are not simple," says Senator Kay Bailey Hutchison (R-Texas). "It makes it difficult for people to know the issues as well."

Some say televised hearings promote grandstanding, while other members of Congress see it as beneficial. Senator Dianne Feinstein (D-California) said she didn't like the way her colleagues promoted themselves in front of the C-SPAN cameras, while Hutchison says C-SPAN "has helped more than anything" to inform people about the legislative process and the issues. "People can hear the whole debate, the good and the bad and make up their own minds, and people do. They're very well informed."

Extended television coverage of legislative activity may have helped inform a portion of the electorate, but in another way television has contributed to passivity among voters. Politics used to be considered a prime source of entertainment in the days before television. Kassebaum, who was four years old when her father, Alf Landon, ran for president on the Republican ticket in

1936, says people used to read the paper, and "even little kids would fight about candidate loyalties. You discussed it at the dinner table, and with neighbors, and people came down to see the campaign train when politicians came to town." Not any more. Because of television, people aren't getting as involved. It has become, she says, "couch potato politics."

If there is increased passivity among voters, then the news media are even more important to politicians because they simplify access to voters, especially for candidates running for statewide or national office. Major news organizations, such as the networks or the *New York Times*, which influence the national agenda, are important to politicians, and so are national magazines. *New York Times* reporter Martin Tolchin summed up an important function of the national press for politicians when he said that national news coverage provides an antidote to insecurity: A member of Congress "can say 'I'm in the *New York Times*, therefore I am.'" Access to the media also leads to credibility with various interest groups and other legislators. Journalists covering Washington "possess a power beyond even their own dreams and fears," said William Rivers, author of *The Other Government.* "They are beginning to become aware that their work now shapes and colors the beliefs of nearly everyone, not only in the United States but throughout most of the world."

The influence of network news has waned somewhat with the proliferation of other viewing options, but the number of journalists in Washington has increased: More than 4,000 reporters have congressional press credentials—roughly three times the number that had them in 1960—and the time politicians spend with the media has grown proportionately. Nearly half the federal officials surveyed in one study spent five hours or more each week dealing directly with the press. Even more time was spent considering press coverage. Nancy Kassebaum says she is astounded at the amount of time consumed by dealing with the media. News is twenty-four hours a day, "constant and immediate. I'm amazed that the media take up so much time," she says. "It just kills you." Marjorie Margolies-Mezvinsky says that while her experience as a network reporter prepared her for dealing with the news media after she became a congresswoman, she didn't realize how much time it would eat up. "Everybody wants an individual interview and everybody wants to talk to you about something."

Public officials do not have direct control over what is reported, but they try to use the media to gain publicity for their work and ideas. Almost all members of Congress employ public relations staffers to "handle" the media. Public officials have several options in trying to manage the news. Their press secretaries may provide information through news releases, news conferences, regular briefings, exclusive interviews, and videotaped news segments. They may limit media access by reducing the amount of time reporters have with the official or by turning down requests for interviews altogether. Press aides frequently respond to requests for interviews on the basis of whether the resulting press is likely to be beneficial. They are experienced in utilizing such traditional news values as unusualness, timeliness, human interest, and conflict to get the candidate or official mentioned in the newspaper or given a few seconds on the television news. News organizations that serve readers and viewers in the congresswoman's district or state are high on the pecking order. Many members of Congress send tapes to local broadcasters and columns to small dailies and weeklies in their home states and cultivate home state media by holding special restricted news conferences for reporters from those organizations. They know that the resulting news stories will legitimize what the member of Congress is doing.

Being a woman is both an asset and a liability in politics. The higher a woman aims, the riskier it gets. Women have been elected as governors and to seats in the House and Senate, and a majority of Americans have told pollsters they would vote for a woman president if the right candidate came along. Yet women running for any public office know their gender is as likely to turn off voters as it is to attract them. And polls show a minority still don't think a woman—any woman—should be president. Journalists sometimes seem to play to the sentiments of that small minority in the way they frame stories, in the facts they select, and in the language they use to describe women politicians. As long as the media continue to emphasize gender at the expense of other qualifications, they are sending the wrong signals to voters. It's worth mulling over the answer that Christine Todd Whitman gives reporters who ask her what it's like to be a woman governor: "I am a governor who happens to be a woman."

❖ *Chapter 2* ❖

THE FIRST AND ONLY

AS FIELD SECRETARY FOR THE NATIONAL AMERICAN WOMAN SUFFRAGE ASSOCIATION, Jeannette Rankin was no stranger to public life. Yet when she ran for the U.S. House of Representatives from Montana in 1916, the press ignored her. Women couldn't even vote in most states, so journalists must have thought it ludicrous for a woman to seek election to Congress. Even the *New York Times* thought it such a dim possibility that editors returned Rankin's biographical material before the election. Yet Rankin's candidacy caught the imagination of many, who saw in her a symbol of the right to vote and be heard. Montana had allowed women to vote in 1914, but Congress would not approve a constitutional amendment providing suffrage nationwide until 1918. Ratification by the states wasn't finished until 1920.

Rankin ran as a Republican because her father and brother were Republicans, but her campaign platform differed somewhat from that of the Republican Party. Her main interests were in preserving peace, passing an amendment to the Constitution to give women voting rights, and enacting legislation to protect children. Montana was sparsely populated and represented in Congress by two members-at-large rather than by district representatives. So Rankin had to promote her candidacy in small towns and villages spread over a vast area.

The press could have helped her spread her message, but she had a hard time getting any media coverage at all. Montana newspapers were controlled by the powerful Anaconda Copper Company in league with liquor interests. They suspected Rankin of siding with the labor union and also saw that Rankin might not be an easy politician to control. But they also thought she stood little chance of winning, so basically newspapers ignored her campaign. In so doing, the newspapers reflected the views of many people, who refused to believe that a woman could be capable of serving in Washington.

As Rankin's brother Wellington, also her campaign manager, wrote to her, "I am shocked at the prejudice that exists against a woman going to Congress." One of the few papers to endorse her candidacy strongly was the *Montana Progressive*, which felt that Rankin shared its editorial beliefs. In fact,

Belle Fligelman, editor and manager of the *Progressive*, later quit her job to become a campaign aide to Rankin.

Elsewhere in the country, her candidacy was given little or no media attention. With the election just days away, the *New York Times* and the *New York Sun* mentioned for the first time the possibility that a woman could be elected to Congress from Montana. The assumption that a woman couldn't win was apparently so deeply ingrained in the press that her hometown paper in Missoula rushed to report that she had lost before the votes were counted. It took several days to tally the returns, but it soon became apparent that Congress would have its first woman member. What put Rankin over the top were the efforts of many volunteers. Montana women mailed thousands of postcards in support of Rankin and on election day conducted a telephone campaign. Prospective voters were greeted with, "Good morning. Have you voted for Jeannette Rankin?"

After the election results were in, there was a dramatic shift in the way newspapers dealt with Rankin: the press couldn't get enough of her. Reporters and photographers camped out at her house in Missoula. Advertisers wanted her endorsement for their products: An auto business offered her a free car, and a toothpaste firm offered $5,000 for a photo of her teeth. She became front-page news, but that meant she could no longer control what was written about her. If she refused to speak with reporters, they would make things up. If she did grant interviews, her words might be distorted to fit a certain image the press held of the first congresswoman.

Reporters clustered around her house, waiting for a comment or an opportunity to shoot a picture. Rankin went into hiding and refused to come out until the "boys" of the press had dispersed. Because she was the first and only woman ever elected to a high national office, papers all across the country were hungry for news about her to feed their readers. Her actions were sensationalized; she was made out to be a symbol of every woman. Many reporters seemed intent on assuring their readers that in spite of her election to the male bastion of Congress, she was skilled in the womanly arts.

The *New York Times* noted Rankin's victory in a paragraph that came as a footnote to the front-page state-by-state analysis of the vote for President Woodrow Wilson. Montana's new member of Congress was described as "Miss Jeannette Rankin, a tall and red-haired Republican." Nowhere else on a page crammed with election results ranging from Alabama to Wisconsin was any other candidate's height or hair color described.

Rankin's election may have been a breakthrough for women, but the men of the press had a hard time portraying her as an astute, well-informed legislator-to-be. She had gained political savvy as a worker in the women's suffrage movement, traveling from coast to coast, yet the press most often framed her through a set of traditional values. Women belonged at home; they were expected to marry and raise a family. Politics was for men.

Montana was only the tenth state to grant women the vote, with national suffrage still six years away, and journalists were slow to catch on to the changes occurring in the country. After Rankin's election in 1916, the press basically reinforced the presumption that women were not suited for high public office by sensationalizing Rankin's actions and trivializing her role in national politics. She became what we would now call a celebrity, but, far from being universally celebrated, she was regarded as an anomaly—an oddity. She had strayed too far from the cultural norm.

Montana Republican Jeannette Rankin was the first woman elected to Congress, in 1916, four years before ratification of the constitutional amendment allowing women to vote.

The leaders of her own party in Montana foresaw what would happen, warning her not to talk to reporters because they were sure to portray her as a freak. Even eastern newspapers had a hard time dealing with the phenomenon. On November 11, after most of the Montana returns had been counted, the *Times* reported Rankin's acceptance speech but first commented on her appearance and her supposed feminine attributes. In two days she had evidently shrunk and the color of her hair had changed. "Miss Rankin is small, slight, with light brown hair. . . . [She] makes her own clothes and hats, and she is also an excellent cook."

The Sunday *Times* expanded its description of Rankin. Articles were not always bylined in those days, but it's likely that the reporter was a man, since women journalists were largely confined to writing for the women's sections. Rankin's hair was definitely light brown, not red, the paper said, and she was about five-foot-four and slender. A female reporter for an evening paper in New York who had known Rankin was quoted as saying she was "a very feminine woman" who danced well and sewed her own hats. The newly-elected member of Congress "has won genuine fame among her friends with the wonderful lemon meringue pie that she makes when she hasn't enough other things to do to keep her busy," the reporter said. As a seeming afterthought, the *Times* noted in a final paragraph that Rankin planned to fight for extension of the child labor laws, national woman suffrage, mothers' pensions, and universal compulsory education. A sidebar followed with the promising headline "Equal

Pay for Women." The brief article quoted Rankin as saying she planned to represent the women and children of the West and would work for an eight-hour day for women and equal wages for the same amount of work. But the reporter couldn't let go of traditional notions of a woman's role. "She was sewing as she said this today," the article continued. "Even after entering politics she refused to forsake the old household arts, cooking and needlework."

Rankin said after her election that she was acutely aware of her responsibility as the first woman to sit in Congress, and she promised to represent the women not only of Montana but also of the whole country. What would this symbol of womanhood be like? Some publications made her out to be a Wild West rough-riding pioneer. Headlines had her campaigning on horseback, although she had actually traveled across the state by train and car. But the *Times* seemed determined to reassure readers that Rankin's election did not signal a new role for women in American politics, and that she would surely continue what were considered appropriately feminine pursuits.

Meanwhile in Montana the state's newspapers initially reported that Rankin had lost as Democrats made what appeared to be a clean sweep, winning the other at-large House seat, the Senate seat, and the governor's office. Ballots were counted by hand in those days, and results trickled into newsrooms. Not until three days after the election did the state's newspapers declare Rankin a winner. After this initial period of doubt, some in the Montana press recognized Rankin as an effective organizer. The *Helena* (Montana) *Independent,* for example, seemed less concerned about her mastery of household arts than about explaining that her election to Congress would also make her leader of the Montana Republican Party.

In sharp contrast to the treatment of her election by the *Times*, the strongly supportive *Independent* defended her campaign organization, touted her political experience as a suffrage leader, and rebuked those who would question her ability on the basis of her gender: "There are naturally some republicans [sic] who will object to having a woman as the party leader. But Miss Rankin is not an inexperienced politician, as she has demonstrated. . . . In the fights for women suffrage carried on in the east since the suffrage was granted to women in Montana, she has gained more political experience than many of the would-be republican leaders in Montana will ever have the opportunity of gaining." Her campaign was also the best organized of the Republicans', the paper said: "Compared to the system, consistency, persistency and efficiency of her organization, that of candidate Edwards, run by men who were supposed to have political astuteness, was a joke." Other newspapers were effusive. The *Louisville Courier-Journal* noted her courage, asking, "Breathes there a man with heart so brave that he would want to become one of a deliberative body made up of 434 women and himself?" The *New York Times Magazine* published this bit of doggerel by Christopher Morley:

"We'll hear no more of shabbiness
Among our legislators
She'll make them formal in their dress;
They'll wear boiled shirts and gaiters."

After months of neglect by the media, this sudden deluge of publicity came as a shock to Rankin. On the advice of Republican Party leaders, she refused to go out of her house until the newshounds waiting for her had left. It was a curious decision by a woman who had eagerly campaigned in the toughest and most primitive parts of Montana, a woman who reputedly could talk to the loggers and haulers and factory workers. In refusing to feed the media's frenzied curiosity, Rankin left them to their own imaginations. She feared that she would be portrayed as an oddity, and in some ways she was right. Unusualness or uniqueness was one of the fundamental news values of American journalism—and Rankin fit that mold.

Occasionally a more restrained voice emerged in the newspapers. Louis Levine, a University of Montana economics professor, praised Rankin's capability in a *New York Times* article. But his comments suggest the stereotypes of women that were prevalent at the time:

> There is a great surprise in store for the members of the new Congress when they convene in Washington next year and meet their first woman colleague, "The Lady from Montana." They will have to throw overboard a lot of mental baggage which they may have valued very highly for many years. They will find in their midst not that impulsive, irrational, sentimental, capriciously thinking and obstinately feeling being which many imagine women to be, but a strong and well-balanced personality, scientifically trained, accustomed to strict reasoning, well versed in the art of politics, inspired by high social ideals, tempered by wide experience.

When Rankin finally traveled to Washington on April 2, 1917, for a special session of Congress convened to vote on a declaration of war, she did agree to an interview with a reporter from the *Washington Times*. But her responses suggest just how wary she was of being given a label by the media. "I have so much to learn that I don't know what to say," Rankin told the reporter. "So I have just decided not to say anything at all, for the present at least."

Newspapers vied with each other to give readers a picture of this novelty, but Rankin's reticence gave them little to go on. One newspaper report referred to her as a "slip of a girl," while other accounts had her packing a gun. A magazine christened her "The Girl of the Golden West." A *New York Times* reporter informed his readers that her office in the Capitol was directly opposite that of "the most confirmed bachelor in Congress." And he expressed surprise at the lack of flowers or "feminine knick-knacks" and the fact that there was no "fluffiness" in her dress. One of the first detailed descriptions, by the Tattler for the *Nation* after Rankin was sworn in to Congress, emphasized her feminine appearance:

> In spite of Jeannette Rankin's unusual position and surroundings, she remains the typical woman from top to toe. The top is especially prominent, crowned as it is with a mass of brown hair slightly streaked with gray, worn *a la Pompadour* in a fashion that emphasizes its abundance. The next most noticeable feature is the nose, which is large, straight in outline and fairly dominates the face, particularly in profile. The chin stands out well, but is round and reduced in conspicuousness by a fullness of the cheeks which extends down to the line of the jaw. Her small, rather slight figure, clad in well-fitting garments . . . adds to her thoroughly feminine effect. The V-shaped opening at the neck and the use of lace and tulle wherever a man would use flat linen stiff with starch, differentiate her completely from the background against which she is projected. . . . Her face is mobile, her motions lithe, and her manner has all the vivacity comportable with her seriousness of purpose.

Rankin's purpose became clear almost immediately. On her first day in the House of Representatives, President Wilson asked Congress to declare war against Germany. On April 6, 1917, after a sixteen-hour debate, the House clerk took the roll call. Rankin was a pacifist, and it was a cruel irony that her first vote in Congress was to be on a declaration of war. She shed tears as she voted no, saying, "I want to stand by my country . . . but I cannot vote for war." Many of her male colleagues also wept openly during the roll call, and 49 of them voted with Rankin; 9 abstained and 374 representatives voted for the resolution authorizing America's entry into the war. But the next day the papers focused on the congresswoman's actions, especially her tears. The *New York Times* said it was possibly the most dramatic scene ever staged in the U.S. House of Representatives and gave a detailed description. "Did you intend to vote no'? (the clerk) asked. Miss Rankin nodded in a tired sort of way and sank back into her seat. Then, she pressed her hands to her eyes, threw her head far back and sobbed." Other papers also reported that she sobbed and/or fainted. Both apparently were considerable exaggerations. The *Times* even editorialized that she was "drawing from unsound premises a false conclusion" and questioned what it described as her conditional allegiance to her country. Her vote, said the *Times*, came close to being "final proof of feminine incapacity for straight reasoning." Even the liberal *Nation* commented that it might not have been such a good idea to allow women to vote.

Rankin was both praised and castigated for her stand, with much of the criticism centering on the fact that she wept as she cast her vote. Even reporters who had not witnessed the scene wrote about it. Not widely reported was the fact that some men were crying too. In fact, it seemed that Rankin was singled out for her actions. The *New York Times*, for example, listed the names of the congressmen who voted against the war in a box at the top of the page, but only Rankin's vote was singled out in the lead story.

After the initial hoopla over the physical features and private life of the newly elected congresswoman died down, the press continued to trivialize her actions. She was asked by a reporter whether she had found any boyfriends among members of Congress. She told him, "I expect to put in my time here learning the ropes." She found a couple of ways to get around dealing with the press. One was to ignore them or turn them away. There was the time an Associated Press reporter came to her office seeking comment on legislation to establish a national draft. When her secretary told Rankin what the reporter wanted, the congresswoman shouted from behind a partition, "Tell him to go to hell!" The reporter left in a hurry.

A second maneuver was to try to counterbalance generally negative or trivial press coverage by writing her own articles on such subjects as child workers on the farm and wage problems of women working in defense plants. These appeared weekly in the *Chicago Herald* under Rankin's byline. Rankin also wrote for women's magazines such as the *Ladies Home Journal*. In one such article, "What We Women Should Do," Rankin promoted new roles and responsibilities for women outside the home, noting that the first revolution to follow from the World War could be said to have occurred among women rather than in the Russian Empire. She urged women not to return to primitive housekeeping customs as a way of carrying out the mandate to economize. "Clearly what we need to-day is to reach out for forward-looking and not backward-looking methods," she wrote. Praising the government-controlled public food kitchens established in Europe, Rankin said women should prepare themselves "not only for a thrifty administration within their own kitchens, but *also for professional and paid work* [italics added] which must be done in connection with public food kitchens, free school lunches and other forms of community feeding."

Rankin understood the power of the press. She knew the adverse publicity she had received after her vote against the war would make it difficult for her to be reelected. But in spite of her knowledge that the press could crucify her, she continued to act on her convictions. One such instance came in August 1917 during a strike by workers for the Anaconda Copper Mining Company. Rankin introduced legislation asking Congress to authorize the president to nationalize the mines because they were essential to the war effort—a direct attack on Anaconda. She was aware, and candid with the press, about what she expected the company to do to her in return. She told the *Washington*

Times that she expected the same treatment accorded anyone who opposed the company. "They own the State. They own the government. They own the press. . . . First I'll be roasted from one end of the state to the other. Every newspaper will print my shortcomings, real or fancied, in the largest type. They probably won't assassinate me. They use more subtle methods now. . . . If the Anaconda Company prevents my ever returning to Congress, I'll at least have the satisfaction of having done what I could for my constituency while I was here."

Two years later, knowing she had little chance of reelection to a second term, Rankin campaigned for the Senate but was defeated in the primary by the publisher of the *Montana Record-Herald*. She then ran for the House in the general election as a third-party candidate but was written off by most newspapers in the state and came in a distant third. When Congress voted to enfranchise women in 1919, Rankin would not be able to cast her vote.

But more than twenty years later Rankin again filed for Congress, making no bones about being a pacifist. Montana had been divided into two congressional districts by this time, and she went directly to the voters of the western district, bypassing the press just as she had done in 1916. In her first campaign she had stressed the right of women to vote, and in 1940, she urged that women use the vote to keep America from entering a second world war. She was elected as a peace candidate and took her seat on January 3, 1941, but by the time she got to cast a vote on war, public sentiment had changed. The Japanese had bombed Pearl Harbor on December 7, and the House voted 388-1 to retaliate. The Senate was unanimous in its support of war. As she cast her lonely vote, Rankin said, "As a woman, I can't go to war and I refuse to send anyone else." Public outrage over what appeared to many as an unpatriotic vote erupted in a torrent of letters and telegrams, but a few letter writers and a few newspapers took a different view. The *Evening Kansan-Republican*, for example, portrayed Rankin's vote as a "symbol of martyrdom to an eternal principle residing in the hearts of women"—to oppose war and violence.

Many years later, Rankin was one of three "women of courage" whom then-Senator John F. Kennedy profiled for *McCall's*. Noting that courage is generally perceived as a "manly" virtue, Kennedy wrote, "Most of us do not associate the quality of courage with women in public affairs. We neither expect it nor reward it. But courage in public life is not a monopoly owned and controlled by men."

When Alice Mary Robertson won a seat in the House of Representatives in 1920, as only the second woman ever elected to Congress, news stories mentioned her gender but didn't make it the primary focus of every article. Times hadn't changed dramatically, although it was the year the Nineteenth Amendment was finally ratified by two-thirds of the states. But several factors apparently overshadowed her femaleness—her age, the Republican tide of 1920 that captured more than sixty seats in the House of Representatives, and the fact that she dissociated herself from the suffrage movement. At age sixty-seven, Robertson defeated a three-term Democrat in Oklahoma's Second District. Her victory was part of a Republican sweep and was most often noted as such. The press focused less on another woman being elected to the House than on the fact that a Republican had ousted another Democrat from Congress.

Robertson didn't get much coverage from the Muskogee dailies, so she bought ad space to tell voters what her positions were. In the weeks leading up to the election, people turned to the classifieds to read about "what the woman candidate has to say tonight." Robertson's age, her marital status, and her substantial life experience also made a difference in how the press perceived her. This was not a woman whom the press could easily stereotype. She was not of childbearing age, nor did she have a husband to care for. Born in 1854 to missionary parents in the Creek Nation in Indian territory, Robertson was the first woman clerk of the Office of Indian Affairs in Washington, and later taught at an Indian school in Indian Territory, in Carlisle, Pennsylvania, and at a mission she founded in the Creek Nation. She held administrative and teaching positions at what is now the University of Tulsa and served as postmaster of Muskogee, Oklahoma. Later she operated a dairy farm and cafeteria there.

Another key reason the press played down her gender was that she distanced herself from the women's movement of her day, opposing the work of such organizations as the League of Women Voters and the National Women's Party. Whenever possible the press personifies issues, and if Robertson had supported women's rights it is likely the press would have thrust her into a role as a spokeswoman for the movement. But Robertson made it difficult for the press to stereotype her. Even her mode of dress and the way she wore her hair—pulled back in a knot—seemed to cause consternation among journalists. "One never knows quite what Miss Alice has on," wrote a *Washington Herald* reporter. "Her costume is always black, and of a cut behind the prevailing mode." She told reporters she had no intention of shortening her ankle-length skirts to conform to the new style of the 1920s.

Robertson didn't conform in other ways either. Her campaign slogan had been "I cannot be bought. I cannot be sold. I cannot be intimidated." She spoke her mind. In office she was criticized by women's political groups for her failure to support legislation seen as beneficial to women. In 1921 she spoke against the Sheppard-Towner bill to provide the Labor Department's Children's Bureau with one million dollars a year to promote maternity and infant care. The *Times* saw it as an example of man biting dog and headlined the story "Woman Assails Maternity Bill." But Robertson was not against women; rather, she saw it as an example of meddling by the federal government. She feared the bill would create an "autocratic, undefined, practically uncontrolled, yet federally authorized, centre of propaganda." She approved other legislation benefiting women, such as an increase in the subsistence rate and rent money for Army and Navy nurses.

Robertson's gender did make front-page news on June 21, 1921, when she became the first woman to preside over a session of the House of Representatives. She was applauded by her colleagues as she ran the show briefly during a roll call vote on funding for a U.S. delegation to the centennial celebration of Peru's independence. "Woman Presides in Congress; Precedent Broken Amid Cheers" said the headline at the top of page 1 in the *New York Times*. The story reported that Robertson "banged the gavel in approved style and announced in a clear voice" the results of the vote. So much for women's power in Congress.

Also serving in the 67th Congress was Winnifred Sprague Mason Huck, a Republican from Illinois. Huck was elected to fill the remaining four months of her father's term after he died. She was known for quotable remarks on a range of topics. Even in those days, reporters were drawn to public officials by the promise of good soundbites. Following her single term in the House, Huck joined the political council of the National Women's Party, wrote a syndicated newspaper column, and worked as an investigative reporter for the *Chicago Evening Post*. Articles based on her undercover investigations of the criminal justice system, prison conditions and the rehabilitation of criminals created a stir. Ohio Governor Vic Donahey arranged for her to stand convicted of theft under an assumed name, spend four weeks in a women's prison, and then look for a series of odd jobs in the Northeast and Midwest. She wrote several articles describing her experiences, including being discharged as soon as her employers discovered she had a criminal record.

Meanwhile, eighty-seven-year-old Rebecca Latimer Felton was sworn in on November 21, 1922, as the first woman to serve in the U.S. Senate. It was a grand symbolic gesture—symbolic because Felton served for less than forty-eight hours—and the Senate gallery was filled with women who had come for the occasion. The outspoken Felton was no stranger to the workings of the press. Campaigning with her husband, who had served three terms in Congress in the late 1800s, she was accustomed to responding to editorial criticism with her own stinging articles. The anti-Felton Democratic press announced that her articles had lost her the immunity to criticism traditionally accorded southern ladies. "There is a nobler, higher sphere for women," one paper editorialized. "Fill it!" Another newspaper editorial sarcastically asked: "Which Felton is the Congressman and Which the Wife?"

She and her husband had also started a weekly newspaper in Georgia, the *Cartersville Free Press*—later renamed the *Courant*. Felton wrote columns supporting woman suffrage, public education, especially vocational training for girls, and prohibition. She attacked conditions in prison camps and the confining of women and juveniles in institutions where hardened male criminals were also housed. She also attacked Jews, Catholics, and blacks, in one case advocating mass lynching of blacks as a deterrent to rape. In spite of her bias, Felton was prescient about the importance of race relations to the future of the country. In an interview with the *Atlanta Sun-American*, she was quoted as saying, "Over fifty years of hard experience since the Civil War demonstrates one fact only: that the Negro is in the United States to stay, and according as he is dealt with depends our own peace or disaster in his association with the whites."

The first woman senator, Rebecca Felton of Georgia, posed for news photographers before her swearing-in in 1922. With her are her successor, Walter F. George (left), and Georgia Senator William J. Harris.

In appointing Felton to the vacant Senate seat, Georgia governor Thomas Hardwick hoped to appease newly enfranchised women but didn't expect Felton actually to serve. Newspapers praised his choice of Felton, but many were critical of his motives, calling it a purely political action designed to enhance his own eligibility for a seat in the U.S. Senate. Perhaps it had been simply a political ploy on the part of the governor, but Felton acted on it, convincing Senator-elect Walter George to delay presenting his credentials so that she could serve for two days. Felton took her seat on November 20 and was sworn in the next day, turning over her seat to George on November 22.

Although some senators grumbled about the inappropriateness of Felton taking a seat in the upper chamber, expressing fears that it might set a precedent, the press was generally upbeat about her. She was referred to in news stories as Georgia's "grand old lady," and descriptions of her campaign to be seated were sympathetic. Of course, Felton didn't represent real change in the social or political order. If she had, the press might have characterized her very differently. Instead, they could relish the story of a determined old woman from the Deep South who would give up her seat to her successor, a man, and go home almost as soon as she was sworn in.

In brief remarks on the floor before giving up her seat, Felton said millions of women voters had been heartened by what she called a "romantic . . . historic event." She predicted to her male colleagues, "When the women of the country come in and sit with you, though there may be but a very few in the next few years, I pledge you that you will get ability, you will get integrity of purpose, you will get exalted patriotism, and you will get unstinted usefulness." Felton's legacy is an odd trio of distinctions: she was the first woman sworn in to the Senate, the oldest senator at the time of her swearing in, and the senator with the shortest term of service.

It was relatively easy for the press to ignore many of the women who served in Congress during the first half of the century because so many of them, like Felton, were seat warmers, temporarily filling congressional seats for a few days or months until men could assume their "rightful" place. The press reflected the common assumption that politics was for men and women's place was in the home, not the House.

But some women were active participants in the legislative process and were reelected on their own merit, although they invariably were tagged with the fact that they first got into office by succeeding their husbands. As Jeane Kirkpatrick wrote in *Political Woman*, the media often emphasized that a particular congresswoman ran for office or was appointed only after her husband died—making her a sort of surrogate no matter how many elections she subsequently won. This assumption that women couldn't have gotten there on their own hung on into the 1970s.

"Curiously," continues Kirkpatrick, "this implication of ineptitude and incompetence often hangs on even though the women may have won five subsequent elections. The fact that Margaret Chase Smith was initially appointed to serve out her husband's term seems more important to many than the fact that Walter Mondale was first appointed to the Senate to finish out the term of then Vice President Hubert Humphrey. Why? Because stereotypes persist, especially stereotypes that involve fundamental notions about the nature of reality—such as what women are like and what they want. Seeing political women as husbands' surrogates is a way of denying they are really political actors in their own right."

When women demonstrated that they could be elected to subsequent terms on their own merits, the press characterized them as different from most other women. They were often portrayed as tougher, more independent, more savvy about legislative processes than the "typical" woman. In short, they were seen as more like men. Florence Prag Kahn, for example, was elected on the Republican ticket in 1925 to succeed her late husband as California's Fourth District representative and won reelection to the five succeeding Congresses. She was effective in securing expanded military installations and other federal construction projects for her home state and was a strong supporter of the FBI. In fact, her support was so great that she became friends with J. Edgar Hoover and earned the nickname "mother of the bureau." But the fact is that she was as effective as a man. At least that's what the *Pictorial Review* said: "Congress treats her like a man, fears her, admires her and listens to her."

Another early congresswoman, Edith Nourse Rogers, a Massachusetts Republican, retains the distinction of being the longest-serving woman in the history of Congress. Like so many other women representatives, she succeeded her husband in the House in 1925 but won another seventeen elections before her death in office in 1960 at the age of seventy-nine. She had intended to run for a nineteenth term but died after checking into a Boston hospital three days before the primary. Rogers was known for her legislative skill—something many reporters considered a male attribute. "On the floor, despite her effervescing femininity, she conducts herself like a man," observed a reporter in the press gallery. "She doesn't get on her mark, get set and then recite her speech in school girl fashion. Bouncing out of her seat, she shoots a question in a high-pitched Boston accent and leaps in where other gentlewomen fear to tread."

There was a "new type of woman leader" coming into party prominence in the 1920s, according to the *New York Times*—"the woman of maturity and leisure, often of wealth, whose children are grown and who now turns to politics as in a former generation she might have turned to philanthropy or the women's club as an outlet for her civic energies." One of the women mentioned by the *Times* was Representative Ruth Pratt of New York. Many women have silently tolerated unfair or inadequate press coverage, but Pratt, a Democrat who served from 1928 to 1933, castigated the political press for "perpetuating the myth that women have a different role to play in public life than men. One of the flagrant weaknesses of our political system is that it draws this sharp line between men and women candidates. . . . Sex has no place whatsoever in politics." In an article published in the *Ladies Home Journal* in 1928, Pratt wrote:

> A man enters public life and not the slightest attention is paid to the fact that he is a man. A woman runs for office and there is more interest in the fact that she is a woman than in her qualifications for the job she seeks. It is then she learns how tenacious the tag woman is—how palpably she is a woman, how completely shackled by her sex. At every turn she is confronted with the fact that the activities of the world have been cut from a he pattern, that it has always been a man's universe and that while she isn't exactly an interloper she's different. The woman label follows her around like a faithful dog. . . . She is a woman candidate, not merely a candidate, as a man is. If elected, she becomes the woman this or that, not simply the title. Where the masculinity of her *confreres* is taken for granted, her femininity always causes mild surprise and is good for an old-fashioned debate on whether women generally are not miscast when assuming roles which have heretofore

been reserved for the other sex. . . . Men and women should be put on
a parity, the sole issue being which candidate is best qualified to perform the duties of the office concerned.

While the *Times'* description of the "new woman leader" of the 1920s
may have been accurate for a few individuals, such a blanket description failed
to cover many other women in politics. Kentucky Republican Katherine Langley, for instance, provided an irresistible story for the press when she ran for
and was elected to Congress in 1926 to replace her husband, who had been
convicted of illegally conspiring to transport and sell whiskey. Her goal, she
said, was to clear her husband's name and continue his work. After her election, she persuaded President Coolidge to grant her husband clemency. In return, Langley promised he would never again run for public office. But not
only did he renege on his promise, he announced publicly that he would run
for his old House seat—without first informing his wife. She in turn said she
had no intention of giving up her seat to him. The dispute provided lively
fodder for the Kentucky newspapers, and even though her name remained on
the ballot, it cost her the election after two terms in office.

Two women were elected governor during this period—the only women
governors for forty years, until the election of Lurleen Wallace as governor of
Alabama in 1966. Nellie Tayloe Ross of Wyoming and Miriam A. Ferguson of
Texas were both elected in 1924, but Ross was sworn in earlier, making her
the first female governor. Ross had no experience in politics but was elected to
succeed her husband, who had died in office. Her election came as a surprise
to many. "The opposition treated her gently," Eleanor Roosevelt later wrote,
"basing their campaign, it can be assumed, on the polite assurance that she
was a fine woman and all that, BUT—being a governor was a man's job."

Ross served one term and was defeated for reelection but achieved a
certain national prestige. In 1928 she received thirty-one votes for vice president on the first ballot at the Democratic National Convention. Roosevelt notes
that because Ross was attractive and feminine, women were reassured that a
successful woman politician didn't have to be aggressive and masculine. This
was reflected in newspapers. The *New York Times* assured its readers that this
wasn't a woman who aggressively sought the governorship. Rather, party delegates "practically forced the nomination on her." Before the nomination, Ross
had not been involved in politics and had "devoted herself principally to her
home and family," the newspaper said. After being nominated, she "did not
campaign as strenuously as the average candidate but left most of the work in
the hands of her party managers."

Governor "Ma" Ferguson received more national press than Governor
Ross, but she was never taken very seriously by newspapers outside Texas.
She had been put up by her husband, James E. Ferguson, who had been im-

peached while governor and was therefore unable to run. She campaigned on two main issues, vindication of her husband and opposition to the Ku Klux Klan. Despite her strong stand against the Klan in one of their original strongholds, she was always considered a ringer for her husband, who had coined the campaign slogan "Two Governors for the Price of One." Ferguson had made it plain from the outset that he would advise his wife. When the opposition charged that he, not his wife, would be the real governor, he reportedly replied, "I ask you, if your wife was governor, would you get mad and leave home? Or would you stick around and help her?"

An Associated Press story shortly after her election began: "The advice of her husband will be taken by Mrs. Miriam Amanda Ferguson, Governor-elect of Texas, 'just as I will take the advice of any citizen of Texas interested in the welfare of the state.'" The reporter asked the governor-elect questions that are still asked by reporters every time a woman is elected governor. Who would serve as first lady? Who would run the governor's mansion? Who would do the cooking? ("She declared that she does not do all the cooking for the family and does not intend to do it while she is governor.") The story also quoted her as saying, "I expect to be Governor, just as any man." And her title? "Just Governor, I guess, for no other title would do," she was quoted as saying. "The title 'Madam Governor' would be out of place."

In fact, what to call a woman governor was a new enough question that the *New York Times* addressed it in an editorial titled "'Governess' Never Would Do!" The editorial writer rejected "governess" as well as "governorine," "governorette," and "gubernatrix" in favor of just plain "governor." "And why not?" said the *Times*. "If they make good governors, it will be not because they are women, but because they have sense, intelligence and character, and if they make bad ones—but of course they will not, and to give any thought to that abhorrent contingency would be discourteously premature and worthy only of a woman-hater."

Miriam A. "Ma" Ferguson received extensive press attention when she was elected governor of Texas in 1924.

Although extensive press coverage made Ferguson known nationwide, it was never particularly favorable. The most serious charge against her during her first term was that she freed some 3,600 convicts from the state penitentiary. But even seemingly minor occurrences brought down the wrath of editorial writers. A newspaper photograph that showed her canning peaches raised a furor in Texas because in theory she should have been so busy carrying on state business that she would have had no time to think about the peach crop. But it turned out that the canning incident had occurred early in her campaign, months before she became governor. Eleanor Roosevelt, herself well acquainted with the ways of the press, observed: "She fell victim to the conviction universal among newspaper photographers that the frying-pan routine gets a woman public official off to a good start, shows she's human. More sophisticated lady politicians resist it."

Meanwhile, the influence of women voters was beginning to be felt during this time. The press took note of women's involvement in politics, especially after they proved to be a force in the 1928 election, the third presidential election since the suffrage amendment was ratified in 1920. In 1924 it was estimated that women's votes totaled ten million, but there was no indication that their vote had a profound effect on the result. In 1928, however, the women's vote increased by 40 to 50 percent over the 1924 vote and was said to be as much as 45 percent of the total vote cast, according to the *Woman's Journal.* "There is no doubt in the minds of either women or politicians that it had a considerable effect on the outcome."

Women also began to make use of the power of the press. Publicity bureaus were established at both parties' national headquarters and in some states. Well-known women writers and newspaper women were enlisted, including Ida Tarbell for the Democrats and Mary Roberts Rinehart for the Republicans. The publicity bureaus, organized like regular city newspaper offices, supplied news and feature articles, editorials, and weekly "clip sheets" to newspapers all over the country. Yet women's interest in issues and ability to distinguish between candidates was demeaned by the mainstream press, which thought that women's votes would be bought with gifts of candy and kisses.

But no amount of publicity can make up for the lack of power, and few women in Congress ascended to the leadership positions that assure media access. One of the early exceptions was New Jersey Democrat Mary Norton, first elected in 1925, who chaired several committees during her twenty-six years in Congress, including the House Committee on Labor in the closing years of the New Deal and during World War II. As chair, Norton oversaw the passage of the Fair Labor Standards Act of 1938 and used her position to be a vocal advocate for equal pay for women laborers. Norton also got press coverage when she became the first representative to propose a repeal of prohibition. As the ranking Democrat on the Committee on the District of Columbia when the Democrats took over Congress in 1931, Norton earned the praise of the Washington papers when she slammed a committee member who regularly opposed appropriations for the District. She said that while he was always preaching economy for the nation's District, he didn't seem to mind spending the taxpayers' money to have his endless speeches printed in the *Congressional Record* at sixty dollars a page. The press nicknamed her "Battling Mary" and dubbed her the "Mayoress of Washington."

Norton was also ranking majority member of the House Labor Committee when the committee chairman died. In spite of protests by the Washington newspapers, Norton resigned the District committee and took on the Labor chairmanship when the committee was in the middle of hearings on the Wage and Hour bill. The bill—a "must" for the Roosevelt White House—was sent back to committee the first time but passed four months later, causing Mrs. Roosevelt to comment, "Mary Norton had accomplished what had appeared to be an impossibility."

Nearly a decade after Rebecca Felton's two-day tenure in the Senate, Hattie Wyatt Caraway became the first woman actually elected to the upper chamber. Initially appointed by Arkansas governor Harvey Parnell in November 1931 to fill the vacancy left by her husband's death, Caraway won a special election in January and then faced four men in the August 1932 primary, one a former governor and another a former senator. Her chances looked slim until Louisiana senator Huey Long gave her his support. The Arkansas papers then began to portray her as Long pictured her—as a champion of poor white farmers and workers and as a senator who could not be bought. She won the 1932 election and was returned to office for a second term in 1938, narrowly defeating John McClellan, who later went on to a thirty-four-year career in the Senate. Caraway rarely participated in debate or gave a speech on the Senate floor, and consequently her opinions were given little national attention in the press. When they did write about her, reporters used phrases such as "Huey's echo" and "conspicuously inconspicuous." Yet her contribution as a female presence in the Senate was noted gratefully by some women in the news business. Rebecca Fulbright, publisher of the *Fayetteville* (Arkansas) *Daily Journal*, wrote that "Our new woman senator is blazing a new trail and a glowing one. Long enough has this old world done without the contribution women are able to make to [solving] its problems." Caraway ran for renomination to a third term in 1944 but ran last in a four-person race won by Representative J. William Fulbright.

The third female senator also owed her election to Huey Long. She was his widow, Rose McConnell Long, who served just a year in office after he was assassinated in 1936. Despite the brevity of her service, her election was significant because it marked the first time more than one woman served in the Senate at the same time. Described by *Time* magazine as a "diminutive, liquid-eyed lady," Long reportedly had an aphrodisiac effect on the Senate, at least according to a reporter: "For years dowdy Hattie Caraway had sat alone relatively neglected in the Senate. Now Senators, leaving the floor, frequently pause to pass the time of day with Mrs. Long. Senators on the Democratic side have taken noticeably more care of their personal appearance since she arrived. Bachelor senators—Rush Holt of West Virginia and Richard Russell of Georgia—have been seen hovering near her desk. As the best-looking Senator her colleagues have ever seen, she is shown special consideration on all sides." Then the reporter couldn't resist this bit of sexist humor: "In the press gallery some ill-bred wag suggested that the parliamentary inquiry most frequently in Senators' minds is "Will the Senator from Louisiana yield?" Long's marriage prospects were also considered newsworthy, especially by the Hearst papers, which periodically reported rumors that she was engaged to be married.

As Long was leaving Washington in 1937, another woman was appointed to the Senate to fill the vacancy left by Hugo Black's appointment to the U.S. Supreme Court. But Alabama governor Bibb Graves' appointment of his wife, Dixie Bibb Graves, was heavily criticized in the press as an act of nepotism that ignored the needs of constituents. Although she served less than five months, Graves made headlines when she delivered a speech on the Senate floor in November 1937 during debate on the Wagner-Van Nuys anti-lynching bill. Graves opposed the bill, calling it an infringement of state sovereignty and an insult to southern law enforcement officers. Graves said lynching had decreased in the South and predicted it might be eliminated within five years without federal interference. The reaction of the press to her comments points up how sharply divided were different regions of the country. Her comments drew angry responses in northern newspapers but enhanced her popularity in the South. In Alabama the governor distributed copies of her speech and white citizens mounted a write-in campaign to have her name placed on the ballot for the January 4 special election. But she declined to run and resigned her seat shortly after the election.

During these decades, newspapers continued to be fundamentally male institutions, employing mainly men, shaped by masculine views and responding to male interests. Although pioneering women politicians were often sensationalized, trivialized, or ignored by mainstream newspapers, women did have an avenue other than the women's page through which they could communicate their ideas and promote issues they cared about—women's magazines.

Although most popular women's magazines have reflected dominant cultural images of women, focusing on fashion, beauty, and home furnishings, they have also introduced successful, interesting women to their readers, including women politicians. In addition, women's magazines have urged their readers to get involved in politics. In the 1930s, for example, *Ladies Home*

Journal ran stories exploring women's role in politics, attempting to galvanize women with articles such as "Whose Country Is This, Anyway?" and "Why Don't You Use Your Vote?" Alternative women's magazines such as the *Woman's Journal* also discussed issues of concern to women in the early part of the century.

In 1928, the *Woman's Journal* ran an article on three new women members of Congress—Ruth Bryan Owen of Florida, Ruth Hanna McCormick of Illinois, and Ruth Pratt—described as "notable for their personality and political leadership who won membership in Congress by campaigns rating with the best of men's." Although two came from political backgrounds (Owen's father was William Jennings Bryan and McCormick's father was Mark Hanna), the article said that "in no case is it the name that has made the congresswoman." In addition to profiling successful women politicians, women's magazines raised fundamental questions about women's role in society and politics.

The question of whether women candidates should emphasize gender was already being discussed in the 1920s and 1930s, and the controversy was reflected in the *Woman's Journal*. Emily Newell Blair, a former Democratic National Committee vice chair, wrote in the January 1931 issue that it had been unwise to "drop the sex line in politics." Agreeing to minimize gender in political campaigns had set back the advancement of women, Blair said. "Even those who ran for office forgot that they were women," she wrote. "'I am not running as a woman, but as a Democrat (or as a Republican)!' How many times have I heard it! No appeal to women to put a woman in office, no argument as to her right to hold office, but a minimizing always of her sex. And yet thousands of votes were cast against her, for no other reason than that she was a woman. Let us not think, because we cease to talk of it, that the prejudice against women in public office has been overcome."

Chapter 3

THE "GLAMOUR GIRLS" OF CONGRESS

BOTH WERE BEAUTIFUL. BOTH WERE ACTRESSES BEFORE BECOMING MEMBERS OF CONgress. And—best of all for the press—the two women represented different political parties. When Helen Gahagan Douglas joined Clare Boothe Luce in the House of Representatives in 1944, it promised to be a juicy ongoing story— the catfight of the decade. Suggestive headlines started appearing almost as soon as Douglas won the July 1944 Democratic primary in California for a seat in the House, beating six male opponents. She was to address the Democratic National Convention in Chicago the same week. Luce, elected a member of Congress from Connecticut two years before, had just been tapped to deliver the keynote address at the Republican National Convention. One Chicago paper bannered a story with the headline: HELEN VS. CLARE: TORCH VS. ICICLE.

Luce, who had been dubbed "Connecticut's gift to the glamour department of Congress" by the *New York Daily News* and the "congressional snake charmer" by a trade publication, wasn't about to buy into the female feud that was being created by the press. She was more interested in getting her message across to the public. It was reported at the time that she refused to be part of the program unless she could speak at an evening session with nationwide press and radio coverage. "Whether she did it for that purpose or not, it served to advance the fortunes of women in both parties," First Lady Eleanor Roosevelt wrote later, "establishing a precedent that has been followed ever since."

But precedents for covering women politicians seemed carved in stone. At a press conference arranged for Douglas in Chicago after she arrived for the Democratic convention, little attention was paid to matters of substance. "Attention was paid to my hat ('It's too large for the photographers—would you mind removing it?'), my knees, which were revealed when I sat down in my narrow skirt, and the color of my eyes (blue)," Douglas recalled. "Some one asked pertly what I would be wearing when I addressed the convention."

A few questions dealt with her political views, notably about women. Douglas said President Roosevelt's New Deal had helped brighten their lives. Noting that women had helped with the war effort, she said that after the war "it will be necessary for them to support themselves, as it is for men to support themselves."

Predictably, the most intense media interest seemed to be in her possible "rivalry" with Luce. "Heads bent over notebooks as I answered, 'I don't like fencing. I have the greatest respect for Mrs. Luce.'" Even the *New York Times*

Connecticut Representative Clare Boothe Luce and her husband Henry R. Luce listened to election returns on the radio in 1944, when she won a second term in Congress.

headlined its story "'Fencing' With Mrs. Luce Barred by Miss Gahagan." Although Douglas was trying to focus on other, more serious issues, virtually the entire Associated Press account—distributed to newspapers across the country—dealt with her prospective relationship with Luce: "Miss Gahagan is sometimes called the Democratic Party's glamour contrepart [*sic*] of the Republicans' Mrs. Luce, who delivered her 'GI Jim' address at the Republican National Convention. 'I'm not going to spar,' she said. 'It is nonsense, with people dying the world over, for anyone to carp. I'm not against debate,' she added. 'I'm against fencing.'"

Despite Douglas's effort to quell the rumors of rivalry before they spread, newspapers took up the theme again after she won the November election, predicting a "battle of the glamour queens." "For reporters short of real news, it was a simple day's work to speculate that we would claw one another," Douglas said. "The implication was that we were frivolous, vacuous women rather than serious, committed politicians. I was determined to clear the air of such insulting innuendo as soon as I could."

Luce, already burned by the press for her public disagreement with columnist Dorothy Thompson, made it a point to see Douglas after the California congresswoman arrived in Washington in an effort to circumvent the press. Luce told her biographer that their conversation went like this: "I told Mrs. Douglas that if she said it was a nice day and I happened to observe that it looked like rain, the press would blow it up into a great big dispute. I wanted to make an agreement with her . . . we would never discuss the same subject on the same day, and we wouldn't under any consideration comment on what the other had said." Douglas agreed, and although they often differed in their opinions and votes, they never gave the press the opportunity to use terms like "catfight" or "hairpulling contests." As Eleanor Roosevelt observed, Douglas and Luce shook hands in public "and spoiled a build-up that would have pictured them as two competing glamour girls ready to tear each other to pieces."

Luce and Douglas were often featured in the press as the most "glamorous" members of Congress because of their association with theater and movies and their society connections. But some journalists tried to paint a similar portrait of a third female member of Congress elected in 1942, who had a very different background. She was thirty-three-year-old Winifred Stanley, who had witnessed gender discrimination as a trial lawyer during a time when jury panels and criminal trials were routinely closed to women. A magna cum laude graduate of the University of Buffalo law school and an assistant prosecutor in upstate New York, Stanley beat seven candidates to win her congressional seat. She came to Congress with impressive credentials, but journalists focused on her looks. Columnist Drew Pearson said Stanley was "Mrs. Luce's chief competitor for Congressional 'glamour girl' honors." And *Newsweek* described her as "pretty enough to 'twitterpate' some of her colleagues."

The press may have had to manufacture the battle among the congressional "glamour girls," but they didn't have to invent the feud between Luce and journalist Dorothy Thompson. In fact, Luce's disagreements with Thompson during the 1940 presidential campaign were even more highly publicized than the anticipated catfight with Representative Douglas. Luce and Thompson had worked together for Wendell Wilkie's nomination, but Thompson abruptly changed her mind, writing a column in support of Roosevelt that said his reelection was essential to the future of America. Luce likened Thompson's about face to the girl in an Apache dance team who passionately succumbs to her partner's brutal treatment. The newspapers loved it, calling it—what else?— a catfight, and egged them on, publishing charge and countercharge. Luce called Thompson the "Molly Pitcher of the Maginot Line," while Thompson dubbed Luce "the Fisher body of politics" and said Luce had "torn herself loose from the Stork Club to serve her country."

Perhaps the most widely quoted newspaper hyperbole about the Luce-Thompson argument was the comment that it was "a confrontation between two blonde Valkyries on the prows of opposing ships of state." Columnist Walter Winchell reportedly quipped that when he encountered Luce and Thompson in the same room at a night club, he urged them to refrain from fighting. "Ladies, ladies," he said, "remember there are gentlemen present." The standoff was capped by a well-publicized radio debate. After the election, however, Luce sent Thompson a conciliatory telegram, and two years later Thompson supported Luce's bid for reelection.

As a result of the press hoopla over her disagreement with Thompson, Luce said she learned one great truth: Men can disagree violently and the press will acknowledge the possibility of a reasonable difference of opinion. If women disagree, it immediately becomes a catfight, a fingernail-scratching or hair-pulling contest. Her biographer said she resolved never again to engage in a public dispute with another woman.

In 1944 Douglas, Luce, and Stanley were among only nine women in the House, and there were no women in the Senate. Only two women had ever been elected governor, twenty years before, and both had succeeded their husbands in office. It would be twenty years more before another woman became governor. Few women wrote for the nation's dailies, and most of those were assigned society news.

Because so much of the news about women politicians was reported and edited from a male point of view, it is startling to read a 1944 *New York Times* story by Kathleen McLaughlin that assesses newly elected congresswomen in a tone both respectful and optimistic. McLaughlin says "informal comment" (a way of indicating anonymous sources) was "almost universally approving of the caliber and background" of the three Democratic women who would be sworn in January 3, 1945. McLaughlin mentions Douglas's theater background, but does so in the context of telling how Douglas became involved in politics. (She encountered Nazism while on a concert tour and as a result canceled a contract to sing in Germany.) Just as male reporters typically did, McLaughlin injected her own sentiments into the story. And that's precisely where it made a difference to have a woman writing the story. A male reporter typically might have focused on women politicians' looks, family, or cooking skills, but McLaughlin looked at their prospects for legislative success: "Women who are particularly concerned about obtaining qualified representatives in Washington are well pleased with their prospects for the Congress of 1945-46, especially since the holdovers, one Democrat and five Republicans, will have acquired additional seniority on important committees."

One of those incumbents was Luce, who was serving her first term in Congress. She had won the Republican party nomination against five male candidates and one woman—but it was the other woman in the race who made the best copy. *Washington Times-Herald* columnist Helen Essary forecast in July 1942 that Vivien Kellems, owner of a Westport industrial complex, would block Luce's nomination: "For a breathless while Connecticut knew only that Clare Boothe Luce was bound for the capitol of the U.S.A. and the House of Representatives. Now it is Vivien and Clare—as quick-stepping, fast-murdering girls as any civilization, primitive or modern, ever stood up under: Vivien and Clare—what a battle! 'The Women' in real life," Essary wrote, a reference to Luce's play about a group of catty women. Kellems repeatedly attacked Luce, describing her as a pawn of special interests for her marriage to Henry R. Luce, head of the *Time-Life* publishing empire, and suggesting she was "running on a platform of sex appeal," but Luce did not respond. In fact,

Luce's marriage was a double disadvantage for her. During the 1940s Henry Luce's magazines were among the most influential and yet most heavily criticized publications in the country. Clare Luce was christened the "Empress of *Time-Life*" and was criticized for her association with Henry Luce but actually got little mention in the pages of *Time*. "The boys at *Time* Inc. (there were no girls to speak of) emphatically did not want Mrs. Luce to become a congresswoman and disgrace the magazine," said her longtime friend Wilfred Sheed. "For a woman bent on making a career, the *Time* connection was as booby-trapped as any other big company connection. . . . Clare could thenceforth count on a certain number of back-room hecklers with a way with words, whose influence with Harry might be expected to grow as his infatuation with her cooled. Whether the pressure on him came from without or within, Clare now says that 'for a publisher's wife, I got less support from the publisher than any character in history. . . .' Harry was proving a point, which was that he could be objective, even about his wife."

Eleanor Roosevelt also commented on Luce's situation, saying, "It is naturally assumed that her rise in politics is due to her position as the wife of the publisher of *Time, Life,* and *Fortune.* The assumption, however, is not entirely fair." Well before Clare married Luce she demonstrated, Roosevelt said, "more than ordinary ability and a kind of toughness" and rugged honesty that won respect.

Only after Luce stepped down from Congress did *Time* publish an extended and flattering article about her. More common in the press was criticism like that leveled by the head of the New York University school of journalism, Dr. Gregory Mason, who was quoted in the *New York Times* as saying that the best way to insure the reelection of Democrat Le Roy Downs was to nominate Clare for his seat. "She is bound to be influenced by her husband," Mason said, "whose yellow journals are doing all they can to keep alive the disunity and acrimony which marred American discussion of foreign affairs before Japan's wanton attack on us."

In fact, not only was Luce not mentioned in the pages of *Time*, she was kept away from the organization of the new magazine, *Life*, even though it was her idea. "*Time* Inc. in those days was a very stag affair and it wanted no part of the boss's wife from the first," says Sheed. "So although Clare could send all the memos she wanted . . . she wasn't allowed any piece of the magazine she'd dreamed up." Later, however, Luce went abroad as a roving reporter for *Life*.

Despite the criticism, she won the GOP nomination handily on September 14, but almost immediately she was betrayed by her own cleverness. She told reporters her opponent had given the district rubber stamp representation and called him a "faceless man," apparently unaware that he had been wounded in World War I and had required plastic surgery to repair his face. He, of course, seized the opportunity to embarrass Luce. Realizing that anything she said would only keep the matter alive, she said nothing. The matter died down in about a week but caused her to adopt one of her basic political principles, according to biographer Stephen Shadegg: "Never explain."

Regardless of whether she responded to allegations in the press or not, she was continually stereotyped as a cold, calculating woman with ice in her veins. Wilfred Sheed said that image wasn't true and that she may have acquired her reputation for icy aloofness as a way of counteracting the effect of her beauty: "No doubt a serious woman had to be very no nonsense indeed (or else very plain looking) to get a fair hearing in those days."

Luce was an outspoken critic of Roosevelt's foreign policy and was often criticized in turn. Her rebuke of FDR at the Wisconsin state Republican convention in 1943 for engaging in "windy, high flown talk" of mechanisms to achieve global security—"dazzle dust terms thrown in people's eyes in order to be able to complain that the people do not see"—brought heavy criticism in the press. Even *Time* called her speech "a model of partisan politics." "It is not surprising that she has made almost the classic fool of herself," said *New Republic* magazine. But a few papers praised her. The *Salem Capital-Journal*, an influential western newspaper, editorialized that the Republicans might well have discovered in Luce "their ablest campaign orator, next to Wendell Wilkie, and she is perhaps more subtle than the latter, a better master of satire, invective and phrase coiner—using the rapier rather than the broadsword."

Apart from her political views, it seemed just about anything Luce did was of interest to the press. She always could be counted on for a sharp quote. For example, seventeen newspapers including the *New York Times*, the *New York Herald Tribune,* and the *Washington Times-Herald* ran lengthy news stories about her troubles with a domestic servant. The maid in question had gone to a reporter after a short time at the Luce house in Connecticut, complaining that it was too hectic. Luce's response to reporters' questions was, "We have lost an old family retainer who has been with us for almost two weeks." And when Luce toured Europe in the early 1940s as the only female member of a sixteen-member congressional committee, her associates were reportedly furious with her because she received so much personal publicity. Throughout the trip, newspapers published her comments and ran photos of her. It had been agreed that the committee chairman would handle all press contacts and issue all public statements, but Luce stole the show. When reporters asked her to comment on the trip and its purpose she told them she had been forbidden to talk to the press—which of course produced more headlines. The *Washington Times-Herald* topped a column with "War Department Denies Any Knowledge of Gag," while the *New York Mirror* gave it a three-column head, "Army Gags Clare Luce in War Zone; Permits Others to Talk."

Luce was in a continual battle to refocus attention on her ideas rather than her looks and gender. So it probably didn't help much when a public opinion poll published during this period said her legs were among the most beautiful in America, second only to Marlene Dietrich's. In his column, Walter Winchell reported Luce's reply to a congressman who asked if she didn't think her latest distinction was beneath the dignity of the House: "Don't you realize, Congressman, that you are just falling for some subtle New Deal propaganda designed to distract attention from the end of me that is really functioning?"

When Luce announced for reelection in 1944, the Democrats nominated a woman to run against her, Margaret Connors, twenty-nine, a Bridgeport attorney who had served as deputy secretary of state, special agent for the Department of Justice, and counsel for the American Civil Liberties Union. Rumors continued to circulate that Luce owed her position to the publicity she got from the *Time-Life* magazines, even though she was rarely mentioned in them. But her reelection campaign was given prominent coverage by more than a hundred newspapers all over the country. Luce drew the most heat when she attacked President Roosevelt and was quoted in the newspapers as saying he was "the only American president who ever lied us into a war because he did not have the political courage to lead us into it." She had told the 1944 GOP convention that Roosevelt's isolationist foreign policy had fueled the war and that a "more forthright American foreign policy" might have saved the lives of millions. Afterward, during her reelection campaign, she was attacked by a number of journalists, including Dorothy Thompson, Dorothy Parker, and Quentin Reynolds, who wrote, "Representative Clare Boothe Luce's charge that President Roosevelt 'lied' us into the war is not the first time a person named Booth treacherously assaulted the President of the United States." Reynolds was speaking for a Broadway for Roosevelt Committee that included a number of well known singers and actors.

One of the stinging published attacks of that campaign was a two-page ad in New York's *PM*, edited by Ralph Ingersoll, a former *Time-Life* employee who had objected to Luce marrying Clare and had tried to keep her away from *Life*. The ad pieced together paragraphs from speeches she had made, articles she had written for *Vanity Fair*, and editorials in the magazine, whether she had written them or not. One of her light satirical pieces was included as evidence that she engaged in untruths. The press disseminated other phony stories. The *Bridgeport Herald* accused Clare of being anti-Semitic, although she had publicly supported the Zionist movement, and anti-Negro, although she had introduced a resolution calling for racial equality in the armed services and had publicly condemned the D.A.R. for refusing to let singer Marian Anderson use its Washington hall.

Luce won reelection but retired from Congress in 1947 after two terms, following her teenage daughter's death in an auto accident. She later served as

United States ambassador to Italy. Eleanor Roosevelt commented on Luce's uncomfortable relations with women reporters, telling of watching her at a party given by the New York newspaper women just before Luce left to assume her post as ambassador. Luce, said Roosevelt, stood apart from the crowd and seemed a little defiant as she talked with the women and responded to their speeches. There was "something that suggested she was not at all sure they had meant what they said," Roosevelt observed, "or that she could command the backing of newspaper women in general." The press women's coolness toward Luce may have resulted from the legend that she was at war with all other women, which stemmed, Roosevelt said, from her play *The Women*, "in which the only moderately nice woman is the least interesting." Part of Luce's legend was that she was invariably successful with men, but Roosevelt said her male colleagues in Congress were not comfortable with her. "Many of them, it was said, were afraid of her. A rumor went the rounds that she was there to get material for another play."

Remnants of the legend that Luce was an icy man hater or, alternately, a woman-hating femme fatale surfaced in the press periodically and tended to overshadow Luce's keen mind and strong ideas. One extreme media view of Luce, which makes her sound like the Lorena Bobbitt of Washington, is represented by a story told by public relations agent Vic Gold, who had gotten her to agree to host a "Coffee Day" reception just after Luce's confirmation as U.S. ambassador to Brazil. Gold had promised the State Department that the event would not only promote coffee consumption but would give Luce favorable publicity in Brazil. Gold calls Luce "the archetypal mid-century male emasculator, verbally desexing her masculine adversaries when Germaine Greer was pre-pubescent." Luce arrived late for the reception. "SHE swept into the room the way only a Clare Boothe Luce or Katharine Hepburn can sweep into a room: brisk, well-groomed and surrounded by a bevy of clucking young male assistants. She was all hard business in a chiffon package." Gold also described her "gleaming frost smile."

As Gold tells the story, the coffee reception was Luce's last public appearance as ambassador. She had just been confirmed after weeks of scrutiny by the Senate Foreign Relations Committee chaired by Wayne Morse. Asked by a reporter why her confirmation had moved so slowly, Luce replied, "I would have been confirmed weeks ago. My difficulty, of course, goes some years back and began when Senator Morse was kicked in the head by a horse." Morse, a horse breeder, had in fact been kicked by a horse some years before. But while Luce was promoting coffee, Morse was on the Senate floor defending his reputation, and within a week Luce submitted her resignation.

The woman portrayed as Luce's Democratic counterpart in Congress, Helen Gahagan Douglas, was involved in her career as an actress and opera singer and didn't become interested in politics until the late 1930s. She first became active in California politics as a Democratic state committeewoman and then was named director of the women's division and vice chair of the state Democratic organization. In her autobiography she recalls that many women came to her with the same complaint—that they were used by the party for manual labor but never appointed to influential positions. "I had approximately the same story for every one of them. I explained that I was raised in a household of dominating males . . . and that I learned early on that men guard their authority over women jealously," Douglas says. "As for politics, they sincerely believe public life to be a male bailiwick. They reason that men have been running the country for the past two hundred years and are meant to continue to do so for centuries to come. In short, men would never share power with women willingly. If we wanted it, we would have to take it."

Take it she did, running a successful no-frills campaign for a House seat from California in 1944. It was wartime, and resources were limited, so a few days after her election some of her women supporters threw a surprise party and presented her with a Washington wardrobe. They had gotten the keys to her theater trunks and had her dressmaker do some alterations. The black velvet evening dress that Representative Douglas wore to Washington parties that winter was the same dress she had worn to her beheading in the West Coast production of *Mary of Scotland.*

Because of her good looks and her background in theater, journalists expected her to provide colorful copy. Columnist Heywood Broun, for example, once described her as "the ten most beautiful women in the world." But Douglas initially proved a disappointment to the press. Eleanor Roosevelt, who became her good friend, wrote that she was a hard worker and seemed determined to live down her Broadway and Hollywood background.

During her three terms in the House, Douglas learned how the media could benefit her and the causes she believed in—and also

California Democrat Helen Gahagan Douglas served three terms in the House but was defeated by Richard Nixon when she ran for a Senate seat in 1950.

how it could be used to damage her. She was ultimately forced from public office by a media campaign orchestrated by Richard Nixon that painted her as a Communist sympathizer. An example of how she learned to use the media involved decisions that were being made about future use of atomic power. Douglas says she became aware that a bill was quietly being ushered through Congress that would give control of atomic power to the military. So she contacted newspapers around the country and mailed copies of the legislation to them, asking them to write editorials if they agreed that the Military Affairs Committee should recall the bill and reopen public hearings. The editorial response was thunderous. And in 1946, almost a year after Hiroshima, Congress passed the Atomic Energy Act placing atomic energy under civilian control.

Douglas knew that if she could gain the support of the press, she could win public support. She put that theory into practice in an effort to restore wartime price controls on food. Food and housing costs were skyrocketing after World War II, and she had secured data on grocery prices and regional income levels. "It was my job to put the material together in a speech that wouldn't cause waves of boredom in the House and in the press," she said. "I lay awake worried that the data I had taken from charts and graphs would be stupifyingly dull. The congressional press gallery would ignore it and I would lose my valuable opportunity to gain public support." By the time she took the House floor the next day, she had come up with an idea to capture the attention of the press. She walked in with a basket of groceries and a couple of sales slips as evidence that decontrol had led to a 50 percent increase in the cost of basic foods such as bread, milk, flour, eggs, and meat—even while corporate profits were going up. Douglas wasn't successful in getting Congress to reimpose price controls on food, but she believed her speech helped delay removal of rent controls.

Douglas was reelected to Congress in 1946 and 1948 but decided not to seek a fourth term in 1950 in order to run for the Senate. Her timing couldn't have been worse. The Soviets' test of an atomic bomb in 1949 had caused widespread anxiety in America. There was a general sense that Communist spies had infiltrated government and were trying to destroy Democracy. Meanwhile, Communists took control of China, driving the Nationalist government off the mainland. During the primary campaign, Douglas's main Republican opponent, Representative Richard Nixon, cast Douglas as a liberal sympathetic to communism and said voters had a choice between freedom and socialism. She was opposed also by Democrat Manchester Boddy, publisher of the *Los Angeles Daily News. Newsweek* commented just before the primary that the paper "has read as if no one was running for senator except Manchester Boddy. He brought his Washington correspondent, Frank Rogers, back to Los Angeles to serve as his chief press agent, while writing daily communiques on the campaign for the *News*, and his political writer, Leslie Claypool, also is busy filling the paper with reports of Boddy's doings. Just to make the coverage of Boddy's campaign complete, the publisher is himself writing a column—about himself."

Although the *News* and other California newspapers began referring to Douglas as "decidedly pink" or "pink shading to deep red" or even "the pink lady," she won the Democratic primary. But almost immediately afterward the North Korean Communists invaded South Korea and the United States had to return to war as part of a United Nations force.

Nixon dug in, attacking Douglas as a Communist sympathizer. The Nixon campaign distributed hundreds of pink sheets at campaign events trying to show that Douglas had been soft on communism because she had opposed the House Committee on Un-American Activities and other bills requiring Americans to take loyalty oaths. Douglas had opposed the popular committee's tactics, saying it was taking on powers that should be exercised only by the attorney general's office, and that individuals' civil rights were being violated. But Nixon's repeated attacks wore her down. "It made me feel I was standing in the path of tanks," she said. In response to the Nixon campaign's pink sheets, Douglas's staff put together a record of her and Nixon's votes, taken from the *Congressional Record*, that showed Douglas's strong stands in favor of civil rights and social justice. But as Douglas acknowledged, the book was "expensive to produce, laborious for anyone but a dedicated liberal to read, and quite unsuccessful in matching the flair and focus of the ubiquitous Pink Sheet."

Although she always took the book with her, it became clear that voters were not interested in legislative details. "People would point to something in a newspaper, a report of a Nixon speech, and ask me to explain it," she said. "When I did, I felt they closed their ears to rational comment. The fabricated stories came at me like a mudslide; I couldn't keep up with it." At least Nixon never made gender an issue, she later said. "Even Richard Nixon did not say that I was a lightweight because of my sex."

California voters were manipulated in the 1950 campaign in a way that Judge Learned Hand had predicted many years earlier when he warned of the danger the mass media pose for Democracy. "People can be stampeded," Douglas says, "especially when they are fearful as they were in California that year, by a clever and cynical campaign waged in the media." "Even though I used a helicopter, something new in campaigning, I couldn't get enough places in such a large state to keep ahead of what was being done to my reputation."

It was more difficult for Nixon to influence media in the East, where newspapers did not have the same vested interest in the race as those in California. The magazine *Liberty*, for example, said there were few in Congress who knew more than Douglas about world affairs and social economics. And some major East Coast papers, including the *New York Times* and *Washington Post*, ran balanced stories about the bruising California Senate race.

Columnist Drew Pearson also wrote a sympathetic piece refuting the allegations contained in the Pink Sheet and saying that powerful forces "have combined in a skillful throat-cutting campaign." But Douglas's supporters were no match for the *Los Angeles Times*, the largest newspaper in the state, which went so far as to publish an appeal for volunteers to work in the Nixon campaign to "keep left-wing Helen Gahagan Douglas out of the Senate." In fact, the *Times* was in even deeper than it appeared on the surface. According to David Halberstam, *Times* political reporter Kyle Palmer had coaxed Nixon into entering the senate race in the first place. And once the primaries were over, the *Times* helped redefine campaign issues. "Instead of tidelands and the rights to offshore oil, the central issue of the campaign and the principal one upon which Mrs. Douglas was running, it became Communism," Halberstam says. "It was all red-baiting. Pink lady. If anything, the editorial voice of the *Times* was even harsher than that of Nixon. Mrs. Douglas's voice was never heard. She was never covered; she was only attacked, that was all that was permitted. Any conservative Democrat who backed Nixon made page one." Douglas couldn't even get her schedule in print without buying an ad, and there weren't any reporters to hold the candidates accountable for what they said and did. The paper never reported that Nixon falsely implied in speeches to civic clubs that there was something sexual going on between Douglas and Harry Truman. "Thus the candidates were unusually free to say what they wanted without any real accountability."

Douglas later acknowledged that she might have lost even if the California newspapers had backed her. The Korean War meant almost certain defeat for her candidacy because it renewed the public's fear of communism, and Nixon was able to exploit that fear. Somewhat ironically in view of its earlier support for Nixon, the *Los Angeles Times* praised her political courage in an editorial on July 1, 1980, after her death. "Her service in Congress coincided with the Cold War and although she had no sympathy with communism, she refused to be stampeded into voting for measures that she was convinced would undermine democracy." Mentioning the 1950 Senate race, the editorial said Nixon's campaign was "a model of its kind—innuendo piled on innuendo."

Luce and Douglas demonstrated that it is sometimes possible for women to outwit and outmaneuver the press. They understood how the game was played, and they pulled the rug out from under journalists eager to write about a catfight or glamour girl competition. Luce chose not to run for reelection, but Douglas was forced from public service by a campaign that drew much of its power from a heavily partisan newspaper. Douglas had media savvy. She was able to circumvent media sexism, and she had learned how to attract media attention for legislative matters. But her knowledge of the press was useless in the face of the steamroller tactics used by the major newspaper in her home state.

Chapter 4

A ROSE BY
ANY OTHER NAME

SHE ALWAYS WORE A SINGLE ROSE IN HER LAPEL. BUT A ROSE IS FRAGILE AND SHORT-lived, unlike the strong-willed, independent Margaret Chase Smith, whose career spanned thirty-two years in the House and Senate. A woman of few words, she had a reputation for doing her legislative homework, and people listened when she spoke. For nearly a quarter-century she was the only woman in the U.S. Senate. Frequently mentioned as a potential vice presidential candidate, she aimed higher, running for president in 1964. But she couldn't break through the glass ceiling of her gender. The media didn't help much.

Although she was adamant that being a woman made no difference in the way she did her job, news stories always seemed to make Smith's gender her primary attribute. She was universally referred to in the press as the "Lady from Maine." After she was elected to the Senate in 1948—the first woman elected in her own right and the first female to occupy a Senate seat in six years, news accounts of her legislative activities often implied astonishment that the little woman showed so much courage. Sometimes she was singled out for coverage simply because she was a woman. Even after twenty-four years in the Senate, she was still depicted as a novelty.

Smith wasn't naive about the news media. In fact, she understood news very well. She had worked for a newspaper as "the girl around town" when she was growing up in Skowhegan, a small industrial town in central Maine, in the early part of the century. Later she was circulation manager for the weekly *Skowhegan Independent Reporter*. She knew what kind of information reporters needed, and she understood the pressures they were under to compete with others for exclusive stories and to meet deadlines.

Smith went to Washington in 1936 and served as assistant to her husband, Clyde, who had been elected Representative from Maine's Second Congressional District. But at reelection time two terms later, Clyde Smith had a heart attack just before the primary filing deadline, and asked his wife to file

Maine senator Margaret Chase Smith served in the House and Senate for thirty-two years and campaigned for the Republican presidential nomination in 1964.

in his place. The plan was that she would withdraw and he would replace her when he recovered. But he soon suffered another heart attack and died, and she was elected to the House.

From her first days in Washington she became friends with May Craig, Washington correspondent for the Guy Gannett newspapers in Maine—one of a handful of women covering the Hill. Smith says she made a special effort to help out Craig, letting her read the office mail to get material for her daily column. Because of her own experience as a newswoman, Smith says she had a special empathy with Craig's work and also recognized that cooperating with Craig would pay off at reelection time for her husband and later for herself. Craig proved to be an invaluable press ally, writing thousands of words about her for homestate papers. A profile in *Colliers* said Craig "has become a sort of unofficial female Boswell to the Lady from Maine."

Smith recognized the value of maintaining relationships with journalists, listened carefully to their advice, and in several instances sought out their counsel. Newspapers were still powerful institutions during this period, and the opinions of newspaper columnists played an important part in shaping public opinion and influencing Congress.

In 1948, Smith decided to run for the Senate when one of Maine's seats came open. Since she was the first woman to seek a Senate seat on her own merits, there was widespread interest in her race. Running a characteristically low-budget campaign, Smith traveled around Maine whenever she could get away from the House, often driving her own car. She made good copy. In September, for example, the *Saturday Evening Post* ran a story about Smith's hardships on the icy Maine campaign trail, written by Beverly Smith, the magazine's Washington editor. Smith was running against three male candidates and hoped to squeak by with a plurality. Instead, she garnered more votes in the June primary than all of her opponents combined. After she won the November election she got almost as much press attention as the president during Truman's inauguration festivities.

Smith wasn't the first woman elected to the Senate, but many thought she was because of all the media attention she was given. The Women's National Press Club gave her its Politics Achievement Award in 1948, and the Associated Press named her "Woman of the Year." In 1949 the United Press radio editors voted her their "Woman of the Year," and the AP for two years running called her "Woman of the Year in Politics," while the Mutual Broadcasting System placed her among the ten Americans who had done the most for their country in 1948.

But Margaret Chase Smith had only begun to demonstrate what she was capable of. Senator Joe McCarthy's vicious campaign to eradicate what he said were Communists in the State Department ultimately moved Smith to take a stand on the Senate floor against his tactics that garnered her national praise and press attention. She was the first member of McCarthy's own party to denounce him. Former CBS correspondent Nancy Dickerson noted in her autobiography that most senators had shown a "remarkable lack of courage" and "had not been anxious to condemn one of their own." Smith had served in the Senate just over a year when McCarthy gave his now-famous speech on February 9, 1950, in Wheeling, West Virginia, saying "I have here in my hand a list of 205" men in the State Department known to be members of the Communist party. His speech was widely covered, and McCarthy was asked to defend his charges on the floor of the Senate on February 20. An ad hoc committee headed by Senator Millard Tydings began hearings into his charges a few days later. They continued all spring and gave McCarthy a forum in which to continue and expand his charges with congressional immunity. The hearings helped inflame the nation's already highly charged anticommunist mood. State department employees were accused and slandered through guilt-by-association tactics that paralyzed Washington to the point where people were not only afraid to speak up but afraid of whom they might be seen with. Smith says the atmosphere of political fear was such that many people refused to accept dinner invitations out of concern that McCarthy might level unproved accusations at someone who had been a guest at the same party. McCarthy's power grew as journalists reported what he said without questioning whether it was true.

In the face of widespread public support for McCarthy, generated by such uncritical news coverage, it became extremely difficult to challenge him. It was even more daunting for a first-term senator. Initially Smith had been impressed with what McCarthy was saying and the fact that he seemed to have proof. She made a point of going to the Senate floor to hear his speeches, but when she asked to see the papers he was waving around as "proof" that his accusations were true, she didn't think they were relevant to the charges he was making. She says she became convinced that he had nothing to back up his charges.

One of the most influential liberal columnists, Doris Fleeson, had been especially critical of the Democratic leadership in the Senate for failing to challenge McCarthy. Now Fleeson urged Smith to speak out, as did radio commentator Ed Hart. But Smith was reluctant. She was a freshman, the only woman in the Senate, and she was not given to making long statements on the Senate floor. It was politically risky to challenge McCarthy during a time when the tide of McCarthyism was sweeping the land. And it was more appropriate for Democratic senators to challenge McCarthy than someone from his own party, which would split Republican ranks. She was aware of all the negatives, but Smith knew what needed to be done. Finally she called Walter Lippmann for advice.

Lippmann, probably the most powerful political columnist of his day, strongly approved of her desire to oppose McCarthy on the Senate floor. She says Lippmann didn't suggest any themes or wording, but his words of encouragement helped her decide. One week later, Smith and her executive assistant, William Lewis, made their way to the Senate floor, carrying 200 mimeographed copies of her speech for distribution in the press galleries. As Smith rose to speak, McCarthy sat two rows behind her. She began: "Mr. President, I would like to speak briefly and simply about a serious national condition. It is a national feeling of fear and frustration that could result in national suicide and the end of everything that we Americans hold dear."

Smith said the deliberative character of the Senate had been "debased to the level of a forum of hate and character assassination sheltered by the shield of congressional immunity." Without mentioning McCarthy's name, she made it clear who she was talking about. She said those who shout the loudest about Americanism in making character assassinations are often those who forget America's basic principles, such as the right to criticize, to hold unpopular beliefs, to protest, and to think independently. "I am not proud of the way the Senate has been made a publicity platform for irresponsible sensationalism. . . . I don't like the way the Senate has been made a rendez-vous for vilification, for selfish political gain at the sacrifice of individual reputations and national unity. I am not proud of the way we smear outsiders from the floor of the Senate and hide behind the cloak of congressional immunity and still place ourselves beyond criticism on the floor of the Senate." Smith said she was speaking as a senator, a Republican, an American—and a woman. "As a woman I wonder how the mothers, wives, sisters and daughters feel about the way in which members of their families have been politically mangled in Senate debate—and I use the word 'debate' advisedly."

Six Republican senators co-sponsored what Smith called her Declaration of Conscience. Her speech was lauded by the press, who seemed to love the fact that a woman had rebuked her male colleagues and criticized McCarthy. "What many a bewildered citizen had waited to hear for a long time was said by a woman last week," reported *Newsweek.* ". . . Her precise, restrained phrases worked as neatly as a broom sweeping out a mess." The magazine also referred to Smith variously as "the diminutive lady from Maine," as "the pert little lady [who] got up and said right out loud," and as a woman "attractive and self-possessed—but with a man-sized will."

That praise was echoed by newspapers and other news magazines. *Time* was far more restrained than *Newsweek,* describing her only as "Maine's earnest, handsomely grey Margaret Chase Smith." The *Washington Star* said it had been a long time since there had been "a finer or more pertinent address" in either chamber and that Smith had brought "a much needed breath of fresh air in the fetid . . . atmosphere." The *New York Post* said her remarks were "proof that decency and tolerance are bipartisan qualities in American life." And political guru Bernard Baruch said that if a man had made the Declaration of Conscience, he would be the next president of the United States.

Smith also was criticized by some publications for being weak or for tilting at windmills. The *Saturday Evening Post,* for instance, called her and her six co-signers "the Soft Underbelly of the Republican Party," while *Life* said they were "Quixotic." Sometimes articles condescended even as they praised her courage. The subhead on *Colliers'* profile of Smith began, "Maine's charming lady senator got up for her first big speech."

But Smith's words seemed to fall into a dark hole in the Senate. Most Republicans continued to avoid crossing McCarthy. Instead of being censured, he was given a committee chairmanship when the Republicans assumed control of the Senate after the 1952 elections, a position unheard of for someone with so little seniority. Smith was a member of the same committee—Government Operations—and of the Permanent Investigating Subcommittee. But once McCarthy was in power he booted Smith from the subcommittee and appointed California freshman Senator Richard Nixon in her place. "McCarthy . . . got his revenge" *Time* reported in an article headlined "McCarthy Gets His Lady."

McCarthy also tried to get her ousted from the Senate by backing a candidate to oppose her in the 1954 Maine primary. That was her first campaign for reelection to the Senate, and Smith stayed in Washington doing Senate business for much of the campaign period, relying on her performance in office to win reelection and expressing disdain for McCarthy's candidate, whom she called "Joe's boy." She won the primary handily but was surprised with a challenge in the November election from Colby College History Professor Paul Fullam. After her rough primary election, Smith wasn't about to give up her seat in the general election. So she pulled a fast one on her opponent, using the new medium of television. She basically ignored Fullam until 11:05 the night before the election, when she made a live television appearance on Station WCSH and accused him of lying about her record and making personal attacks. The station went off the air after her speech, and Fullam had no opportunity to respond. The polls opened the next morning. The station did provide Fullam equal time to respond to Smith's allegations—four days after she had won the election.

Much press coverage of Smith's congressional service focused on her achievements, although it was often implied or explicitly stated that what she was doing was a rarity for a woman. But Smith was successful at projecting a no-nonsense image of herself as straightforward and honest, a serious legislator. She made herself accessible to journalists and says she rarely kept anything a secret. "I was always direct with them. They knew I wasn't hiding anything. I answered their questions as they wanted and if they didn't like [my answers], then it was too bad . . . they could go somewhere else." As David Broder noted in a 1990 *Washington Post* column, "Margaret Chase Smith was always herself: a strong independent voice of conscience in the Republican Party and in the United States Senate."

Asked if newspapers were a help in getting her message across to constituents, Smith replied, "Well, they were no damage to me," although she acknowledged getting annoyed at editorials she considered unfair. Sometimes coverage of trivial matters seemed overblown. That was the case when Smith joined Representative Frances Bolton of Ohio in sponsoring a bill to adopt the rose as the national flower. Their male colleagues offered alternatives such as the Easter lily and stinkweed, and the resulting debate was played up in the press as the latest "War of the Roses." Yet when Smith subsequently broached a more serious topic—that any reduction in military spending would leave the United States a second-rate power "incapable of assuring the future security and freedom of its people"—her warning was given minimal coverage and relegated to the back pages of newspapers or not covered at all.

The influence of radio and television on politics grew during Smith's time in office. The story she tells about how she planned for a televised debate with former First Lady Eleanor Roosevelt before the 1956 presidential election is a good illustration of the way television had brought to politics a new emphasis on appearance. Roosevelt was to speak on behalf of Democratic presidential nominee Adlai Stevenson, while Smith was asked to take President Eisenhower's side. The debate was to be held on CBS's *Face the Nation* the Sunday before the election. Smith's first task was to anticipate questions and issues and prepare for them, but just as important was to anticipate Roosevelt's appearance and style.

Smith figured Roosevelt would wear a tweed suit and hat and would project self-confidence and speak at length. To underscore the differences between the two presidential candidates visually, Smith decided to present herself as a contrast to Roosevelt, in a simple dark dress without a hat, speaking briefly and to the point. Smith figured it right. On camera, Mrs. Roosevelt looked bulky in her suit and top-heavy in her hat, Smith said, and the contrast in their appearance was reflected in their style of speaking. "Mrs. Roosevelt was caught by surprise as I refrained from tangling with her. The more that I spoke softly and smiled faintly, and the less I said in reply, the more Mrs. Roosevelt seemed to be put off balance. And this made her talk more." It was an early harbinger of the effect television would continue to have on politics.

But Smith was not one to toe the party line at all costs. One of the best publicized encounters of her second term in the Senate was over President Eisenhower's proposed promotion of the popular actor Jimmy Stewart to brigadier general in the Air Force Reserve. Stewart had had an exemplary combat record in World War II and the Korean War, but Smith discovered that his postwar attendance at Reserve meetings and drills had been poor. She was also concerned about the fact that he would become chief of staff of the Strategic Air Command's 15th Air Force Division in case of hostilities. She successfully argued for denial of Stewart's promotion by the Armed Services Committee, of which she was a member. Three years later, after Stewart had completed the requisite training, Smith voted for his promotion. This time his mobilization assignment in the event of hostilities was to be in public relations.

Although she was telegenic, Smith relied mainly on her reputation and her grassroots support in Maine to stay in office. She was strongly opposed to taking large campaign contributions for fear she would be beholden to special interests. Doris Fleeson is reported to have asked a Maine resident if he knew how important Smith was in the Senate. "We know," he said. "And she did it without kissing anybody's backside either." Her campaigns for reelection were always low budget. She didn't have the money to pay for televised political advertising, which was becoming increasingly important for candidates in the late 1960s and early 1970s, and that contributed to her defeat in 1972. Televised images of the aging senator reinforced her opponent's assertions that it was time for a younger person to represent Maine voters in the Senate.

Smith had told a reporter for the *Chicago Tribune* earlier that year that she had seriously thought of retiring instead of running again, "but I hate to leave when there is no indication another qualified woman is coming in. We've built a place here for quality service. If I leave and there's a long lapse, the next woman will have to rebuild entirely." Although Smith took note, in this and other public statements, of the importance of having a woman in the Senate, she said she always considered herself a public servant first, a woman second. "I never thought of women being women. I always thought of women as people," she later said. "Women should be judged by their achievements, not their sex."

During her years in the Senate, Smith sought and received committee assignments that were considered male territory, such as Naval Affairs and Armed Services, because they would be handling issues of importance to Maine.

When she campaigned for reelection, it was as a public servant. "I was not a woman campaigner; I was not a woman candidate," she said. "I was someone who was running for office—just like you would be." Did the press get the message? "If they wanted to," she answered. "I did everything a man did; served on the same committees, was chairman of several subcommittees. It never occurred to me that I should act any differently if I were a man," she says. "I was Margaret Chase Smith. The only difference was I was Mrs. instead of Mr. if they wanted to put a handle on it."

Smith was the only woman in the Senate during her four terms, but several women were elected to the House during that quarter-century. Even though their numbers were growing, they still encountered amazement and disbelief. The media often reflected the cultural assumption of the day: women were expected to be at home caring for their husbands and children. And some in the press clearly thought women were a passing fad. *Harper's* magazine reflected the status quo in 1955 when Oregon Representative Edith Green took the oath of office in the presence of her husband and two sons: "Few husbands will go as far as Mr. Green. He is moving his electrical heating business to Washington. Perhaps most callings are less mobile than electrical heating. But since the election of a married woman to national office usually involves uprooting or forfeiting a valued male, there is a chronic shortage of good female candidates."

Green took issue with that assessment, blaming the shortage of women candidates on a political climate fostered by men who think politics is exclusively their arena. "When I entered politics, a thousand and one times in a condescending tone I heard: 'How did it ever happen that you [as a woman] are running for office?'" But Green was also able to use the media in her favor. In the closing weeks of her 1954 campaign for Congress, Green—who had spent most of her life as a teacher and PTA official—was charged with being "the puppet and mouthpiece of Eastern labor racketeers." So Green challenged her opponent to appear with her on television. When he refused, she taped his speech, played it on a program of her own, and then sent him a check, at union rates, for his services as a recorded TV performer.

Among Green's contributions in Congress was her work to end discrimination against women. She sponsored the Equal Pay Act of 1963, which required that women be paid the same salary as men for identical work. She also pushed through landmark education legislation, including the Higher Education Acts of 1965 and 1967 and the 1972 Omnibus Higher Education Act, which prohibits institutions that receive federal financial support from discriminating on the basis of sex. Referred to as "Mrs. Education" in the media, Green also initiated work study and grant programs for needy students. Her spirit and independence belied her gentle image, as the *Wall Street Journal* noted in a story headlined "Rep. Edith Green, a Bareknuckle Fighter." The reporter set up a contrast between Mrs. Green's appearance and what she was really like: "The diminutive Mrs. Green, a grey-haired grandmother, speaks softly and certainly seems gentle. Rarely have appearances been more misleading. Strong men quake with fear and fury when Mrs. Green opposes them, while those on the side she favors will gladly let her take the lead in bruising legislative battles."

Michigan Democrat Martha Griffiths came to Congress the same year as Green and also worked for legislation prohibiting discrimination on the basis of sex. It was she who pushed for the addition of the word "sex" to "race, color, religion and national origin" in the 1964 Civil Rights Act. If "sex" had not been included, white women discriminated against by an employer would not have been entitled to protection under the law. "In my judgment, the men who had written the Equal Employment Opportunity Act had never even thought about women," Griffiths said.

Griffiths also was responsible for legislation that allowed divorced women married twenty years or more to draw on their former husband's Social Security; that made motherless children eligible for the Social Security benefits their widowed fathers had been unable to collect from their working wives' accounts; and that made widowers eligible for their wives' Civil Service pensions. But Griffiths is perhaps best remembered for her tenacity and legislative skill in pushing the Equal Rights Amendment through Congress in 1972.

Griffiths was also the first woman ever to sit on the twenty-five-member House Ways and Means Committee. She said her participation was useful. "A feminine voice removes a proverbial blind spot in the thinking of male lawmakers. Men think of women as wives or widows, but never as workers." Her perspective did make a difference as legislative language became inclusive. A term like "widow," for example, was replaced with "surviving spouse."

If it was rare for a woman to run for Congress, it was even less

Representative Martha Griffiths (D-Michigan) worked behind the scenes for passage of the Equal Rights Amendment, which had been stalled in Congress for close to fifty years. Courtesy of the State Archives of Michigan.

common for one woman to challenge another for a congressional seat. So when Marion Sanders challenged Katherine St. George for a New York congressional seat in 1952, it made good copy. Sanders says that at the beginning of her campaign St. George pretended no one was running against her, giving Sanders a brief lock on the headlines. "Word was then leaked from her headquarters that a shocking disclosure about me would soon be unveiled." What St. George had discovered was that Sanders had once edited a U.S. government magazine that was sold in the Soviet Union. "The Russians," St. George intoned suggestively, "must have liked it." An irony was that Sanders had included the editorship in her campaign biography and it had been praised in such publications as *Time,* the *Washington Star,* and the *Wilkes-Barre Record.*

Sanders says at first she spoke of many issues but was advised by "seasoned counselors" to stick to women's issues. "Friendly reporters also thirsted for 'women's angle' copy, preferably double distilled since this was a two-woman race," she says. "Price control, middle income housing and other housewifely topics were not the burning issues of 1952, so most of my speeches were pretty dull." She shed what she terms her "spiritual hobble skirt" a month before the election when she campaigned in upstate New York in a blizzard, getting to a hotel for a rally three hours late. When she got up to speak, she decided to bag the "women's angle" and tackle the issue of war and peace in the atomic age. Afterward the district Democratic Party chairman stood up. "Fellow Democrats, I must confess I wasn't anxious to come out on a night like this to listen to some housewife," he said. "But our candidate is better than Lowell Thomas." Sanders says she knew she was accepted in the masculine society of politics when he turned to a waiter and said, "Bring this lady a Seven-up and applejack."

The term "housewife" hung like an albatross around the necks of many candidates in the 1950s. And no matter how serious their purpose, women politicians could be trivialized through media jokes exploiting their family situations. What happened to Minnesota Democrat Coya Knutson is a case in point. Knutson defeated a six-term incumbent in 1954 to begin a congressional career devoted to saving family farms. She was elected by farmers in her district, and she demanded and won a place on the all-male Agriculture Committee. "This is subversive stuff and was so noted in the political section of the New York Times," Marion Sanders later wrote. "Lady politicians more commonly land on the woman's page, when, like Representative Leonor Sullivan of Missouri, they bemoan the high price of coffee." Knutson was responsible for several major pieces of legislation, including a bill to create a federal student loan fund that became Title II of the National Defense Education Act of 1958.

But a ruse by her alcoholic husband Andrew—the well-publicized "Coya Come Home" letter—put an end to Knutson's congressional career after only two terms. Since her election to Congress, "Our home life has deteriorated to the extent that it is practically nonexistent," her husband wrote in an open letter. "I want to have the happy home that we enjoyed for many years prior to her election." His complaints, and a subsequent press release he signed that accused his wife of improprieties with her thirty-year-old administrative assistant, drew reams of publicity.

The Knutsons had operated a hotel and restaurant in Oklee, Minnesota, before Coya's election, and *Time* magazine was one of the publications that had a field day describing their domestic dispute. The magazine described the congresswoman as "the innkeeper's

Representative Coya Knutson (D-Minnesota), shown here with Sam Rayburn, was a strong defender of farmers but lost her House seat after her husband wrote a plaintive letter to a newspaper saying he needed her at home. Courtesy of the Minnesota Historical Society.

blonde, comely wife [who had] cooked hearty food, waited cheerfully on tables and made the guests feel right at home." Under her picture was the caption, "No one in the kitchen with Andy." Knutson eventually apologized to his wife, and his apology was published in Drew Pearson's syndicated column—but not before the damage was done. Knutson was defeated in her bid for a third term in the House. According to later testimony before the House special elections subcommittee, the press release was actually the work of the campaign manager for the GOP candidate who unseated Knutson in 1958.

Amid all the media snickering, columnist Doris Fleeson's voice stood out. She pointed up the double standard in a column: "Many in Washington, not all of them women . . . feel that [Knutson] was marked down as 'fair game' simply because she was a woman and roughly treated in a manner that the men in her business are not. . . . There are many better stories here than *l'affaire* Knutson and they are about much more prominent people, but it is not considered cricket to use them as a political weapon. The lesson is that, as a practical matter, women are held to a far higher standard of accountability in politics than men are. Women clearly cannot count on the club spirit for protection."

Women were especially vulnerable to attacks transmitted through the media, as Marion Sanders noted in *The Lady and the Vote*: "To link their opponents with a major sin or conspiracy is, of course, the overriding goal of political gutter fighters. Since heavy artillery is not always available, they often resort to minor buckshot," Sanders wrote. "Even this can be pretty disconcerting when fired at short range, on the local scene. Women present particularly inviting targets, for Caesar's wife has been worrying about her reputation for centuries."

Stereotypes of women persisted in the press in the mid-1950s, even though a record sixteen women had been elected to Congress in 1954. One example was this line from the post-election story distributed by the International News Service: "If the gentlemen of the 84th Congress appear a little better shaved and a little better mannered than usual, there'll be a reason: women."

Some women members of Congress played right into these media stereotypes. Margaret Chase Smith and Frances Bolton's effort to establish the rose as the national flower is an example. Martha Griffiths argued for enriched flour; Gracie Pfost of Idaho worked to improve the visitors gallery by distributing a card with rules on smoking, applauding, reading, taking notes, and hanging coats over the railings. Her Michigan colleague, George Dondero, responded that visitors were less uncouth than congressmen who smoked, jabbered, and propped their feet on desks.

There's nothing inherently wrong with such actions, but, as Marion Sanders has written, the attention given them by the media blacks out "the many sensible efforts of women in office to behave like public servants as well as females. And the ladies themselves seem reluctant to jettison the tired stereotypes of yesteryear. . . . Perhaps we take for granted the rights another generation won for us. Women in our time seem less eager to expand their horizons than were their mothers and grandmothers."

Finally, however, enough women were elected to the House during the 1940s and 1950s to be able to provide support for one another. Instead of Alice Robertson dressed in black, sitting by herself, women had come to Congress and had stayed. A story told by Mary Norton illustrates this newfound camaraderie. One afternoon in the House a member "noted for his vilification" cast a slur on the patriotism of actor Melvyn Douglas. Norton was seated a few rows away from the actor's wife, Representative Helen Gahagan Douglas. "I glanced around at Helen and saw that she was white as a sheet. I wanted to go to her, but I didn't dare risk it. I was too angry myself. It wouldn't have helped her for me to blow up," Norton said. "Then I saw something I shall never forget as long as I live. Quietly and with great dignity, Mrs. [Frances] Bolton got up from her seat on the Republican side, came across the aisle and sat down beside Helen. Never was I so proud of being a woman in politics."

The camaraderie and support shining through that story are evidence of the steady gains women were making in Congress. By the early 1960s women seemed entrenched in the House and Senate. More women ran for Congress in 1960 than ever before, and, though not all were successful, a record number served in the 87th Congress. No matter. Their presence on the national political scene still dumbfounded some journalists. *Time,* for example, ran a cover story on Margaret Chase Smith's 1960 Senate race, giving it such fanfare because it was the first time two women had vied with each other for a seat in the Senate. The magazine called it "the nation's biggest, most eye-catching feminine contest." The publisher of *Time,* in a letter at the front of the magazine, said the editors, all men, "find women politicians—and women—an always fascinating, sometimes baffling and ever-changing story." But from a record high of twenty, the number of women in Congress declined each year, falling to eleven in 1969. Was women's participation in high-level politics only a passing fad? "Are lady lawmakers facing extinction?" asked the *Chicago Tribune.* Its answer: "Possibly." Associated Press newswoman Frances Lewine said the reason for the decline wasn't clear: "Politicians aren't sure if it's faint heart or fading interest." But as the women's movement grew in influence, things didn't turn out to be as bleak as the 1969 numbers suggested.

Chapter 5

THE PUSH FOR
EQUAL RIGHTS

THE 1970S WERE A DECADE OF MANY CONTRADICTIONS, AS WOMEN SOUGHT EQUAL opportunities with men and the news media wrestled with fair coverage. Congress finally approved the Equal Rights Amendment in 1972. Women were elected to the governorship of Connecticut in 1974 and of Washington state in 1976 without succeeding their husbands in office. Women who advocated women's rights were elected to the House of Representatives, and a woman was elected to the Senate in 1978, which had been without female representation since voters retired Margaret Chase Smith in 1972.

Women began to organize into political groups, a sure sign that they intended to stick around. The National Women's Political Caucus was founded in 1971, and the Women's Campaign Fund was started in 1973, at that time the only bipartisan national organization giving financial support to women candidates. Women journalists were moving off the women's pages and into the city rooms, where a few were reporting politics and government. Awareness was growing of the sexism that had pervaded news stories, and some made efforts to correct it. There was also a rapid increase in the use of so-called "paid media"—televised political advertising—to supplement the news and feature stories that politicians call "free media."

By the end of the decade, some things had changed but others stayed the same. As Pat Schroeder said in 1979, "We are still novelty acts." Several highly visible women had given up their seats in Congress, including Democrats Patsy Mink of Hawaii and Elizabeth Holtzman and Bella Abzug of New York, who left the House to run unsuccessful Senate campaigns, and a number of others who simply stepped down, such as Barbara Jordan (D-Texas), Shirley Chisholm (D-New York), Martha Griffiths (D-Michigan), and Edith Green (D-Oregon).

Even as the public became more accepting of women holding public office and being given wider opportunities in journalism, there remained an undercurrent of fear of what was viewed as potentially destructive social change.

Women had proven they could succeed in what had traditionally been considered male areas, but many people worried that women's success would come at the expense of children and family and that women would take men's jobs. The media often seemed to reflect this concern for preserving the status quo. Women's issues were not seen as a legitimate area of concern in the early 1970s, and in fact were often ridiculed in the press and on the floor of Congress. Female candidates still were portrayed in the media as exceptions and anomalies. Sometimes these stereotypes helped them. As outsiders, women were considered likely to be more honest and idealistic and less corruptible than men. "Because you are a woman you may have the ability to gain more than your fair share of press and media coverage," Schroeder told the National Women's Political Caucus convention in 1973, "because you are the different candidate. But the other side of the coin is that you will often be more severely cross-examined on your views and statements by news people than is the average male candidate."

Of course, as Jeane Kirkpatrick has written, a woman running for office by necessity must run as a woman because she *is* a woman. "Sexual identity is an irreducible, ineffable part of the self. We are all either male or female." Women who say they don't campaign as women mean, Kirkpatrick said, "they don't emphasize female identifications any more than male candidates emphasize male identifications." Although women candidates may not emphasize their female attributes, the media often do. Journalists' questions relating to physical appearance or dress and/or family responsibilities may be considered irrelevant by women candidates yet will help shape a candidate's image. "That image often exists in spite of the candidate's stand on issues, qualifications, merit, ability or intelligence," observed Suzanne Paizis, who was unsuccessful in her effort to become the first woman elected to the California Senate.

Some things were changing. Kirkpatrick says that in the past, women more frequently felt compelled to reassure voters that they could be as rational as men. But in the 1970s women candidates would no longer be caught dead saying they "could work like a horse and think like a man." Yet they still walked a tightrope, searching for the right balance of qualities. They knew, for example, that "too much aggressiveness is not acceptable in a woman." It was an era characterized by extremes. On one hand, women were riding a tide of opportunity, moving into the work force with expectations of equal opportunities and equal treatment. But a strong undertow of fear of social change was pulling society the other way. Patsy Mink's encounter with Edgar Berman could be considered emblematic of the struggle to define a woman's role in politics.

Mink was arguing before the Democratic National Priorities Committee in 1972 that the right of women to be policymakers should be at or near the top of the party's list. Edgar Berman, a committee member, objected, saying that "physical and psychological inhibitants" limit a woman's potential to move into the upper echelons of business and politics. In particular, he cited "raging hormonal influences" relating to women's menstrual cycles and menopause. Mink demanded—and got—Berman's resignation from the committee. She called his statement a "disgusting performance," saying the effect was to caricature all women as neurotic and emotionally unbalanced. She said Berman's words were "as indefensible and as astonishing as those who still believe, let alone dare state, that the Negro is physiologically inferior." Berman resigned but got the last word. He said Mink's anger was a "typical example of an ordinarily controlled woman under the raging hormonal imbalance of the periodic lunar cycle." *Time* magazine headlined its story "Hormones in the White House."

Meanwhile, Martha Griffiths was engaged in one of the great success stories of Congress—passage of the Equal Rights Amendment after it had been stalled for nearly fifty years. The amendment, intended to outlaw discrimination based on sex, had first been introduced in 1923. It was reintroduced every Congress thereafter, but for decades it had been bottled up in the House Judiciary Committee chaired by Emanuel Celler, who had refused to hold hearings on it, much less bring it to the floor. Griffiths managed a rarely tried parliamentary maneuver to bring the measure to the floor without committee approval and won passage by the House in 1970. The measure died in the Senate, but Griffiths was back at work the next year. She again persuaded the House to pass the amendment, and the Senate approved it on March 22, 1972. The second time around, Griffiths was joined in the fight by her newly elected colleague Bella Abzug, who not only urged support for the amendment but criticized the House for discriminating in committee assignments. "It is absolutely indefensible that the committee which considers the questions of equal rights for women—the Judiciary Committee—has not a single woman member to represent our interest."

Although Griffiths fought discrimination in job practices and inequitable laws, other women—such as Abzug—often got headlines while Griffiths remained relatively unpublicized. "It doesn't bother me when they say I'm not militant enough," she told an interviewer later, "but how could anyone say I'm 'not with' today? What do they mean? I *made* today." Sometimes when she was mentioned in the press, the words used to describe her were not exactly flattering. Jack Anderson, for example, wrote in his syndicated column that Griffiths had "nagged" the Equal Opportunity Commission until it agreed to crack down harder on job discrimination against women, that she "has kept carping" and "complained" to the commission about inequality.

Some journalists seemed to want to reassure readers that even though Griffiths was a feminist, she was also a traditional woman. *Time*, for example, called her a "graceful feminist" and "firm but not fiery on the subject of women's rights." The news magazine reported that when her husband sent a dozen yellow roses to her office after the House passed the ERA, "Martha smiled and said quietly: 'It's nice to know my husband still loves me.'" *U.S. News & World Report* said Griffiths was "a soft spoken woman" who was "described by colleagues as reasoned in argument and modest in dress."

Women politicians had to perform a balancing act, trying to show themselves as assertive without being aggressive, committed without being emotional, confident without being pushy, and attractive without being too sexy. There was always the risk of being labeled a "women's libber," which had the same connotation of radicalism as the term "feminist" does today in some quarters. "On the issue of 'women,' female candidates walk through a minefield," wrote Ruth Mandel in her 1979 classic *In the Running*, "never knowing when a seemingly mild reference, or a personal decision to retain one's own professional name, or an old speech dredged up by the opposition will set off headline explosions."

Mandel illustrates her point with the story of Carolyn Warner's 1976 Senate primary campaign in Arizona. Warner played down feminism during her campaign, fearful it would cost her votes. She campaigned as a businesswoman and fiscally conservative administrator who had reduced paperwork and increased efficiency during her first two years as state superintendent of education. She played up her image as a wife and mother and played down her support of the Equal Rights Amendment—so much so that she failed to get enthusiastic backing from the state's feminist groups. But when Warner did make a feminist-sounding remark, the media pounced on it. Warner told a businesswomen's group that since the U.S. Senate was all male, "It's time a qualified woman was elected to the Senate." Her chief opponent, Dennis DeConcini, charged that "a political campaign has reached a new low when a candidate finds it necessary to appeal to race, religion or sex." The story made page 1 of the state's largest newspaper, the *Arizona Republic*, with the headline "DeConcini says Mrs. Warner begs election because of sex." "For those who had watched Warner's careful maneuvering around feminist issues, the headline could not have been more ironic," Mandel commented. Warner lost the primary to DeConcini by twenty thousand votes.

Newspaper headlines didn't always reflect it, but there was much talk among journalists during this period about how to cover women more fairly. Guidelines issued by the Stanford University Women's News Service in 1974 suggested ways to make media coverage more equitable—and thereby suggested the myriad ways in which the media were covering women differently from men:

> 1. A woman's marital status should not be indicated by a prefix attached to her name. First reference should include a person's title, if any, and given name. For example, Rep. Bella Abzug, D-NY, said today. . . .

Abzug stated. . . . Use of Mr. and Mrs. is limited to discussions which include a married couple where the last name only rule might cause confusion. Miss and Ms. should not be used at all.

2. Females over the age of 18 are "women," They are not "girls," "gals," or "ladies." Words like "homemaker" and "housewife" are not synonyms for "woman."

3. Gratuitous physical description, uncommon almost to the point of absence in news stories about men, should also be eliminated from stories about women. This rule does not apply with equal force to feature writing, especially profiles in which physical description is often an essential aspect. However, care should be taken to avoid stereotypical descriptions in favor of describing an individual's unique characteristics.

4. Similar considerations apply to the mention of an individual's spouse and family. In a news story, a man's wife and family are typically mentioned only in passing and only when relevant; the same practice should apply to news stories about women. And again, the practice is slightly different for feature stories and profiles but the test of relevance should always be applied.

5. Most achievements do not need sexual identification; those which do should be so identified for both men and women.

6. Avoid sins of omission as well as commission. If, for example, an expert is sought in a given field, or if an example is needed to make a point, women should be used in those cases as a matter of course—not simply as "oddities" or representatives of "a woman's viewpoint."

7. Women's professional qualifications or working experience should always be acknowledged.

8. The term *women's libber* should not be used. It has no informational content and is simply a blanket pejorative.

9. When you have completed a story about a woman, go through it and ask yourself if you would have written about a man in the same style.

Those suggestions were controversial in the 1970s. It was a struggle, for example, to get editors to abandon use of the traditional courtesy titles Mrs. or Miss. Reporters thought they shouldn't have to ask women their marital status if it wasn't relevant to the story. Eventually most newspapers began to refer to women in the same way as men, by last name without a courtesy title.

The changes slowly worked themselves into journalism conventions. As the women's movement helped change the political climate, newspapers changed too. When Connecticut representative Ella Grasso ran for governor in 1974, she was described by journalists as a "gubernatorial candidate" and a "congresswoman," not as "mother and housewife," which had been used during her campaign for Congress in 1970. And when Ann Richards was working on Sarah Weddington's campaign for the Texas legislature, she was described by the *Texas Observer* as the campaign's "political brain trust." Weddington said Richards was happy to be referred to in the media as a brain trust instead of a housewife.

In 1977 the Associated Press and United Press International issued a new joint stylebook prohibiting stories belittling the ambitions of women and forbidding gratuitous descriptions of women when a journalist offered no similar descriptions of men. "Women should receive the same treatment as men in all areas of coverage. Physical descriptions, sexist references, demeaning stereotypes and condescending phrases should not be used." Even so, newspapers and the wire services often violated their own rules against sexism. "We find many papers are internally inconsistent," said Bobby Ray Miller, who edited the stylebook. "It seems to be left up to the person in charge at any given time."

Similarly, for every example of more equitable news coverage, there was coverage that trivialized women and suggested strongly that if they were in politics, perhaps they were out of place. Three months before the Connecticut Democratic Party convention at which she would be nominated for governor, Ella Grasso told the *New York Times* her gender would not be a factor for voters, who would judge her on her accomplishments. Evidently that's not what the *Times* copyeditor thought. The front-page story was headlined "Woman Odds-On Favorite for Connecticut Governor." Although she was an established politician who had held public office without interruption for twenty years, the article downplayed her platform and record and contained several references to her height, weight, and what she wore. At one point the reporter described her voice as "trilling, as it sometimes does."

After a paragraph devoted to a description of her face, eyes, hair, and "rather toothy" smile, the reader encounters this: "Straight backed, 5 feet 8 inches tall and full figured, she fights to keep her weight at 135 pounds despite an unappeasable appetite for risotto, polenta and tortellini. In the Connecticut manner, her campaigning clothing is unobtrusive, suggesting garden clubs. This day, she was wearing a black velvet jacket, a white turtleneck sweater, gray slacks and buck walking shoes. Her only jewelry was her plain gold wedding band and a thin gold necklace."

Grasso tried to get the press refocused on the issues by giving facetious answers to questions about her clothes, but the *Times* reporter didn't seem quite sure how to take her response. This was his account: "'Oh I love clothes,' she said in reply to a question, 'but I never get a chance to go shopping.' Mrs. Grasso gives the impression of not taking herself with total seriousness at all times. Her voice took on a bantering tone when she said, 'That blue suit I was wearing the other night in Fairfield was a Halston. Didn't you notice?'"

In Congress, freshman Pat Schroeder had to fight two dragons in 1973—the chairman of the House Armed Services Committee, who attacked her for her lack of knowledge on military matters, and the news media, which sometimes trivialized her role. Determined to get up to speed on national defense, Schroeder went to the Middle East with a special congressional subcommittee over Thanksgiving recess. Although committee members met with Egyptian President Anwar Sadat and Israeli prime minister Golda Meir during the ten-day visit, the only footage that appeared on one television network showed Schroeder and some other members riding camels at an Egyptian horse show. She says it was the only tourist event of the trip.

On the other hand, television news did provide viewers with a glimpse of some strong women politicians—images that did much to counterbalance the media's sometimes stereotypical coverage of women. The presence of Barbara Jordan and Elizabeth Holtzman on the House Judiciary Committee during the 1974 Watergate hearings, for example, brought them into people's living rooms as serious and articulate investigators. The speech Jordan gave on July 24, 1974, as the Judiciary Committee opened its public deliberations on whether to impeach the president, in which she measured Nixon's actions against constitutional mandates, is still used to teach communications students about powerful speechmaking.

Jordan was also in demand as a guest on televised news programs throughout the spring as the committee met behind closed doors to review the evidence against President Nixon. After her speech, her photograph appeared in both *Time* and *Newsweek,* and the text of her speech was the only one carried in full the next morning on the *Washington Post* editorial page. Through the media—especially television, which could capture her deep, resonant voice and measured delivery—Jordan became a national figure. She appreciated the phenomenon. It was the first time, she says, that she had reached her audience with no one in between. Before that she had "long since been stereotyped by a press used to summing up secondary sources." Typical, she says, was a feature in the liberal *Texas Observer* in November 1972, which included this observation: "Aside from the vicarious kick a white lib can get from watching Jordan speak to a

Barbara Jordan (D-Texas) served on the House Judiciary committee that voted to impeach President Richard Nixon and earned a national reputation for public speaking.

new audience—they tend to snigger and assume that anyone who looks that much like a mammy is going to be pretty funny to hear—she's not much use as a token." Even the imperial Jordan could be taken down a notch or two with sexist and racist writing.

But for the most part, the news media treated Jordan with respect. She intimidated even veteran journalists. The *Wall Street Journal* termed her "majestic" and said in a front page profile that she had achieved "more honor and perhaps more power than most members . . . can look forward to in a lifetime." Meg Greenfield, now the *Washington Post* editorial page editor, said she couldn't remember ever being more apprehensive of an interview with a public figure. "The message is conveyed in her every word and gesture: Don't tread on me," Greenfield wrote. "And she is also known for a certain brusqueness associated with another minority group to which she belongs: that of very smart people who see the point long before others have finished making it and who have a low threshold for muzzy argument or political blah."

In 1976, Jordan was asked to be one of two keynote speakers at the Democratic National Convention. She was the first black and the first woman ever to keynote the gathering. "There is something different about tonight," she began. "There is something special about tonight. What is different? What is special? I, Barbara Jordan, am a keynote speaker. . . . I feel . . . that my presence here is one additional bit of evidence that the American dream need not forever be deferred." She received a standing ovation.

Almost immediately and throughout 1976, there was speculation in the media that Jordan might be the first black and female vice president or president, governor of Texas, speaker of the House, or member of the Supreme Court. Jordan did nothing to stop the speculation. In fact, she fueled rumors by answers such as the one she gave on a spring 1976 *Meet the Press*, when asked if the country was ready for a woman—particularly a black woman—as a vice presidential candidate. "The country is not ready, but it's getting ready," she said, "and I'll try to help it."

The media seized on her convention role as the personification of the American dream. The *New York Times*, for example, called it "a classic American success story," referring to Jordan as "a poor child of extraordinary intellect, driven by parents who sought a better life for their offspring." The *Washington Star* said Jordan bore "witness to a dream [Democrats] yearn to claim." And the *Houston Post* said, "A poor kid from Houston's Fifth Ward sealed her destiny as a national superstar." Jordan's appearance at the convention also provided an opportunity for millions of viewers to see a confident, articulate woman politician commanding the attention of party delegates.

But in addition to the upbeat poor-kid-makes-good kind of stories, inevitably some stories focused on everything but Jordan's message. A good example of trivial coverage appeared in the *Houston Chronicle*. After gaining weight in office, Jordan had dieted in preparation for the convention, and a few days after her speech the *Chronicle* ran a brief story about her weight loss headlined "A Svelte Jordan," with side-by side before and after photos of her. The story referred to her as "the trimmed down Jordan." Some politicians say any press is good press because it leads to enhanced voter recognition, and Jordan didn't complain about the photos. But her Republican opponent in the upcoming November election, Sam Wright, let the *Chronicle* have it for what he considered unfair and trivialized coverage. Wright wrote:

> During my uphill fight to unseat Rep. Barbara Jordan, I have had to sit by while my opponent has received national coverage as a vice presidential candidate, watched while she has been featured as a symbol for blacks and women and read her opinions on topics varying from Nixon's trip to China to Ford's chances for reelection. But when you recently printed a story focusing on her tremendous weight loss, and illustrated it with before and after photos, that was the last straw!
>
> How can a responsible candidate from a major political party get a fair hearing when his opponent's every word and action is splashed across the newspapers and his own candidacy is ignored? . . . I hardly think it is significant whether my opponent has lost weight or not—or at least it shouldn't be significant as regards her qualifications as a congressperson.

By 1977, at the start of her third term in the House, Jordan said she had finally gotten to the point where she could read that she was a national figure and not flinch, because people had heard of her all over the country. But she began to feel her future was not in politics. "I had a real sense that ultimately a woman or a black would be the President or the Vice President, but not now." So Jordan decided not to seek a fourth term and subsequently became a professor at the University of Texas at Austin.

Jordan's only female colleague on the thirty-eight-member House Judiciary Committee during the Watergate hearings was Elizabeth Holtzman, who had defeated the "unbeatable" Emanuel Celler, a New York institution who had sought reelection to a twenty-sixth consecutive term. Holtzman won the 1972 Democratic primary by a margin of only 610 votes out of more than 30,000 cast. In something of an irony, she was appointed to Celler's old place on Judiciary, even though she didn't want the assignment. At the time, no one knew that the committee would be overseeing Nixon's impeachment proceedings. As chairman of Judiciary, Celler had not only succeeded in burying the Equal Rights Amendment for years but he was also a fierce supporter of the war in Vietnam. Holtzman was both an ardent feminist and a strong opponent of the war. She was only thirty-one and a political novice when she filed to oppose him, and Celler commented, "As far as

I'm concerned, she doesn't exist." That summed up the overall media reaction to her candidacy as well.

Although she was basically ignored by the press for most of the campaign, she says it didn't hurt. "The newspaper and television people had to do stories on all the congressional races in New York, but they decided that all the others were much more interesting than mine . . . so what happened was that all the media coverage on my race appeared virtually in the last week of the campaign and that was really very helpful. In fact, we couldn't have planned it better." The *New York Times* endorsed her in the final days of the campaign. "Otherwise I wasn't endorsed—or newspapers endorsed my opponent," she says. Holtzman attributes her victory largely to the fact that she was a woman and a political outsider. Since she was the only woman campaigning on the streets, people remembered her, she says. When Jack Anderson wrote a column saying her opponent had received contributions from defense contractors, she had it reprinted and distributed on the streets and at subway entrances. Women were perceived as outsiders, not as politicians, and people were disgusted with politicians, she says. "They didn't see a woman as a politician, so that I was never perceived as being part of the backroom cigar-smoking machine."

Newspaper columnist Jimmy Breslin records this exchange with Meade Esposito, boss of the Brooklyn Democratic political machine, in his book *How the Good Guys Finally Won*, which deals with Nixon's downfall—and suggests just how male-dominated the machine was:

> I stopped into Woemer's Restaurant on Remsen Street in Brooklyn, just downstairs from Esposito's headquarters. And Meade, in a back booth, waved for me to sit down.
> "I don't know what to do, I can't get this freakin' Liz Holtzman out of the race."
> "Who is that?"
> "The broad running against Manny Celler."
> "Well, is it a fight or what?"
> "Nah. Shouldn't be a fight. It's just that this Manny, you know, he never comes around. And I hear this girl, she's got all kinds of young girls running around her. Indians. Freaking squaws. I've tried to talk her out of the race, but it looks like I can't do it. Maybe Manny better get his ass up here and see some people."

After the election and during her four terms in the House, Holtzman's relationship with the media was consistently "very professional and respectful." But she says it degenerated when she ran for the U.S. Senate from New York in 1980. New York changes reporters, she says. "They lose human perspective." But Holtzman also thinks that some reporters felt she had aimed too high, that "maybe it was okay if I was going to stay in my place [in the House]—but maybe I didn't know what my place was anymore."

Standards of acceptable behavior were different for women politicians than they were for men when she served in Congress, and she says they are still different. It's harder for people to accept women politicians asking tough questions, for example. Holtzman discovered that when she questioned President Gerald Ford about why he had pardoned former President Nixon for his role in the Watergate burglary. She was attacked by the *New York Daily News*. "I was respectful and polite," Holtzman says of her questioning. "But part of it is that you're not being feminine by doing it. I was not in my place. You don't do that."

Things hadn't changed much by 1992 when Holtzman again ran for the U.S. Senate and raised questions during the Democratic primary about her opponent's background. For targeting frontrunner Geraldine Ferraro, she was also harshly criticized. The media are "not helpful at all," she says. "To the contrary, the media is one of the big problems." Holtzman had been optimistic that stereotypes about women were changing in the early 1970s. "I thought when I was first elected to Congress in 1972 that it would be a very short process, but it's one of the deepest things—gender stereotyping, prejudice, bias. There's a lot of anger and resentment [at women]. I don't know how long it will take for that to change."

Holtzman says it doesn't seem to make any difference whether journalists are male or female. "I've seen situations where women reporters, to prove they're 'one of the boys,' would be sent in deliberately to do a negative story on their first big assignment. I saw that a few times. . . . I was the target." She prefers not to name reporters or newspapers, saying it happened at different papers and involved more than one reporter. But it has been difficult for her to become inured to critical stories and editorials. "I used to quote Eleanor Roosevelt that 'if you're going to be a woman in public life, you've got to have a skin as thick as a rhinoceros.' But even a rhinoceros's skin can be pierced. You take a cannon and you can get through that," she says. "Sometimes it feels like cannon balls coming at you. Some of it you can laugh off, but you realize it's very destructive and distortive."

Holtzman was the driving spirit behind formation of the congresswomen's caucus, an effort to bring together all women members of Congress in an informal structure, regardless of party, and she helped plan the national women's conference held in Houston in November 1977. Several other women's political organizations were founded during the 1970s, including the National Women's Political Caucus in 1971, to increase the number of women in elected and appointive office nationwide.

The caucus lacked resources to supply women candidates with funds or workers but was able to help with publicity, speakers, moral support, and occasionally political expertise. Perhaps as a result of women's increased visibility and their consensus on issues of particular concern to women, the media often lumped women together as a category. But some felt that was a step forward. "Some women candidates may object to being referred to in a collective bloc, but it is progress of a sort," said Jane McMichael, who was then executive director of the National Women's Political Caucus. "For the first time, they were around in enough numbers even to be noticed."

Numbers are relative. At mid-decade women represented more than half the national vote but had only token representation on the national level. No women served in the Senate between 1972 and 1978, when Nancy Kassebaum was elected. Only eighteen women were in the house in 1975, one less than the high of nineteen during 1961-63. By 1976, gender appeared to have become less of a factor in election campaigns, particularly in state legislative races, wrote Susan Carroll in her study of women candidates. "While gender was perceived as an important problem by a sizable proportion of women candidates, the overall effect of gender on women's campaigns appeared less one sided than the effects of money, people, time and party support. . . . In the aggregate, gender probably was not a major determinant of the outcome of women's campaign efforts."

Indeed, the novelty of being a woman proved to be more of an asset than a disadvantage to Nancy Kassebaum when she announced she would run for Kansas's open U.S. Senate seat in 1978. Kassebaum's theme was that, as the lone woman senator, she would bring a "fresh voice" to be heard in Washington. Kassebaum was candid with reporters about her relative inexperience, saying, "In a way, I'm sure I looked like Mary Poppins dropping out of the sky with her umbrella." Senator Bob Dole campaigned for her, telling voters that a woman would have immediate celebrity and instant clout, unlike other freshman senators. Local newspaper editorials and her own political ads promoted the idea that her victory would be a positive symbol for the state.

As the daughter of Alf Landon, Roosevelt's Republican challenger in the presidential election of 1936, Kassebaum was a member of one of the state's best known political families. But even her father discouraged her from running. "I think he worried about the publicity," Kassebaum said, "because my husband and I were separated. . . . He thought it would be very costly." As it happened, the breakup of her marriage was never an issue. And along with name recognition she apparently benefited from her gender. Commenting on her election, a *New York Times* op-ed piece said the "desire to make history in a respectably dramatic fashion and develop a new image may well explain the apparently successful projection of Nancy's womanhood and inexperience as assets." The *London Daily Mail* put it another way, saying Kassebaum had been elected not from a "trendy East Coast or West Coast state but from conservative Kansas, where a man's a man and a woman's his cook."

But some writers couldn't seem to get over the womanhood angle. *Christian Science Monitor* staff correspondent Louise Sweeney was one who squeezed it for every drop of femininity. "Senator Nancy—it is difficult not to call her that—is the sort of woman other women want to give their salt-rising bread recipes to, and men want to protect," the story began. Sweeney described Kassebaum as a "frail looking, soft-voiced brunette," spoke of her "fluffy, helpless image," and said she would be "a sole doe among 99 well-antlered stags, this woman with the soft brown eyes and gentle, unassuming manner."

There was novelty in the gubernatorial races of the 1970s too. For the first time, women ran for chief executive of three states on their merits—not as surrogates for their husbands, as their predecessors had. But beyond playing up the novelty of their candidacies, the news media did not necessarily help them get elected. Ella Grasso had served two terms in Congress when she defeated her House colleague, Robert Steele, to become governor of Connecticut in 1974, the first woman elected in her own right. The three previous

Ella Grasso served two terms in the U.S. House before being elected governor of Connecticut in 1974. Courtesy of the Connecticut State Library.

women governors—Alabama's Lurleen Wallace, Ma Ferguson in Texas, and Wyoming's Nellie Tayloe Ross—all succeeded their husbands in office. Grasso was the highest ranking woman official in the country and the only female governor. Although she tried to play this down, she attracted nationwide media attention, much of it focusing on the "woman" angle. But Grasso was also careful not to be labeled a feminist or to be too closely associated with the women's liberation movement. Her opposition to legalized abortion ran counter to the women's movement stance, although she swore to uphold the law. She was a moderate on most other issues.

In her favor was a squeaky-clean image. Like many of the post-Watergate candidates, male or female, Grasso was perceived as being an honest politician. Her gender worked for her too. Polls showed that many voters thought women were more honest than men. Grasso maintained her popularity despite imposing a series of spending cuts as a way of forestalling a state income tax. She was reelected in 1978 but resigned at the end of the year because of illness. She died a little over a month later.

Dixy Lee Ray of Washington, the second woman elected governor in her own right, in 1976, felt that she had been persecuted by members of the press. She was often attacked for being too eager to encourage development. "Ray feuds with local political writers, charging unfair treatment," said an article in *Time*. "At times, the *Seattle Post-Intelligencer*, which supported Spellman [her opponent] during the election, does seem to delight in baiting her." Ray, in turn, refused to grant interviews to two of the newspaper's correspondents, saying they fell into the category of "radical extremist environmentalists." One of her biggest public fights was with university administrators and academicians, who criticized her for supporting the legislative movement to cut the budgets of state universities. Ray had charged that Washington was acquiring a reputation as a "degree mill state" where faculty tenure protected "the mediocre and incompetent." In fact, she herself was a marine biologist with a Ph.D from Stanford who had been a zoology professor at the University of Washington until her election.

Ray had also served as chair of the Atomic Energy Commission, where she was known for her outspokenness. She attributed her appointment by Presi-

Dixy Lee Ray battled with the press throughout her term as governor of Washington state. She was elected in 1976.

dent Nixon, for instance, more to the effect of the women's liberation movement than to her scientific qualifications. "I was appointed because I was a
woman and that's all right with me," she told an interviewer soon after she was
nominated. Being a woman—and a single woman at that—seemed to make
her a media curiosity. The *Wall Street Journal*, for example, implied she was a
mystery because she was "a single woman, now aged 63" and said Washingto-
nians were trying to figure out what to make of "the portly woman with the
close-cropped hair." *Time* described her as a "stubby and sturdy woman" and
said, "When she is in the mood, she radiates a charm that makes her seem like
a benevolent pixie, a chubby (5 ft. 4 in., 165 lbs.) Peter Pan." But *Newsweek*
got it right in a story headlined "Lady with a Chainsaw," which started: "When
Dixy Lee Ray left her mobile home on Puget Sound to run for governor of
Washington, the major newspapers opposed her, her foes chuckled, and just
about everyone predicted the state was not ready for an unmarried woman
who gave herself a chain saw for Christmas."

Ray didn't exactly cultivate members of the press. In fact, following a
feud with the media during her first few months in office, she declined to hold
press conferences, though her predecessors had made a point of having them.
She also refused to give interviews over the phone and had only a part-time
press aide whom reporters found hard to contact. *U.S. News & World Report*
said the governor sent reporters a pink cake with a "Love and Kisses, Dixy"
note after one blowup. "Some say it was a let-them-eat-cake expression."

Her press secretary, Duayne Trecker, quit and charged her with failing
"to consider her obligation to the public, to keep the public informed." Ray
countered that she made herself available to constituents at town meetings.
"The average person in a town hall doesn't ask tough questions," Trecker said.
"It's really not opening up the governor's office to the people. The governor
won't get over her insecurity until she learns to face the press, slug it out with
tough questions and go away with a smile."

Near the end of her term, the governor got in a lick at journalists, naming
a litter of eleven pigs after members of the press corps. "Dixy Calls Pigs Newsmen," read the headline in *Mother Jones* magazine. She named one of the
piglets Al Gibbs after a *Tacoma News-Tribune* reporter, telling the press "with
a chuckle" that he was already auctioned off for slaughter. But the governor
didn't name a piglet after *Seattle Post-Intelligencer* reporter Shelby Scates,
who had been a relentless critic, saying, "Any pig farmer comes to love pigs."

Ray expressed her feelings about the media at a news conference a week
after she was defeated for renomination in Washington's Democratic primary.
She said she had been "victimized by a deeply biased press that opposed me
from the day I filed for office and never let up." Her anger at the press was
prompted in this case not by her electoral defeat but by publication of a made-
up article about her in the *Portland Oregonian*. The story purported to be an

account of an exclusive interview that *Oregonian* reporter Wayne Thompson had with the governor after the primary. Both had tape recorders going. Hers worked. His didn't. Thompson pieced together the story from memory and his handwritten notes. But most of the statements attributed to Ray in the story turned out to be *his* statements. After the governor's press conference, the *Oregonian* checked out the matter and ran a front-page story apologizing to Ray and retracting material it considered "false and distorted." Thompson also wrote an apology, carried on the front page, and was suspended for two months. He attributed his mistakes to overstrain. The governor later commended the *Oregonian* for its speedy corrective action, calling it "the only honest paper in the Pacific Northwest."

Ray and Grasso had proved that women could be elected as governors without following their husbands into office—and without necessarily being somebody's wife. The public would not have to wait another fifty years for a woman to be elected governor in her own right. Nor would Nancy Kassebaum remain for long the only woman in the Senate. By the end of the 1970s the stage was set for what would be billed by pundits as a new "decade of the woman."

❖ *Chapter 6* ❖

BATTLING BELLA

ONE OF THE HEROINES OF THE WOMEN'S POLITICAL MOVEMENT, NEW YORK REPRESENtative Bella Abzug, is outspoken and assertive and regularly challenges the status quo. When she ran for Congress in 1970 she had a clear idea of her objectives, which included trying to stop the war in Vietnam and changing laws to provide equal treatment for women. She hit the floor running, introducing a resolution on her first day in the House that demanded an immediate end to the war. But much of her press coverage created a stereotype of her as strident and bellicose. She was frequently described in terms that might not have been used for a man. "I've been described as a tough and noisy woman, a prizefighter, a man-hater, you name it. They call me Battling Bella," Abzug wrote in a journal of her first year in Congress in 1971. "But whatever I am . . . I am a very serious woman."

Looking back, she says the news coverage she received couldn't have been any other way because the media tend to caricature people and exaggerate things. "So that if they see you're a strong woman, you're abrasive and aggressive and so on, and if they see a man he is courageous and dynamic and bold. Those are entirely different adjectives for the same person, male or female." Abzug says that happens because journalists "are largely spokespersons for the status quo. They're not spokespersons for change."

More women had begun working in the media at that time, but not enough to make a difference, says Abzug. She was the first woman member of Congress invited to address a luncheon of the National Press Club, but the club had not yet opened to women journalists, who were made to sit in the balcony if they were covering a speech. Club members presented Abzug with the traditional gift they gave speakers—a necktie with the club seal on it.

Some of the women who covered her were very conscious of being women and reflected a woman's point of view, while others tried to be objective in their reporting. But Abzug believes women journalists should promote women's issues, and she calls the word *objective* "pure nonsense." She knows most reporters don't agree with her, but she feels strongly about this. "It doesn't matter what area you're in, if there are things you care about, then you care about them through your profession."

It wasn't that Abzug lacked press attention. Quite the reverse—the media buzzed around her. "I did a lot of things, so there was a lot of press coverage. . . . I came in pretty determined to stand for the things I thought were crucial and I continued to do it," she says. "I don't think there's any question that the media attention made me very well known, and made it clear what I stood for, to my constituents and to people all over the country." But at the same time, she believes she was stereotyped. "The press tends to be very one dimensional, think in one dimension—and nobody is one dimensional."

Much of her coverage focused on her unconventional demeanor. Journalists generally seemed fascinated with her tough veneer, which included conversation liberally sprinkled with four-letter words—unusual in women's speech in those years. Norman Mailer reportedly said Abzug's voice "could have boiled the fat off a taxicab driver's neck. It was as full of the vibrations of power as those machines which rout out grooves in wood." But many trivial references to her appearance or behavior diverted attention from her legislative work. In fact, Abzug's media coverage represents a mind-numbing example of how women who don't fit stereotyped notions of femininity are distorted by the media and judged by different standards than men.

Abzug provoked extreme reactions, apparent in this *National Review* article: "Say it softly under your breath, abzug, abzug. Bella wallows out of the sound, her mammoth, sluggish hips ridiculing a body's natural ball and socket litheness. Abzug, abzug: the strange, hooded, leering, Mongoloid eyes. Abzug: the too many teeth, which are certainly all there, yet seem gapped, now above, now below. Abzug: the demagogue's rhetoric, husked out in a voice which cannot be categorized by sex, gross and shameless as the thing itself. This grossness is a tool, used as Belle Barth used grossness. To shock. After all, what you can't cosmetize must be made a virtue." The author, D. Keith Mayo, also refers to Abzug's "always male hats, with the testosterone sucked out of them. The butch haircut. She wears a necklace *underneath* her drab, brown dress; you can see one or two pearls at Bella's thick nape. Introduced as 'wife and mother,' Bella Abzug looks like Jacob Javits in drag."

Abzug was a liberal Democrat, on the other end of the political spectrum from *National Review,* but that doesn't excuse such savage writing. Abzug took a battering because she had so clearly stepped over the line defining appropriate female behavior and keeping women from speaking out. She was a wife and mother who didn't act like Donna Reed. She was a legislator who pushed hard for her bills. She used profane language that was considered unladylike, the same language many male legislators routinely used. She didn't make an effort to charm her male colleagues; she had her own forceful and direct style.

Abzug clearly made some men uncomfortable in the 1970s. But former president George Bush's comment about her in 1995 indicates the persistence of old fears about women who step out of traditional roles. During a visit to China that coincided with the United Nations Fourth World Conference on Women, Bush said he pitied the Chinese for "having Bella Abzug running around China." In a speech, Bush said Abzug had "always represented the extremes of the women's movement." Abzug said it was a cheap shot. "Bella-bashing may be good old boy sport, but in this case he's denigrating the work of 35,000 women and 180 governments dedicated to making the lives of half the world's population better. . . . George Bush stands forever in what used to be. The very thought of this conference succceding, which it is, must be terrifying to him."

Representative Bella Abzug (D-New York) was an outspoken member of Congress who often made news.

Bush's comment was reminiscent of former vice president Spiro Agnew's effort to demean Abzug at a Maryland fundraising dinner twenty-five years earlier. UPI reported Agnew's remark: "Republicans should work for adoption of environmental programs, welfare and revenue sharing and most importantly, we have to keep Bella Abzug from showing up in Congress in hot pants."

Sexism permeated stories about Abzug even without the help of prominent newsmakers. But she doesn't blanket-bash the media. For one thing, extensive coverage improved her name recognition among voters. "I swear I could run for anything in the Bronx and get elected," she said after being mobbed on a shopping trip during the 1970s. "Those people obviously do a lot of TV watching. How else do you explain strangers coming up to you as if they had known you all their lives?" And she says the media came close to being accurate. "They got a part of it. They got the fact that I was honest and forthright," she says, "and the rest was an exaggeration of style which always tends to negate the more positive."

How did she respond to unfair or exaggerated news reports? "I didn't even try," she says. "If asked to comment, I would." Occasionally she would write an op-ed piece circumventing the filtering mechanism of the press. The *New York Times* headlined her March 1972 commentary, "The House of Semi-Representatives." She began this way: "If a man from Mars were to visit Capitol Hill and take the term House of Representatives literally, he would conclude that the United States is a prosperous land of small towns, farms and suburbs occupied by middle-aged and elderly white men who are lawyers, bankers, businessmen, and occasionally, teachers or journalists. Many are quite rich. No one under thirty lives there. No veterans of the Vietnam War. It has an insignificant number of women and black members."

Because she was so outspoken, she was quoted often, and some of her colleagues resented her taking center stage. She was also criticized for being a media darling and not attending to the details of legislative work. "Many of her male colleagues, jealous of her ability to attract press coverage, regard her as a creature of the media, more interested in showboating than in doing the hard, anonymous behind-the-scenes work," wrote two journalists who studied women in politics in the 1970s. Abzug shrugs off such criticism. "You haven't got much choice if you're a powerful, active person," she says. "You don't determine if the press is going to cover you or not. They're obviously going to cover you if you're doing things." In fact, Abzug had become so well known by the end of her first year in Congress that she made it into the *New York Times* Sunday crossword puzzle. She was 66 across. Hint: "Bella Abzug is one." Answer: "Woman of the House."

Abzug first ran for Congress in 1970 with the goal of ending the war in Vietnam. She challenged incumbent Leonard Farbstein for her party's nomination and won both the primary and the general election. She didn't have money to buy television ads, and the media were slow to realize that she was a viable candidate. So, using the catchy campaign slogan "This woman's place is in the house—the House of Representatives," Abzug campaigned in the Greenwich Village neighborhoods of her district. As she tells it, she would stand on the sidewalks near a big housing project with a microphone and speak up to the windows. "People would open their windows and listen to me and that's how I won the election." She was helped by hundreds of volunteers from Women Strike for Peace and members of the Democratic Club where she lived.

Her success in the primary attracted national media attention—a hint of the publicity she would soon attract on the Hill. Abzug herself acknowledges that her bid for a major office was "sufficiently novel" to attract press attention and volunteer workers. She understood the value of symbols for the media, and so she was rarely seen without her trademark wide-brimmed hat. Much has been made of the symbolic value of Abzug's hats, which enhanced her name recognition. But she was anything but a traditional hat-and-white-gloves woman. She started wearing a hat after graduating from law school because there were so few women lawyers that she was often mistaken for a secretary. Since professional women wore hats, she says, "they always knew I was there for business." She kept on wearing one simply because she liked to wear hats, she says.

It was so rare to see Congresswoman Abzug without her hat that such a sighting led a campaign roundup story in the *New York Times*. It seems that Abzug's straw hat—the summer version of her usual floppy felt headgear— was snatched from her head by a man who identified himself as a Republican. Abzug was only briefly bareheaded as campaign workers chased the man into a café, retrieved the hat, and replaced it on Abzug's head. Later that year one of her hats was again in the news when a man purchased it at a fundraiser for the Manhattan Women's Political Caucus.

A good illustration of Abzug's media savvy came on January 3, 1971, the day she was sworn in as a member of Congress—two times. The first was an official ceremony in her office. But Abzug understood how to make the most of the moment. After the official swearing in, she went to the steps of the Capitol, where her colleague from New York, Representative Shirley Chisholm, swore her in again with hundreds of supporters looking on. Abzug dubbed this the "people's oath," gaining nationwide media coverage. It was a strong state- ment, she says, designed to focus attention through the mass media on the fact that women were in Congress. Abzug and Chisholm were among only twelve women in the U.S. House while Margaret Chase Smith was serving her last term, the only woman in the Senate.

In her acceptance speech, Abzug promised to work toward ending the war in Vietnam and refocusing the nation's resources on solutions for domes- tic problems. On her first day in Congress she introduced a resolution calling for the withdrawal of all troops from Southeast Asia by July Fourth. Later that year the House finally passed a watered-down resolution to require the war to end within two years.

Abzug often made news as she introduced bills but was not always suc- cessful in getting them passed. She tried unsuccessfully to end the military draft, for example, and a bill she co-sponsored with Chisholm to fund twenty- four-hour affordable child care was passed by both houses but vetoed by Presi- dent Nixon. Her style tended to be confrontational ("I took off the gloves a long time ago") and she was labeled "abrasive" and "strident." A hurricane was named "Bellicose Bella" after her. "Had I been a male politician with my record of accomplishment in Congress and the movements for social change, the adjectives would have been transformed into 'strong,' 'courageous,' and 'dynamic,'" she says.

Actions that seemed out of the norm for a member of Congress were extensively covered—to the point that legends grew up about her. One story, which she vehemently denies ever happening, involved House doorkeeper

William "Fishbait" Miller. The Associated Press reported that Abzug told the doorkeeper to perform an "impossible sexual act" when he told her she couldn't wear her famous floppy hat on the House floor. "What the Associated Press doesn't understand, besides the fact that this is absolutely untrue," said Abzug, "is that I'm not there to fight about my hats, and if I were, the last guy I'd fight with is Fishbait Miller."

Other brief articles appeared about Abzug's use of profanity. She "responded to a suggestion that she take a spot on the Agriculture Committee with an expletive meaning male animal manure," the Associated Press reported. "I suppose I should deny it, but who would believe me?" she wrote in her journal. "I'm a very spontaneous and excitable and emotional person, and I do have a way of expressing myself pretty strongly sometimes. Big deal. I don't see where it matters. What matters—all that matters—is that I say what I feel, and I always do *that*. The press is stupid to get all excited because I'm prone to use a few choice words now and then." She says the stories about her grew out of the press's tendency to exaggerate and stereotype women politicians. "The press is always the good Bella; the bad Bella, the loud Bella, the talk Bella," she says. "That's all baloney. The press has to try to caricature people." While this is true for both men and women politicians, Abzug says it has been more of a problem for women because the press has dealt with such things as their appearance, tone, style, hair, and personal lives.

The same sort of thing happened at New York's Inner Circle Press Club annual dinner during her first term in Congress, when she was spoofed along with local male officials. It wasn't her politics but her figure that was satirized. The *New York Post* reported the lyrics of the song about her: "I guess I've never been the high-fashioned kind, Mother Nature gave me a big behind. Wherever I go, I know I won't fall flat. When I just wear my hat. . . ." Abzug said she was willing to have her political views parodied, but that she was the only official whose physical appearance was joked about. It is a "reflection of a male approach to women that dictates that if you're not gorgeous, svelte and sexy, you're somebody to make fun of. And if you are gorgeous, then that's all they see." Abzug said none of the men were lampooned for their looks but for what they stood for and what they believed in. "But I as a woman was considered fair game to be ridiculed for what I look like."

The media emphasis on her appearance and behavior tended to obscure her achievements. One of her successful legislative endeavors, opening up government records, has had a significant impact on the press. The 1975 Freedom of Information Act, which had languished in a committee for twenty years until Abzug helped push it through, gives all citizens the right to see files the government has been keeping on their activities. It has proved to be a boon to writers, historians, and reporters who want to examine the workings of different branches of government. Abzug was also a strong supporter of the

Equal Rights Amendment to the Constitution, which was approved by Congress but died after failing to win ratification by enough states.

Abzug's reform efforts were not limited to legislative matters. One famous story concerns the time she and Representative Edith Green were swimming in the House of Representatives pool at 6 A.M. Women were not permitted in the pool between 9 A.M. and 9 P.M., when it was reserved for men, who swam nude. One day, Abzug says she remarked to the lifeguard, "I guess this place is really jumping later on." The lifeguard replied that very few people ever swam there. Abzug says she went to the head of the gym committee and said, "Tell the boys to put their suits on. We're coming in." From then on, women members of the house were permitted to use the pool at any time.

The gender issue came into sharp focus in the media in 1972 when Abzug sought a second term in Congress. Her district had been carved up by the New York legislature, and Abzug protested that she was the victim of sex discrimination. So she challenged a six-term liberal, Representative William Ryan, for the Democratic nomination in his West Side New York City district. Ryan's record in Congress was similar to Abzug's in his opposition to the war in Vietnam and support for antipoverty and civil rights legislation, but Abzug made women's rights the primary focus of her campaign. "I speak for a developing political movement that is challenging the right of a small, white, male, upper-class elite to rule our land," she said at a press conference announcing her candidacy. Throughout the primary campaign, Abzug argued that she was the more effective leader because she was an activist for women's and minority issues. "I act as a pacemaker for my colleagues," Abzug said during her first televised debate with her opponent. She said she had helped organize a "new majority" of women, the young, and minority groups to bring pressure on Congress and on the Democratic Reform movement itself, which "has not been sufficiently responsive to change." Ryan believed women should be able to run on an equal basis with men, "but not just because they are women. . . . I disagree with her on this thing. It is paranoid to have to support a woman."

Abzug's strategy divided the women's rights movement, and the conflict was played out in the press—both in the news columns and on the op-ed page of the influential *New York Times*. She was criticized as "predatory" and "power hungry" by the New York newspapers. "Bella Abzug forces women to make a painful choice: to vote against a woman," wrote Jean Faust, founding president of the New York chapter of the National Organization for Women, in a letter to the *Times*. "As much as we would like to see a woman in office, we cannot join in the defeat of a man who has a fine record on women's rights." Faust highlighted Ryan's record on issues of interest to women and noted that his staff in New York and Washington was predominantly female. "Yes, Mrs. Abzug has an 'equal right to run'; but women have the right—and the responsibility—to oppose female chauvinism as much as male chauvinism. As voters, we'll decide on the record and on the issues. We'll vote for the better candidate—even if he was born a man."

One of Abzug's supporters responded, saying the women's political movement "has progressed to the level where it will no longer be content with male surrogates." Elizabeth Harris wrote in a letter published on the *Times* op-ed page that the allegations of female chauvinism were ludicrous in light of the fact that only 12 of the 535 members of Congress were women. It was "not likely that any congressman . . . will voluntarily step aside to make room for women in our national legislature." Harris also pointed to a double standard at work: Only Abzug's challenge of Ryan's seat had generated such animosity, she noted, even though, as a result of reapportionment, liberals were in contest all around the country, including other New York districts. "She is one of the founders of the National Women's Political Caucus, which has attracted a following of thousands of women in 45 states. These women are not playing games, nor will they fade away and leave it to the men to introduce bills or write letters in their behalf. They are fully capable of doing that themselves."

The debate was joined by Betty Friedan, whose book *The Feminine Mystique* had been published in 1963 and helped give rise to the women's movement. Writing in the August 1972 *McCall's,* Friedan urged women to work with men, not against them, and she criticized Abzug and Gloria Steinem, the writer and lecturer who had become a highly visible spokeswoman for women's causes. "The assumption that women have any moral or spiritual superiority as a class—this is male chauvinism in reverse; it is female sexism," Friedan said. Obliquely referring to Abzug, Friedan continued, "Only a female chauvinist would say that no matter how good a man's record—on peace, on women—women must support a female opponent just because she is a woman." Friedan called a press conference in New York to elaborate on her article. In response, Abzug's office issued a statement that said, "Once again, Betty Friedan has exercised her right to be wrong. I've never asked anyone to vote for me only because I am a woman."

Reaction to the brouhaha, reported in the press the next day, included exasperation and indignation from within the women's movement. Women were said to be split over the question of whether to support women in political campaigns just because they were women or because of their stand on issues. "There are women running who just want a piece of the pie," said one woman, "and then there are women who want to change the pie."

It was a natural for media coverage—conflict personified in two strong women. But back of headlines such as "Feminists Scored by Betty Friedan" or "Mother Spanks Offspring" floated two serious questions: How much attention should the media give to gender when women are running in political campaigns and serving in public office? How much responsibility do journalists have for perpetuating stereotypes about women politicians?

Abzug lost the Democratic primary to Ryan, but in an odd twist Ryan died in September and Abzug was selected to take his place on the ballot in the general election. Ryan's widow ran on the Liberal Party ticket. Abzug eventually won the election but poured out her anger at the press during the latter part of the campaign. She told an interviewer the press had been the worst of all, "because it's all-male, baby, and they feel threatened by me." She charged that the press should have reported that Representative Ryan had cancer because everybody knew about it anyway. Actually, even Ryan's physician had denied it publicly. Abzug also disliked the way the press rated her and Priscilla Ryan as equals. But Abzug did receive extensive attention, such as the *Life* magazine cover photo of her captioned "Women in Politics" the weekend before the primary.

Abzug served three terms in the House before declining to run in 1976 in order to seek New York's open Senate seat. After losing the Senate primary to Daniel Patrick Moynihan, she lost a bid for the New York mayoral nomination the next year and was unsuccessful in two subsequent attempts to return to Congress. When she ran for the Senate in 1976, newspapers seemed fascinated by what appeared to be the softening of her image. There were many references in the press to the "*new*" Bella." But two weeks before the primary, the *New York Times* reported that she would not support Moynihan if he won the Democratic primary. (Abzug says what she really said was that she would not support him unless he clarified his position on the Nixon administration.) But the *Times* said the "nearly unanimous reaction of Democratic politicians" was that "after a year of the 'new' Bella biting her tongue and being nice, the 'old' Bella emerged . . . and got the 'new' Bella in trouble." The following year, when she ran unsuccessfully for mayor, she used her "Bad Bella" reputation to portray herself in her political ads as "a fighter," one who knew how to be both tough and soft.

Abzug's style had mixed results. On one hand, her exposure in the news media allowed mass audiences to see a woman politician being confrontational and bold. Her high visibility helped give the idea of women in politics national exposure. But on the downside, other women candidates were compared with her in an effort to make them back off. Ruth Mandel, in her book about women in politics in the 1970s, says that Abzug "more than any other female candidate has been seen as a warning about what happens when a woman cannot escape a negative image after having been labeled as 'too ambitious' and 'too aggressive.' Abzug's aggressive style has been held up as a symbol of bad behavior, and her image as a fighter has caused some backlash for other women candidates."

Actually, Abzug's media image was quite different from the image she presented in person. She was an ardent campaigner and related well to crowds of people. The contrast was especially startling for voters in rural upstate New

York, where she campaigned during the 1976 Senate race. Abzug was able to capitalize on her negative advance image in an area where she was not personally known because, as Mandel wrote, she "came across well in person when people could see there was more to her than her press portrayal." Although she was already known throughout the state and nation, Abzug says her direct one-to-one campaigning and her political advertising "helped show I was more than one dimensional."

After three terms in the House, Abzug says she grew tired of reading articles about how she used four-letter words, was confrontational, and bullied her staff. Although she has not held elective office since, she has remained active in public life. Has she ever developed a thick skin about what the media say about her? "You're always sensitive. You know, we're human beings," she replies. "I've always said if they ever do an autopsy, there are all those little scars. If you're out in the public, you're subjected to certain scrutiny and certain description, and you have to expect that's going to happen. But the press likes to make greater conflict than exists. They like to exaggerate and they're one-dimensional."

Unfortunately the effect of Abzug's media coverage was to cause other politically involved women to steer clear of words or actions that might get them compared with her. Women candidates knew they were better off to refrain from "unconventional" behavior that might reap negative headlines. But until journalists put aside their templates of what is "feminine" or "masculine" behavior, women politicians won't be able to be themselves—bold or low-key, policy makers or detail people. And they may decide it's not worth the effort to get involved in politics.

Chapter 7

ARE WE THERE YET?

THE 1980S WERE SUPPOSED TO BE THE DECADE OF THE WOMAN. "BATTLING BELLA" and others had paved the way. The campaign to ratify the Equal Rights Amendment had been lost, but news coverage of the struggle to get it passed by Congress and then ratified by the states had made more people aware of women's struggle for equal opportunity and equal pay. As Betty Lall, a 1982 candidate for Congress from New York, put it: "A lot of people have been harboring thoughts they didn't articulate because they didn't think they were accepted thoughts. Now they are beginning to act on them. They saw the defeat of the ERA and they don't want to accept that defeat. They also see the country's in a mess and needs new people. Look at the composition of Congress—it's 88 percent men." After awareness comes change. In theory. But it would be 1992 before dramatic change occurred.

Admittedly, some things were different. News coverage began to reflect women in their own right; they were now often referred to by what they did rather than as someone's wife. Three female governors were elected and made national news: Martha Layne Collins in Kentucky, Kay Orr in Nebraska, and Madeleine Kunin in Vermont. Even the seemingly small change in courtesy titles used in news stories—from *Mrs.* or *Miss* to an optional *Ms.* and then to no courtesy title—made a difference in how women politicians were perceived.

Fifty-six women, more than ever, ran for congressional office in 1982. And one of the biggest political stories of the decade was the Democratic party's nomination of a woman for vice president in 1984, which elicited premature press proclamations of the "Year of the Woman." The same thing happened in 1988, when the media again proclaimed that the election of growing numbers of women signaled another Year of the Woman. But toward the end of the decade there was a growing awareness among journalists that an imbalance still existed between coverage of men and women and that coverage of women was still often distorted. In fact, because of changes made in how the media covered women during the 1970s, pressure on journalists to clean up their act had declined. Stereotypes lingered, even though more women were running for office. The number of women journalists was also increasing, but this didn't necessarily guarantee better coverage of women candidates and office holders. The two women serving in the Senate in the 1980s, Republicans Nancy Kassebaum of Kansas and Paula Hawkins of Florida, sometimes were lumped together in news stories simply because they were women and from the same party, even though Hawkins was far more conservative than Kassebaum.

Although women were being considered for top political offices, it was common knowledge that they had to act like men—or the way men were supposed to be—tough and strong. They had to avoid actions that might stereotype them as women. "Female candidates can win national office if they convince voters that they possess masculine traits and are competent on 'male' policy issues," concluded the authors of a study of women candidates. Female candidates have the difficult task of convincing voters, especially male voters, that they are different from the "typical" woman. "It is made more difficult by the media which perpetuates gender stereotypes by portraying male and female candidates differently."

Take the *New York Times* Sunday magazine profile of the three candidates vying for the 1980 Democratic nomination for Senate in New York to oppose Alfonse D'Amato. Four-term congresswoman Elizabeth Holtzman was competing with former New York mayor John Lindsay and former city Consumer Affairs commissioner Bess Myerson. At one point author John Correy differentiates between the female candidates this way: "Miss Holtzman was dining in a Chinese restaurant on the East Side, and she was wearing a cardigan sweater over a blouse with a round collar. It is difficult to imagine her wearing a plunging neckline or a skirt slit to the thigh. Miss Myerson became famous when she was named Miss America in 1945, stretching a size 34 bathing suit the night before her coronation and then getting sewn into it the next day. Miss Holtzman became famous on the House Judiciary Committee in 1974, peering intently through horn-rimmed glasses and asking questions about Richard Nixon and Watergate. Miss Myerson has been surrounded by men. She has competed with them, fought with them, and married and divorced two of them, one of them twice. Miss Holtzman is single. Once, this was a political liability. Now it is part of the political reality. Miss Holtzman is offering herself as a technician with the devotion of a Carmelite. She is supported by feminist groups, and unquestionably she is a woman of today. But a blouse with a round collar under a cardigan sweater says she is June Allyson and it is 1946. This is part of her appeal, too."

This is clever writing but at the expense of the women candidates. The author attempts to justify this sort of description with the paragraph: "What counts may not be so much what the candidates say but how they say it and what they look like. This is image. And as Louis Lefkowitz, former New York State Attorney General, says, 'organization doesn't mean a thing these days. What counts is image and the kind of campaign you run.'" But Holtzman sees Correy's reference to plunging necklines as an example of a double standard linked to female stereotypes. "As though that was a criterion! It was a put-down," she says. "I'd like to see some of the other senators in low-cut evening gowns, from Robert Dole on down to Alfonse D'Amato. Nothing is more threatening than an intelligent, well-educated, independent woman."

Dianne Feinstein, the former mayor of San Francisco who was elected to the Senate in 1992, spoke about the importance of avoiding actions linked to female stereotypes when she advised women who wanted to advance in professions formerly closed to them not to cry. Newspaper photos had shown Feinstein wiping her nose, trying to keep from crying in January 1983 during the announcement of a vote to recall her as mayor. Feinstein's advice was printed in *Working Woman* magazine in 1986: "Do not cry. Ever. If you've got to bite off your tongue or close your eyes so tight that nobody can see what's in them, do it. Because a man can cry and somehow it doesn't bother anybody. If a woman cries, it's an immediate, destructive thing that goes out and that everybody seems to remember."

Feinstein is right that tears reinforce stereotypes of women as the weaker, more emotional sex. Journalists have tended to interpret tears as a sign that a politician can't stand the heat. Maine senator Edmund Muskie's tears, shed in frustration over a newspaper's attack on his wife, contributed to his loss of the 1972 Democratic presidential nomination. The situation has changed some for men, though. Recently it has become "sensitive" instead of wimpy for male politicians to cry in public. Yet while men in the 1990s may be able to demonstrate their sensitivity through their tears, for women crying is still considered an overemotional response.

A decade ago when a male candidate tried to latch onto female traits to gain political mileage it sometimes backfired, as it did in the 1982 Michigan governor's race. Republican Richard Headlee, running against James Blanchard, was responding to claims that he was insensitive to women. Headlee said his opponent had only one child. "I have nine children," he said. "So who loves women more?" A local paper commented caustically: "On that basis, women should prefer to vote for Peter Rabbit."

At their best, the news media point out the ridiculous, the illegal, and the extreme. But media scrutiny of women candidates sometimes has seemed excessive and without justification. Geraldine Ferraro's treatment by the media after she became the Democratic vice presidential nominee is a classic example. *Newsweek* suggested that Ferraro had been "the victim of a hit job" by the press and had faced "one of the toughest media hazings a political candidate ever faced." But Ferraro wasn't the only woman subjected to what appeared to be overzealous media scrutiny during the 1980s. Roxanne Conlin, who ran unsuccessfully for governor of Iowa in 1982, is a case in point. Conlin, a former U.S. attorney who had worked in politics for twenty-two years, encountered many questions about the effect her gender would have on the race. "A party worker suggested, entirely seriously, that I gain a great deal of weight and 'wear sensible shoes and house dresses' in order to enhance my chances of winning," Conlin said. "The editor of a small weekly newspaper urged me, in print, to 'toss [my] pretty bonnet into the ring.'" In the June primary Conlin defeated two male opponents, the former chair of the state Democratic party and the 1978 Democratic party gubernatorial nominee.

Even more daunting was the media scrutiny of Conlin's tax situation, which she said was an example of gender bias. On July 1, Conlin released a financial statement, as promised, which showed that while she and her husband had a substantial net worth, they had owed no state income tax in 1981. Conlin's husband was a real estate broker, and 1981 was an unprofitable year for real estate, she explained. That's when the media dam broke. The *Des Moines Register*, which prided itself on being Iowa's statewide paper and setting the political agenda for the state, took up the issue of Conlin's tax situation. "It weighed in with daily coverage including eight front-page stories and numerous columns and editorials. It demanded that I provide them with copies of our tax returns for several years, which I refused to do. Besides violating my husband's right to privacy, such a disclosure would also have infringed on the rights of his partners," Conlin said. "The fourteen-year incumbent never revealed his tax returns, nor did my opponent until after my disclosure and the resultant furor."

The newspaper's attack on Conlin was so vicious it drew comment from other journalists, inside and outside the state. The *Wall Street Journal*, for example, ran an editorial entitled "*Register*'s Reputation On the Line in Iowa," which criticized the *Register* for setting aside its responsibility for laying out the candidates' stands on issues. "Did Mrs. Conlin's tax flap deserve all the attention it got, or did it become . . . the *Register*'s 'holy crusade'?" The *Kansas City Star* slammed the *Register*, saying it appeared to be punishing Conlin for telling the truth about her finances and that the *Register* was "waist deep" in "hypocrisy." "Despite record-breaking unemployment, low farm prices and a potential state deficit, the continuing stories on the 'tax issue' took their toll," Conlin said. "I dropped in the polls from 45 percent to 32 percent. Those who were uncomfortable with a woman candidate were handed an easy excuse to support my opponent."

Some people remained uncomfortable with the idea of women candidates through the 1980s. But for the majority, as Studs Terkel observed, the woman issue was a non-issue: "The issue is dead. The guys in the bar are ready for a Gerry Ferraro, a Pat Schroeder, or a Barbara Mikulski." Whether or not the public was ready for women, most female candidates were at a disadvantage in terms of media coverage simply because they were challengers, not incumbents.

A 1983 study of congressional campaign reporting said that challengers had a rougher time than incumbents in getting press attention. Candidates in open races didn't fare much better. Journalists avoided news about open races as though they were following two rules, according to the authors of *Covering Campaigns*: When the outcome is in doubt, support the traditional winner, and when newcomers are in an open race, stay away from the contest—don't risk identifying with the loser. The study also found that news coverage was more consequential than editorial endorsement in campaigns for House seats because campaign news runs with entertainment and other news, appears more frequently over a longer period, and carries "the mantle of objective reporting."

Just as women candidates suffered from lack of media coverage because they were challengers or newcomers, they shared another potential disadvantage with male candidates—the generally weak or favorable media coverage of officeholders. The first critical thing voters hear about incumbents usually comes from political advertisements, not the news media, says Timothy Cook in *Making Laws and Making News*. Cook says the Capitol Hill press corps is passive, favors incumbents, and therefore falls victim to incumbents' media strategies that emphasize name recognition stories. As a result of this neglect by journalists, almost 99 percent of incumbents are reelected to the U.S. House of Representatives. There need be nothing conspiratorial about this bias. . . . The information available to voters on candidates is simply too sparse to allow them to cast informed ballots," Cook writes. "Few members' records are scrutinized in the media."

Because women often were running against incumbents, it was particularly important for them to get their names out to voters through news coverage and paid media advertising. Name recognition was—and continues to be—especially important in statewide races where it is not possible to meet every voter personally. Money has long been a Catch-22 for women politicians. They haven't been able to win partly because they haven't had the money it takes to purchase paid media, and they haven't been able to get the money it takes for ads because fundraisers thought they couldn't win. Furthermore, women candidates haven't been able to count on news coverage until their campaigns have been legitimized by campaign contributions. Journalists use financial resources as an important criterion in determining the "viability" of candidates, i.e., whether they merit coverage. Enter Emily's List, a fundraising group founded in 1985 by Ellen Malcolm to try to get more women elected to Congress. Emily's List is an acronym for Early Money Is Like Yeast—and early money is what women candidates have needed to get the media and the voters to take them seriously.

Emily's List helps only pro-choice Democrats, but both parties finally got around to helping women run for office. The Democratic party created the Eleanor Roosevelt Fund, which contributed more than $300,000 nationwide to women running for state and local office between 1982 and 1986. That's a drop in the bucket considering that a single congressional campaign can cost millions of dollars. The GOP counterpart is the National Federation of Republican Women, an independent affiliate of the Republican National Committee that runs regional candidate seminars and recruitment programs aimed at funding and training women.

In 1988 for the first time both national party platforms contained planks endorsing women for office. The Democrats promised "full and equal access of women and minorities to elective office and party endorsement," while the Republicans committed "strong support for the efforts of women in seeking an equal role in government" and promised "vigorous recruitment, training and campaign support for women candidates at all levels." While such promises were only symbolic, they did send a sign that the major parties were ready to support female candidates.

Door to door campaigning had become a thing of the past in national races—unless the television camera was along, wrote Barbara Trafton in her 1984 book *Women Winning: How to Run for Public Office.* Trafton, a former Maine legislator and Democratic National Committeewoman, said that suggested a problem that men didn't have to consider: Women had to decide whether they wanted to appear "cool" or combative as they campaigned. Men didn't need to worry about that because their varying styles were accepted. Men may have had more latitude in style than women simply because of habit—voters were more accustomed to associating men with political office. But men, like women, may bump up against other parameters that limit how far they can go, such as concerns about age or health.

Out of the awareness of an imbalance in coverage came a news research and monitoring project called Women, Men and Media, co-chaired by Betty Friedan and Nancy Woodhull. Their first study in 1989 showed that women reported only 16 percent of the news on the three commercial networks and represented only 11 percent of newsmakers. The study covered women as correspondents on ABC, CBS, and NBC and as experts—including women politicians—on the nightly news. "Those of us who have thought long and hard about the media's impact on society frequently say that it mirrors society, but we know that the American media is not mirroring society," *Washington Post* columnist Judy Mann said at a 1990 journalism conference. "I look at news coverage of women, and I think I've wandered into the fun house at the circus. Women are distorted by the media. We are too tall in our aspirations, too short in our accomplishments, too thin in our talents, too heavy in our personal burdens. And a great deal of the time we simply don't show up in the mirror at all." Mann's comments came after the 1990 Women, Men and Media study showed that the number of women reporting network news had actually dropped to 15 percent while women accounted for 13 percent of newsmakers. Women did better on public television, where they participated in 40 percent of the stories as correspondents and 17 percent as experts.

At newspapers, representation of women had gotten slightly better by 1990, with an April study of the front pages of twenty newspapers showing that females were quoted in stories an average of 14 percent of the time compared with 11 percent in 1989. More women were featured in front-page photos, and there were slightly more female bylines. Another study of news magazines showed a slight increase in the number of female bylines between 1989 and 1990, with a slight decrease in the number of references to and photos of women.

Other studies confirm those findings. A survey of four newspapers by *Christian Science Monitor* staff writer Marilyn Gardner showed 30 percent more front-page women's bylines in a three-month period in 1987 than in the same period in 1982, but front-page articles and photographs featuring women were up only slightly over the five-year period. Of the four papers, the *Washington Post* had the most women's bylines while the *New York Times* had the least. The study found on average that only 6 percent of front-page stories in 1987 pertained to women, compared with just under 5 percent in 1982. Even when women did make front-page news, stories often treated them as victims or problems, the study said. One example: "Patricia Schroeder received more front page coverage for shedding a few public tears than she did for running a brief but respectable 'testing the waters' campaign."

Although the numbers showed slight improvement, they nevertheless indicated women's low visibility. Why weren't women politicians reflected more fully? There weren't very many of them, for one thing, and in Congress they had not attained the seniority that would propel them into committee chairmanships. It was unlikely that most reporters even thought much about gender balance as they looked for sources to interview. They still tended to gravitate first to male "authorities."

In Fairfield, Connecticut, George Dean, a retired advertising executive, founded a bipartisan, nonprofit group, 50/50 By 2000, to push for more women in public office. "I would watch MacNeil/Lehrer [NewsHour] and they would have on all these blue and black suits talking about abortion, education, health care and child care," he said. "Every once in a while they'd bring Pat Schroeder in. I thought it was really ridiculous not to have women participating in the leadership process." Dean's organization pushed for an equal number of men and women in Congress, on the U.S. Supreme Court, and in the president's Cabinet by the year 2000. Dean told a reporter he had not always been in favor of women's rights, and his comment suggested the subtlety of sentiment about women politicians. "I am probably the embodiment of one of the main problems in America: I never thought about it. That's almost worse than being an enemy. The Jesse Helmses of the world—they're easy to handle. You know where they are. They're out front."

Sometimes it seemed that headline writers went out of their way to write misleading heads concerning women. That's the conclusion of the Woman in the Newspaper project, which studied the *Austin American-Statesman* in the early 1980s. On June 20, 1982, for example, an article appeared with the headline "'Stupid' Texans lead fight for ERA." The headline was based on the story's opening paragraph, in which Hermine Tobolowsky described her testimony before the Texas legislature some twenty-five years before. She had supported a bill that would secure women's property rights, but, she said, "The senators said women were too stupid to control their own property."

Differences in the way journalists covered male and female politicians were revealed in a study by two political scientists, Kim Kahn and Edie Goldenberg. Looking at coverage of twenty-six Senate races in 1984 and 1986, they showed that reporters were likely to write longer stories about male candidates than about women and to cover the male candidates' platforms in greater depth. Also reporters were more likely to concentrate on women candidates' lack of campaign resources and raise questions about their political viability or to focus on what were perceived as stereotypically "female" issues such as drug abuse, education, the environment, and health care—even if the candidate stressed issues considered "male," such as foreign policy, defense spending, the economy, and farm issues. (Issues were classified as male and female based on stereotyping research conducted by a number of organizations, including Gallup and the National Women's Political Caucus.)

The study found that journalists tended to play up the "horse race" aspect and in close races wrote about the woman's relative lack of resources, campaign organization, and endorsements. In fact, the study showed reporters wrote twice as many articles about a female candidate's lack of resources as about a male candidate's. Ultimately such media coverage may cause voters to dismiss a female candidate as unelectable and noncompetitive, the authors concluded, saying patterns of press coverage may serve as a "critical obstacle" for women running for the U.S. Senate. The study also found that the reporter's gender influenced both issue and personality trait coverage, and that the presence of female reporters and the accompanying pattern of coverage might encourage more positive evaluation of candidates by voters. But the authors noted that female reporters were relatively rare; only 24 percent of the campaign articles in their sample were written by women.

History was made during the 1980s in governors' races, with the 1986 Nebraska race the nation's first gubernatorial contest in which two women representing major political parties ran against each other. Republican Kay Orr defeated Helen Boosalis, Democratic mayor of Lincoln. Two other women were elected governors, Martha Layne Collins in Kentucky and Madeleine Kunin in Vermont. They had different styles and backgrounds, yet both experienced media coverage that was biased and often focused on different factors than it would have if they had been male. The journalistic sexism they encountered wasn't always the kind that hits you between the eyes. "So much of it is subtle, says former governor Collins. "It's innuendo." When Collins was running for the Democratic gubernatorial nomination in 1983, for example, news accounts would often

Martha Layne Collins was elected governor of Kentucky in 1983.

refer to her appearance. Anyone who gets involved in politics can expect to be labeled, since it's a form of journalistic shorthand that simplifies a situation for the audience. But initially the media more often tagged Collins by her looks than by her other qualifications. "I was 'that icy blonde,'" she recalls. In contrast, the label "physician" used for her male opponent tended to connote professional stature. Even the national media bought the beauty queen label, although Collins was never Miss America; she had won a Kentucky Derby pageant twenty-five years earlier. *Time* mentioned Collins in its story about Walter Mondale's potential running mates: "Kentucky's first female governor is a former beauty queen who belies the old saw that pretty women can't think."

Stereotypes about women's roles carried over into Collins's four-year term as governor. Reporters who had not yet met the governor were likely to march right past her and introduce themselves to her cabinet secretary, Larry Hayes, mistaking him for the governor. "When a man walks into a room or building, he's considered a businessman, whereas a woman is not thought of as a businesswoman—she's a wife," Collins says. And even male reporters who knew who the governor was would frequently bypass her and talk to Hayes, or even seek out Collins's husband, Bill, a dentist, and quote him instead of the governor. "That was one of the most frustrating things to me," Collins says.

Hayes says gender was definitely a factor in the way journalists covered

Collins. "It seemed to me many times that the reporters, many of them, would have an undue interest in 'Doctor Bill'—even when the timeliness of the issues at hand dealt with government matters. If I was an amateur psychologist, I'd say there were some—particularly men—who probably gave a measure of credit of being successful in politics to her husband or [me]. . . . I think there was some question in their minds about how a woman could govern." But Hayes says Collins was actually "one of the best retail politicians" he's ever met—a governor interested in developing policy and in promoting economic development. Hayes says female reporters recognized that Collins was being held to different standards. "I watched them [during press conferences] and I could tell they flinched" when reporters' questions implied that women were not as capable. He noted that when Collins would get angry with male members of the press corps, "they would behave like kids in a classroom—and then they would say to me what was on their minds in language they were used to. . . . They were never in a position to have that kind of conversation [with the governor] because they never felt comfortable talking to their wife and mother that way."

Collins describes herself as a "closed-mouth person. I don't want to say something until I'm ready to say it." And she acknowledges that her reluctance to schmooze with the media probably hurt her in terms of media coverage. "Part of their frustration where I was concerned was that I didn't send up hot air balloons. I announced my game plan and I carried it out," she says. "There were periods of time when I was quiet. I didn't have anything to say to them." A good leader "maps out the strategy and leads. You don't take a poll and then run around in front and lead," she says, adding, "I don't think women bluff like men do. "

Another media practice Collins found frustrating was the way some journalists used remarks she considered off the record, or rushed to print a story without checking it out. "I find myself a bit on the defensive," she says. "As people I like them, but I wonder what their intentions are. I listen to their questions and I wonder what their ulterior motive is, where does this lead?" Collins still has difficulty understanding why the Kentucky media had such a field day with the story about installation of a tanning bed in the governor's mansion. Collins remembers emerging from a meeting with President Reagan early in her administration on issues important to the Commonwealth; the first questions two Kentucky reporters asked her related to the tanning bed. Collins still doesn't understand their news judgment. "Here are all these other [national] reporters with no idea of what they were talking about." Her cabinet secretary observes that it would not have been treated as such a big story if it had involved a man. "If Larry Hayes had had a tanning bed moved from Lake Cumberland to the governor's mansion, it wouldn't have had the same chuckle," he says. "Some reporters allowed themselves to think that defined the governor. If she had brought in a poker table they wouldn't have had a story."

Hayes says he doesn't think reporters intentionally played up the tanning bed story to trivialize the governor, but it's an example of the sometimes subtle ways in which the media defined the governor as a woman. Another example is the way the *Louisville Courier-Journal* referred to the governor as "Mrs. Collins" during the first part of her term. "I talked to someone about not doing that," Hayes says. "I felt like that somehow diminished her—when they used that term that somehow wrapped up everything about the family together, instead of setting her apart as governor." The newspaper dropped the courtesy title after several months.

In Collins's experience, media coverage didn't reflect much difference between male and female reporters. She says she'd like to think that women journalists could help other women succeed. "I'm not asking them not to scrutinize or not to be objective. But I think they should promote women. Lots of times they hesitate. They're afraid it shows a bias that would jeopardize their advancement." Even if a woman reporter wanted to do a favorable story, it would be difficult, Collins said, "because of the guys—they're kind of like Piranhas." For example, she says reporters "would try to catch you in the hall when you had your mind on something else and were least prepared. They would try to trap you," she said. "They were probably testing me to see how weak or strong I really was, how frustrated or confused. But instead of getting back to me, they printed it." Collins says reporters seemed more interested in making her appear indecisive than they were in getting solid answers to their questions. "If they were really interested, they would have said, 'If this is not a good time. . . .'"

Hayes said the governor's relationship with the media was "something that fed on itself. Martha Layne Collins felt like she had to have every answer to every question, that if she fell short she would somehow be the 'know nothing' governor that she assumed the press thought she was. She was much harder on herself because she sensed the press thought she did not have a real grasp on substantive matters of government—but she drove the priorities. She dealt with things at policy level. . . . Any other governor or businessman would be judged on results," Hayes adds. "The truth is anyone else could have been governor and Toyota would never have come to Kentucky. She had the ability to put things together."

Despite her differences with journalists, Collins says it wasn't all negative. "There was mutual respect by the end of my term. Maybe I helped them grow; they helped me grow." But Collins also says she hopes journalists consider the effect of their stories on young people who might be interested in going into politics. "It's not something that should be taken lightly." Journalists question politicians' motives, integrity, and credibility and are a powerful force, she says. "They form public opinion and set agendas. How do you compete with them? Whether its true or not, it's written and it goes down in history—how do you ever correct it?"

Near the end of her administration, Collins's husband was indicted and later convicted on federal extortion and tax fraud charges. She maintains his innocence. Collins says she and her husband didn't discuss running state government, and she is critical of the media for using innuendo to foster a perception that she was involved. She says it may have been done to discredit her. Successful women are sometimes perceived as a threat, she says, and some journalists think they have to put a woman "back in her place. Maybe that's one reason I was targeted. Maybe as a female I have not promoted my experience, my successes enough. I've been pushed back there. I happen to think it was done deliberately because I might be a threat to somebody. How much influence might I have had nationwide when I came out of the governorship? How would things have been different . . . if I had been able to put together a coalition?" Collins became a college president in 1990 and has stayed out of politics.

Madeleine Kunin got involved in politics after working as a journalist, so she has seen both sides of the fence. After earning her master's degree from the Columbia Journalism School she took a job as a reporter for the *Burlington Free Press* in 1957—the first job she was offered that was not on the women's page. Her experience as a journalist helped her anticipate certain kinds of questions after she was elected to public office, she says, but "once you step on the other side, it doesn't help you with the press—they immediately look at you as another kind of human being. . . . You're totally vulnerable." Kunin had served six years in the Vermont legislature and four years as lieutenant governor before running for governor. She was elected on her second try in 1984 and served three two-year terms before stepping down.

When she lost her first gubernatorial race in 1982, Kunin attributed her defeat to Governor Dick Snelling's incumbency but says she knew her gender also made a difference. "Very few people would admit today that they wouldn't vote for a woman—we've moved beyond bigotry," she says. "But it comes down to who is believed when complex technical subjects are discussed, or who is perceived to have managerial ability." Women face gender assumptions "that create certain expectations before you even have a chance to define yourself." One of the common assumptions is that unless a woman has been a CEO or businesswoman, she can't deal with numbers, although she may be able to deal with education or the environment, which are considered the softer issues. Assumptions are also made about women's ability to lead. The underlying question is often, "Can she make tough decisions?" Women politicians are also permitted a smaller range of emotional expression than men, says

Kunin. A man can pound the table and get angry and it's considered normal, where a similarly angered woman might be labeled hysterical. At the other end of the emotional spectrum, a man can earn a reputation for sensitivity by showing a softer side, while a woman risks being stereotyped as overly emotional, she says. "You can't be too warm, you can't be too cold, you can't be too emotional."

In a newspaper interview a week after she lost her first gubernatorial election, Kunin talked about the subtlety of bias against women and was quoted in the press as charging that the news media "treat women candidates as a separate class and have helped perpetu-

Madeleine Kunin served three terms as governor of Vermont before being named to a federal post.

ate the belief women are more emotional and less rational in decision making." As an example, she cited a *Free Press* editorial endorsing the incumbent governor for reelection. It praised Snelling for having stood up to her "hysterical cries that you should be doing more about the shipment of nuclear waste through the state." Kunin says that the word "hysterical," connoting an irrational response, derives from the Greek word for a womb and would never have been used if Snelling's Democratic opponent had been a man. It is difficult to talk about sexism in politics, Kunin adds, because complex issues are reduced to screaming headlines such as "Kunin Says Sexism Played Role in Her Defeat." As a candidate, she learned to keep her answers simple in response to gender-related questions, since talking about gender as an obstacle would likely make it one. She would say something to the effect that it was difficult to gauge the impact of gender on the race because some people probably wouldn't vote for her because she was a woman, while others would vote for her for the same reason—and they would cancel each other out.

Kunin says dealing with the media's power to shape reality is one of the hardest parts of being in public life. From her own experience as a journalist, Kunin knew the press would err. But during her gubernatorial campaigns she felt frustrated by the journalistic practice of substituting the reporter's interpretation for the candidate's words. She was especially annoyed when a reporter covering one of her speeches concluded she had said nothing of substance—without letting the public form its own conclusions. Kunin says she was never able to just shrug off what the press said. "You really do wake up in the morning and wonder how you are defined" by the press. "Sometimes I would ask my husband to read the paper first. You do feel defined by the press even though you tell yourself it's really not how you are. It's impossible to separate the two." Family and close friends who are not in politics and who know you well help counter the effect of the media by reminding you of who you really are, she says.

Of course, the media representation isn't always negative. Sometimes, the media makes politicians bigger than life. "It sort of blows you up into gargantuan proportions. You may feel uncomfortable, but you smile and say, 'Maybe I am that great.' But it may be punctured the next day," she adds. "There's no way, if you have any ego or sensitivity at all, that you can escape it." Being governor meant always being on camera and on the record, and Kunin says she found that emotionally draining. But she says she learned to develop resilience, though she never acquired immunity to what the media said. "On the whole, I was treated fairly by the press, although there were days when I didn't think so."

Kunin broke through the image barrier encountered by so many women politicians during one of the last televised debates before her first successful gubernatorial election. She says she was confident of her appearance and her mastery of issues and command of facts and realized she could be herself instead of measuring her responses, worrying about how she was coming across. "I did not search for the right word, tone or position; I knew it. No longer did I debate whether to be passive or aggressive, cautious or decisive. I had found my stance, my voice, myself." Moments like that don't happen often. "It's an ideal situation," she says. "There's a desire for wholeness, a desire to integrate the inner self and the outer image. When you can find the right words that reflect your beliefs and also resonate with an audience, it's one of the great delights of life." She says it also shows that politicians don't have to pretend, although some people think politicians are always on stage.

After leaving the governor's office, Kunin served as U.S. deputy secretary of education during a time when the Department of Education was being targeted for cutbacks, and she continually had to field questions from the media. Even so, she thinks the press was tougher when she was governor because journalists held her responsible for everything that happened in the state. As governor she was only beginning to learn to deal with the media and has since had plenty of practice. One of the hardest things for her was to learn to simplify her answers. "Sometimes I felt I overemphasized the facts. Women tend to want to answer questions like good students," she says. "You can get too tangled up in the facts and forget to give the soundbite kind of opinion. That's the hardest thing—moving to the soundbite."

As the nation entered the final decade of the twentieth century, media commentators were still asking some of the same questions they had been asking for the past fifty years: Should women candidates emphasize their gender to attract votes? Should women support women candidates because they are women? Do women politicians possess characteristics that are different from those of men? Some politicians played the gender card. During the California gubernatorial campaign, reporters asked Dianne Feinstein to comment on commercials that showed a thank you letter she had written her opponent, Pete Wilson, when she was mayor of San Francisco. In a postscript she had written, "You're wonderful." Feinstein's comment to the media: "I guess men like to be called wonderful. I'm glad he treasures it and wants to keep it." And Ann Richards had a quip ready for the media when she was told that her Texas gubernatorial opponent, Clayton Williams, had met with President Bush and they had commiserated about running campaigns against women. "Even cowboys get the blues," Richards said. "I don't want to be his mother. I want to be governor of Texas."

But for the most part Feinstein downplayed her gender and ultimately lost the gubernatorial race to Wilson, while Richards talked about women's issues the same year and won a tough race. That had at least one columnist peering hopefully into the future, speculating that the 1990 elections showed women could win on their own terms. Kay Mills wrote in the *Los Angeles Times* that while the California race showed women are still shy about running as women, in Texas Ann Richards proved that a woman can talk about family and women's economic issues and win. "If women would run on issues that concern them as women, maybe, just maybe, they would feel a mandate to govern as women and programs benefiting real people might be instituted."

New York Times columnist William Safire saw it differently. In a column headlined "Bad Year for Women," Safire laid the blame on women voters for not supporting women candidates. "Progress is much too slow," Safire wrote, "because women of every political stripe—at home and around the world—are letting down their own sexual side by not demanding more female candidates and not supporting them when they run." Safire said that while sex was not the main qualification for office, the lack of women candidates was dismaying. "All other things being roughly equal, women should strongly support women as women until some parity is reached. Then, secure in a system in balance, they can throw the rascals out, regardless of sex."

Newsweek's Eleanor Clift wrote hopefully just before the 1990 election, "This may be the last election season that women candidates are novel enough to command attention as a group. And that in itself is one giant leap for mankind." Perhaps she spoke too soon. While progress had been made, emphasis on irrelevant gender differences continued to permeate media coverage. "In the national publications we don't see the worst excesses of the cute stories on women candidates," said political analyst Ann Lewis. "But it's clear that we have yet to enter the period where campaign coverage is identical for men and women candidates. . . . I realize we are not going to arrive at the perfect balance [of coverage] overnight, but I cheer the fact that the double standard is crumbling. What we all ought to be aiming for is a single standard. Anytime there is a double standard, we women lose."

Chapter 8

ALMOST A BRIDESMAID

AS THE FIRST WOMAN EVER NOMINATED FOR VICE PRESIDENT ON A MAJOR PARTY TICKET, Geraldine Ferraro knew she would be in the media spotlight. She figured she could handle the media attention in the 1984 presidential race because she had weathered a nasty congressional race six years earlier. But she didn't know how bad it would get. She was scrutinized as a woman and as an Italian-American, and news stories linked her and her family with organized crime. "I hadn't been worried. We had nothing to hide," she says. "Never did I antici-pate the fury of the storm we . . . found ourselves in."

Journalistic investigations into her personal life were the start of the media preoccupation with the so-called "character issue," she says, in which candi-dates' motives and personal life are examined as a way of seeing whether they can withstand the stresses of public life. "They say it started with Gary Hart," says Ferraro, "but it didn't. It started with me." She observes that Dan Quayle appeared to have an awfully short memory when he said no vice presidential candidate had ever been attacked as viciously as he had. And Ferraro's former administrative assistant, Eleanor Lewis, says in hindsight that the media at-tacks on Ferraro were just the tip of the iceberg of media hostility toward political candidates that emerged fully during the 1992 presidential election.

Ferraro was a three-term congresswoman from Queens when a group of five politically active women decided she would make a good vice presiden-tial candidate and began laying the groundwork in 1983 for public acceptance of a female contender. They knew the media would be instrumental in creating a political climate favorable to a woman's nomination. The women, calling themselves "Team A," developed a two-part strategy designed to get the Demo-cratic Party to put a woman on the ticket in 1984. But first they had to per-suade Ferraro to take the idea seriously. Ironically, Ferraro was initially skep-tical that a woman would be acceptable on the ticket. She wasn't alone. Former representative Barbara Jordan, in a National Public Radio interview with Susan Stamberg in late 1983, said she didn't think people were willing to consider a woman for the vice presidency. "We have been so brainwashed with the superiority of white male personalities," Jordan said, "that it is difficult to cut through and perceive a woman as a person of competence." And just a week before Walter Mondale announced his choice of Ferraro, some skepticism was still being expressed. Even India Edwards, whose name had been placed in nomination for vice president by the Democrats in 1952, said in a radio interview that Ferraro was not well enough known to be a vice presidential candidate and would not be an asset to the ticket nationally.

Ferraro and Edwards weren't the only women to be considered for the vice presidency. Former Wyoming governor Nellie Tayloe Ross's name had been placed in nomination at the 1928 Democratic convention, and there had been a move to nominate Margaret Chase Smith at the GOP convention in 1952, the same year Edwards's name was put forward by the Democrats. In 1972, women delegates to the Democratic convention pushed for the nomination of former Texas gubernatorial candidate and state legislator Sissy Farenthold, and she received more than 420 votes, second only to Senator Thomas Eagleton. Eagleton was dropped from the Democratic ticket when his health problems came to light, but Farenthold was never considered as a replacement nominee. With few exceptions, the media never treated her seriously. CBS anchorman Walter Cronkite, for example, told viewers, "A lady named Farenthold wants to be vice president," before the network blacked out her nominating and seconding speeches with commercials. With that experience in mind, Team A's first task was, in Ferraro's words, "to convince the male-dominated media to take the concept of a woman vice president seriously, to legitimize it for the public."

Laying the media groundwork was vital. "It was important that the media take it seriously so that people would take it seriously," Ferraro says. "How many people do you know who say 'I read it in the *New York Times*' as though they read it in the Bible—or say I read it in *Newsweek.* . . . That is an avenue that you have to go to." Ferraro says the old saw about getting your name in print is basically true: it doesn't matter what they say about you—as long as they spell your name right. She said it was important for her to get noticed by the media for several reasons: to get a "buzz" going so people would begin thinking about her candidacy; to legitimize the notion of a female candidate, and to get name recognition.

Soon some women columnists, including the *Washington Post*'s Judy Mann and *Time*'s Jane O'Reilly, began floating the idea. Ferraro quotes O'Reilly as saying her editors thought it was a nice story in a slow political year but were nonplused when Ferraro actually was nominated. "They loved the idea of a woman candidate," O'Reilly said, "but were totally baffled when the concept turned out to be a real woman." Initially the stories were played on inside pages, but the idea gained credibility after public officials such as senators Gary Hart, Walter Mondale, and Ted Kennedy spoke of the importance of the woman's vote and the need for women in national office. Their comments were carried on the front pages of the nation's newspapers and at the top of evening newscasts.

Once the idea had been advanced, the second phase of the strategy was to suggest the names of specific women for the vice presidency. Although she considered it a farfetched idea at the time, Ferraro said she was willing to be the vice presidential nominee if the idea caught on. The idea of having a woman on the ticket *did* catch on, and the month before the Democratic Convention opened in July 1984, Ferraro found herself in the news as one of a handful of con-

Geraldine Ferraro was a three-term congresswoman from New York and the 1984 Democratic vice presidential nominee.

tenders for the vice presidential nomination. Journalist Marie Brenner said Ferraro didn't fully realize the historic nature of her candidacy until the national media started paying attention. "I happened to be traveling with Gerry just as she went from being a rather obscure congresswoman being talked about as a potential vice presidential nominee, right through the swirl of all her national publicity," Brenner said. "But she never believed for a minute that she was famous until Barbara Walters came to interview her."

Walter Mondale's potential running mates included three women, two blacks, a Hispanic, and a white male. Dianne Feinstein was actually the first to be invited to an interview, and the meeting between them was such a novelty it made the front page of many newspapers, including the *New York Times*. Feinstein told the *Times* reporter she was proud to be the first woman and first Jew considered for vice president. "All of a sudden when the call came, it was like one of these flashes and this recognition that there is a historical impact that I'm on that list," she told a reporter. "From now and forever on . . . women will be considered. It's crossing that threshold."

Feinstein was only partly right in her euphoric assessment. In theory, a door opened. In theory, women henceforth would be considered as candidates for the vice presidency, a traditional stepping-stone to the presidency. But in reality, it would be twelve years before a woman was again seriously considered for vice president on a major party ticket. Geraldine Ferraro's disastrous experience with the media may actually have caused the door to swing shut. For women interested in seeking national political office, the price paid by Ferraro may have seemed too high.

Time's June 4 cover story can be seen as a measure of how far women had come in media coverage of politics and how far they still had to go. It showed mugshots of Ferraro and Feinstein above a headline asking "Why Not a Woman?"— a significant and controversial question. The story noted that attitudes had markedly changed for a woman even to be considered—after all, it had been just fourteen years since one of Hubert Humphrey's associates declared publicly that women were unfit for high office because they were subject to a "raging hormonal imbalance" every month. But the story also called it an "unorthodox way" to balance a ticket and reflected on the questionable electability of a woman candidate. Choosing a woman running mate would "carry as much risk as logic," the article said. "If not handled well, it could come across as a political gimmick, a desperation gesture." Mondale clearly needed to do something to freshen his campaign, which *Time* described as sounding like a "large heavy suitcase being tumbled slow motion down an interminable flight of stairs."

The same article quoted a senior Democratic congressman as saying that neither woman had achieved national distinction, and that if Ferraro or Feinstein were nominated it would only be "because they are female." Even though the article wasn't very positive about either of Mondale's potential women running mates, at least their pictures made the cover, legitimizing the possibility that a woman could be a partner in the Executive Office. But *Time* was skeptical that the time was right for a woman. "Is the nation 'ready' for a woman vice president?" the magazine asked. "The answer to the question must be intuitive. It is possible that this barrier passed some time ago, in the psychological sense, and that it is simply waiting to topple. Perhaps."

To some extent, the *Time* article reflected public cynicism about Ferraro's nomination. Polls indicated that 60 percent of the public perceived Ferraro's nomination to be the result of "pressure from women's groups." Only 22 percent believed Mondale chose Ferraro because she was the best candidate. A 72 to 22 percent majority said Mondale chose Ferraro "because he thought having a woman on the ticket would help him get elected." In fact, polls showed that a woman running mate would hurt Mondale about as much as it would help him. But in spite of the general lack of support for the Mondale/Ferraro ticket, a strong majority of Americans said they were glad a woman was finally on a major party ticket. By a majority of more than two to one (62 to 30 percent), Americans said that regardless of who they voted for in the general election, "I'm glad a woman was nominated for vice president—it's about time." Given this level of public support for a female nominee, the media's scrutiny of Ferraro's family finances, speculation about her connections to organized crime, and continual references to her appearance seemed to go well beyond being a reflection of public concern about a female nominee. Perhaps some journalists believed Ferraro had overreached herself.

One curious aspect of so much of the media coverage of potential presidential running mates was that women contenders frequently were compared to each other, not to their male counterparts. Published leaks from Mondale's campaign staff indicated that Dianne Feinstein was seen as more impressive than Ferraro, according to the *San Francisco Chronicle*, while Kentucky governor Martha Layne Collins had "a very clear idea of her own agenda of state and national affairs," according to the *Washington Post*. "That burned me on more than one level," says Ferraro. "Why were we never compared with [Henry] Cisneros or [Lloyd] Bentsen or any of the other male candidates? Were we, as women, just running against each other? How sexist can you get?"

As Susan Carroll notes in *Women as Candidates in American Politics*, Ferraro was often treated differently because she was a woman. One often-told story about Ferraro's campaign involves her first swing through the South after her nomination. In Mississippi, which was developing four new crops, including blueberries, she told seventy-year-old Agriculture and Commerce Commissioner Jim Buck Ross that blueberries grew wild on her family's Fire Island property. "Can you bake a blueberry muffin?" asked the commissioner. "Sure can," Ferraro replied, pausing. "Can you?" "Down here in Mississippi the men don't cook," Ross replied. The widely reported exchange prompted some observers to criticize the media for sexist reporting, but Ferraro seemed more amused than offended.

She was also subjected to labels that wouldn't be used for a man. Ferraro was called "bitchy" by her opponent's press secretary and labeled a "_____, rhymes with rich" by Barbara Bush, the vice president's wife. Mrs. Bush wrote in her diary that she was joking with the press on the campaign plane, assuming everything was off the record, when she made the comment. Later that day, when she discovered her comment was running on television and radio, she called and apologized to Ferraro. "It was an astonishing thing to say to the press," Ferraro commented later, "and, of course, they jumped on it."

Possibly even more astonishing than Bush's comments were the questions put to Ferraro based on the stereotype of woman as the weaker sex. During her televised debate with Vice President Bush she was asked about her ability to serve as commander-in-chief: "How can you convince the American people and the potential enemy that you would know what to do to protect this nation's security, and do you think in any way the Soviets might be tempted to try to take advantage of you simply because you are a woman?" "Are you saying that I would have to have fought in a war in order to love peace?" responded Ferraro. Three days later she was asked an even more pointed question by Marvin Kalb on *Meet the Press*: "Are you strong enough to push the button?" Ferraro replied, "I could do whatever is necessary to protect this country." Her campaign press secretary, Francis O'Brien, says Ferraro grew impatient with these kinds of questions, which stereotyped women as the weaker sex with little knowledge of military defense matters. "How much did she have to prove that she could blow somebody up, that she could be a moll?" asks O'Brien. "Put a magnum in Gorbachev's mouth and pull the trigger?"

More than a decade later, Ferraro still sounds angry about her televised encounter with Ted Koppel, who grilled her about her statement during the vice presidential debate that the U.S. and the Soviet Union were both building nuclear warheads. Ferraro says it was as though Koppel were administering a foreign policy exam, "the way he came at me with all this military information." Koppel, she says, had "bought into the stereotype that women can only deal with children's and women's issues." But she also acknowledges that the questions about her ability to be commander in chief reflected some public concerns. Focus groups showed most women of her generation "totally resented my campaign . . . The press did reflect the personal feeling out in the electorate." But in addition, she says, "they had a predisposition to ask those dumb questions."

It's clear that in many instances the media handled stories about her differently because she was a woman, but her Italian-American heritage also figured in the media scrutiny she was subjected to. She was asked to answer not only for herself but for her parents and husband. Because they were Italian, "she was assumed to be mobbed up," O'Brien says. Reporters also had to deal with a national candidate's husband for the first time, and John Zaccaro was linked to figures with organized crime ties. "Whatever he was purported to have done or not done, she had to answer for," O'Brien says. "They couldn't accept the fact that she wasn't under her husband's identity."

Media pressure nearly caused Ferraro to pull out even before the Democratic convention opened. Continuing leaks to the press that denigrated Ferraro distressed her to the point that she decided to withdraw her name from consideration. On July 8, after reading a *New York Times* analysis, she told Mondale on the phone, "I do not want to be part of this process anymore. I never really did want it." Mondale refused to agree to her request, and less than a week later Ferraro was nominated as vice president at the Democratic convention. Some newspapers couldn't resist framing the historic event in romantic terms: "GERRY, WILL YOU BE MY RUNNING MATE?" the *New York Post* headline blared. "Mondale pops the question and Ferraro says, 'I will.'" It was standard fare for the *Post*, known for its sensationalism and eye-popping headlines. But the *Post* wasn't alone in its touting of the perfect couple. Immediately following the convention, the media were full of stories about the Mondale-Ferraro relationship: Would they kiss each other or touch each other in public? How should Mondale treat Ferraro? Who should precede whom?

Image was important. A Mondale staff memo obtained by NBC-TV outlining convention strategy prohibited the two from performing the traditional victory gesture—joined hands held aloft. Syndicated humor columnist Art Buchwald poked fun at the situation, weighing in with his own rules for correct behavior: "Keep your hands off Rep. Ferraro during the campaign and don't give the public the slightest excuse to think there is anything going on between the two of you other than you trying to find out where she really stands on the nuclear freeze."

In articles reminiscent of those that flooded newspapers after Jeannette Rankin's election to Congress almost seventy years earlier, Ferraro was described as "feisty," "peppery," "charming," and the "pushy but not threatening" mother of three. Articles revealed the name of her hairdresser and that her hair was frosted. Not only was Ferraro a woman—giving her the luster of being a first in national politics—but she also appeared to many reporters to embody the American dream. The daughter of an Italian immigrant, she had been raised by her widowed mother, who sewed beads and sequins onto evening gowns in order to provide her daughter a good education. Ferraro became a teacher, earning her law degree at night, then married and stayed home with her children for fourteen years. She was working as an assistant district attorney when she ran for Congress and won in 1978.

Initially her novelty as a woman and her rags-to-riches background made her irresistible to the media. As Peter Boyer, Atlanta bureau chief of the *Los Angeles Times,* observed, even routine campaign stories in the early days of Ferraro's candidacy "were infused with that 'Golly! she's a girl' wonder." To ice the cake, Ferraro's husband apparently wasn't bothered by playing a supporting role. Zaccaro told the Associated Press he didn't mind being called Mr. Ferraro. "She gets upset," he said. "I get a kick out of it." But news reports during the Democratic convention foreshadowed the intense media scrutiny she and her husband were later to face. The *New York Post* reported that a tenant of Zaccaro's (who turned out not to be his tenant) claimed she had to take her baby to bed with her to keep it warm. Ferraro told reporters her husband had no knowledge of or connection with the situation and shrugged off the incident. "Some nastiness is always expected in politics, and I dismissed those opening salvos," she said. "What I didn't know then was the personal agony that lay ahead, an agony that at times would seem almost unbearable."

Although media attention was flattering, it was overpowering in the early weeks of the campaign. Capitol Hill police had to rope off her office to keep reporters at bay. "The frenzy around my candidacy was almost out of control. . . . It was bedlam." Ferraro had expected the Republicans to bring up the issue of her 1978 congressional campaign loans, which had been investigated by the Federal Election Commission. Sure enough, the day after Walter Mondale announced that Ferraro would be his running mate, wire service stories reported that she had been fined by the Federal Election Commission in 1979 for accepting an illegal campaign loan from her husband. While she may have expected that old news to resurface, she says she wasn't expecting the onslaught of news stories about the financial disclosure statements she had filed while a member of Congress. For the last six years, Ferraro had taken the so-called "spousal exemption" that permitted her to exclude information about her husband's finances. In the two weeks following her nomination, the exemption became a big issue, and the media also questioned her husband's ethics in handling a court-appointed conservatorship of a widow's affairs and several of his real estate transactions.

Although she had thirty days to file a financial report with the FEC, Ferraro remembers feeling hounded as reporters pressed her for details of her family finances. But she doesn't lay all the blame on the media for derailing her campaign. She acknowledges that early on she shot herself in the foot with the way she handled questions about the kind of information her husband would release. The day before her official nomination, for example, she had promised that she would disclose all of her and her husband's financial holdings. But at a news conference following the convention she said her husband was not going to release his tax returns because his business interests would be affected. As soon as she had spoken she saw a ripple move through the journalists and knew too late that she had made a mistake. She tried to change the subject by joking that women married to Italian men "know what it's like," a remark that was widely interpreted as an ethnic slur. "My candidacy had been struck an almost fatal blow before the campaign had hardly begun," she said. "And I had done it to myself."

From then on, Ferraro couldn't avoid media questions about her family's finances. Because she had taken the spousal exemption during her years in Congress and would not release the details of her husband's finances, speculation grew that she was hiding something. She claimed she and her husband led separate professional lives and that their financial affairs were separate. But the media wouldn't let up, not even aboard Ferraro's campaign plane. The pressure was so intense that Ferraro says she stopped drinking water so she wouldn't have to use the bathroom in the back of the plane—thereby avoiding an encounter with members of the press. Less than a week later, Ferraro announced that her husband had changed his mind and would release his tax returns. She held a press conference and released a file of documents that showed they had paid about 40 percent of their income in city, state, and federal income taxes since Ferraro's election to Congress five years earlier. She fielded questions for more than ninety minutes and afterward was praised by many in the media for her candor and poise under pressure. *Time* said she had given a "bravura performance" and that she had shown "an astonishing knack for handling journalistic inquisitors."

Los Angeles Times media critic David Shaw said Ferraro's disclosures caused many journalists to back off and play down subsequent reports of links between the Zaccaro family and organized crime. "Having been 'wrong' once in their speculation, they didn't want to risk being wrong again, on something far more pernicious," Shaw said in a two-part analysis of Ferraro's media coverage published after the election. But other journalists said Ferraro had not answered their questions satisfactorily and had, in fact, raised new questions about her role in the family business and about the illegal 1978 loan to her campaign.

As it happened, Knight-Ridder's Washington bureau had sent out a lengthy story to run the same day as Ferraro's first post-convention news conference, predicting that her finances might become a major campaign issue. The article mentioned Ferraro's failure to disclose Zaccaro's holdings on her financial disclosure statements; her receipt of an illegal $130,000 campaign loan from her husband and children, and her repayments of those loans with profits from the sale of real estate involving her husband's business partner. The *Philadelphia Inquirer*, a Knight-Ridder newspaper, jumped on the story, committing additional staff and resources and not letting up for weeks. On August 14, an *Inquirer* editorial demanded full disclosure, saying it was vital for the public to know how her involvements might affect her judgments in public office. The next day the paper ran a story on the dilemma facing public office holders about disclosing personal finances, and the day after that the paper ran a page-one story about GOP attacks on Ferraro's financial problems. On August 17, the *Inquirer* ran the news that Ferraro—who had said she and her husband were financially independent of each other—was actually a half-owner of one of Zaccaro's firms. And when Zaccaro finally agreed to release his tax returns, the *Inquirer* put the story on the front page, asking whether Zaccaro was trying to hide something.

Even after Ferraro released her and her husband's financial data, the *Inquirer* continued to hammer away at the story, saying details of Zaccaro's business dealings should be revealed. But the *New York Post* topped even the heavy-charging *Inquirer,* pointedly replacing the S in headlines over critical stories with a dollar sign. Ferraro's release of information on the family's finances didn't change anything. The *Post* headline the next day read: "GERRY STILL ON THE GRILL." Other papers also ran the stories but often used wire service stories rather than assigning their own reporters and played the stories on inside pages. Many were less scathing in their editorials than the *Inquirer*. The *Atlanta Constitution*, for example, dismissed the stories about Ferraro's family finances as just a "tempest in a teapot" and said the allegations were a "small and dreary business."

Eight days after Ferraro's news conference, the *Inquirer* began looking into possible mob connections with a front-page story alleging that contributions totaling $1,200 had been made to her congressional campaigns over a six-year period by a man convicted of labor racketeering who allegedly had ties to organized crime. Ferraro later told *Los Angeles Times* reporter David Shaw that she resented the implication in the *Inquirer* story that "because you take a campaign contribution from someone, it influences how you vote [and] . . . you're hanging out with him." In fact, editors at some other major papers, such as the *New York Times* and *Washington Post,* decided that the story was not relevant to the campaign. *Times* executive editor A.M. Rosenthal said that if the *Times* had devoted as much attention to the story as the *Inquirer* did, "the whole country would have been up in arms against us. . . . They would have said we were persecuting her."

But on September 13, two weeks after the *Inquirer* story suggesting Ferraro's link with racketeering, the *Wall Street Journal* ran a story on its editorial page about connections between the Zaccaros and organized crime that proved to be one of the most controversial of the entire campaign. The *Journal*, saying it had been unable to get answers from Ferraro, ran a story on the editorial page headlined "Rep. Ferraro and a Painful Legacy." The piece said Ferraro's father-in-law's pistol license had been revoked twenty-five years earlier because he had supplied a character reference for the brother of a reputed organized crime figure who had applied for a pistol license.

Although the story ran on the editorial page as opposed to the news pages—signifying that it was opinion—*Journal* editors were strongly censured by other journalists. "Writing a story with questions whose implications are mostly sinister, when you can't answer them yourself—there's only one thing to call it—it's a smear," said *Los Angeles Times* Editor William F. Thomas. Syndicated columnist Richard Reeves said there would have been protests about the Ferraro stories if she were a man. "The stoning of Geraldine Ferraro in the public square goes on and on, and no one steps forward to help or protest—not even one of her kind. Especially her own kind. The sons of Italy and fathers of the Roman Catholic Church are silent or too busy reaching for bigger rocks. Other women seem awed and intimidated by the charges and innuendo: Heresy! Mafia! Men are putting women in their place." Reeves concluded: "If Geraldine Ferraro is stoned without defenders, she will be only the first to fall. The stones will always be there, piled high, ready for the next Italian, the next Catholic, the next woman."

Reporters for several papers said Ferraro refused to discuss her husband's business dealings or charges of his alleged links to organized crime throughout the campaign. But Ferraro had a different take on it. "Where there was a legitimate inquiry [about family finances], we answered it," she told the *Los Angeles Times* after the campaign was over. "But some of those reporters asked

questions that were totally irrelevant and insulting." Ferraro said that to answer their questions would invite more questions and more unfavorable stories and would take the focus away from campaign issues she believed important. She also said that to comment on stories about links with organized crime
would only give them legitimacy and credibility.

O'Brien, her former press secretary, says it was a no-win situation. Commenting on unfounded allegations about her family's connections would mean
only that they would be given wider attention and get into the mainstream
media. As it was, reporters ended up writing stories with phrases like "it is
alleged," he says. "There's no way to answer those implications." Would he
have managed her media relations differently, in hindsight? "It's impossible to
manage," O'Brien says. "I would have found out all the questions and answered them at the beginning. You can't do anything when you're in the chute
. . . but survive."

Ferraro's silence may have fueled speculation that she was covering up.
Still, it's hard to understand why she was pursued so relentlessly. As Philip
Seib notes in *Who's In Charge? How the Media Shape News and Politicians
Win Votes*, law enforcement agencies weren't taking the allegations very seriously, "but the press pursued Ferraro with a vengeance." Seib says the reasons
are unclear. He notes that there was no long-standing antipathy between the
press and the nominee, such as existed between President Nixon and the media. Nor was the alleged wrongdoing something that endangered the Republic, as Watergate had by involving tampering with the electoral process and
criminal conspiracy in the White House.

Looking back on the experience, Ferraro says she would not have handled
reporters' questions any differently. She answered questions she felt were legitimate but says some questions went beyond the pale and some were based
on confidential information only in the FBI's possession. "My candidacy posed
the only threat to the Reagan White House," she says. "When I got the nomination the numbers shot up [the Democratic ticket's standing in the polls]"
and the Republican administration made her its target. Citing the newspaper
story about her father's arrest many years before, Ferraro says someone must
have provided reporters access to FBI files, since he was never convicted of
the charge.

By the end of the summer, Reagan's lock on the presidency seemed
unbreakable, and presidential campaign coverage lapsed into routine reports.
Reporters interviewed for an article in the *Washington Journalism Review* pro-
nounced themselves bored. They agreed that the Mondale-Ferraro ticket had
virtually no chance of winning against Ronald Reagan and George Bush and
that there basically wasn't anything new to cover. That resulted in less play for
stories about the campaign—making it tougher in general for the Democrats
to get their ideas across. Yet Ferraro was still experiencing adulation from the

crowds. People were still holding up their baby girls to see and touch her, but she says their excitement wasn't reflected in the press coverage. Had the novelty of a woman vice presidential candidate worn off for members of the press sooner than it had for the public? After a media roller coaster ride from popularity through scandal, Ferraro had become just another candidate. "At first, people were caught up in the symbol. Now what's happened is we're talking on the issues," she said in mid-September, "and people see me more as a candidate than just a symbol."

As a symbol, Ferraro had to be particularly aware of her image—of the way she looked and sounded. Although it seems silly for the news media to have focused on such trivia as whether the two nominees would kiss, it was exactly the sort of thing political consultants told Ferraro was important because it was a factor in her public image. When she traveled to Minnesota for the announcement of her candidacy, she knew that when Dianne Feinstein had come for an interview at North Oaks, Mondale had not kissed her, which the press interpreted as making her a serious candidate. But he had kissed Ferraro when she came to report on the Democratic Party platform, which meant the opposite. "What a pain this gender thing was going to be," she wrote later. "I decided that as the vice presidential candidate, I would definitely not kiss Fritz [Mondale] when we arrived." But when she got there, the problem resolved itself. Both Mondale and his wife kissed her.

"Reporters were totally confused. . . . They didn't know what the hell to do," comments former press secretary O'Brien. Should they cover what she wore or what she said, or both? "They didn't know what to ask," he says, "and she didn't know what to answer." O'Brien says everyone was trying to figure out appropriate roles. He tells about the time he came in and saw that Ferraro's silk dress was wrinkled. When he said it needed ironing, all her female staff members "went into a role playing freeze," O'Brien says. "No one moved." He ironed the candidate's dress himself.

In order to answer some of the questions raised by her gender, such as how something she said or did might be perceived or whether she was being treated the way a male vice-presidential candidate would be, Ferraro created a mental image for herself of a white-haired southern senator. How he would have been treated became the standard for what she expected for herself. She was right about the standard against which she was being measured—the stereotype of chief executive as an older, courtly, white male.

Would she do it over again if she had to undergo the same media scrutiny? She says she didn't like it but understood why it happened. "I instantly stepped into a media whirlwind," she said during her unsuccessful campaign for the Senate in 1992. "I took some shots from the press in that campaign and I will tell you, frankly, I didn't think everything that was written about me was fair. But the vast majority of the coverage was. When you step into the great public arena as I did, you have to be willing to take the heat."

On another occasion, and in a more humorous vein, Ferraro said, "I suppose if God had said to me before I got Fritz's phone call—'Gerry, sit down a minute and put this tape into your VCR. I want you to see what the next six months of your life will be like'—I must tell you that I probably would have said: 'Could you do me a favor, God, and give it to Dianne Feinstein?'"

But Ferraro sees some good coming out of her candidacy. She says she's at least partly responsible for the increased number of women in visible media roles because news organizations began looking for women to put on her campaign plane. More women than ever before covered the 1984 election, and although there are no official statistics, a *New York Times* reporter estimated at the time that about 20 percent of those following the president's campaign, and about 30 percent of those covering the vice presidential campaigns, were women.

Much discussion about reporting assignments took place after Ferraro was nominated. The central question was whether a woman should cover a woman, since it was feared that women might tend to be softer in their coverage of someone of the same sex. That would be all right, said ABC news correspondent Lynn Sherr, "as long as they then no longer allowed men to cover male candidates. It's just a very simple equation. Sherr also said that to some extent "many of the women reporters will be better than male reporters because we will look at her as a person and a candidate. Men are used to looking at women in the news as a 'woman-something.' All the men pundits have been sitting around asking themselves, 'What effect will a woman have on the ticket?' My first question is, 'What effect will Geraldine Ferraro have on the ticket?' I haven't done a so-called women's story in ages, but when I cover women, I cover them as people."

In fact, women were not softer on Ferraro than men, even though it was hard for many to cover the financial disclosure stories. "I don't know any woman reporter who wasn't mortified by what she had to do," said Nina Totenberg, National Public Radio's legal affairs correspondent. "But, it's your job. We couldn't treat her any differently. Perhaps, if anything, we treated her more harshly than we would have a male counterpart." Ferraro might agree. She says many women reporters felt compelled to come down harder than male reporters, and suggested they were looking for a Pulitzer. "They were as confused as anybody. I was brand new and they didn't know how to deal with me. In some cases they were tougher," Ferraro says. "They were trying to find themselves. A lot were torn because they were happy about my nomination but they had to prove themselves by being objective." O'Brien says he was sympathetic to the women assigned to cover Ferraro. "This was their first big break" and they had to prove they weren't soft. "It puts you under a glaring light. You prove your mettle by how hard your questions can be—not by how insightful you can be."

Although Dianne Feinstein's jubilant statement in early 1984 that the threshold had been crossed and that "from now and forever on . . . women will be considered" was echoed widely, there was still a long way to go. Ferraro said the real test would come when the next woman ran for the presidency or vice presidency. "Only then will we know if she, too, will be judged by a standard different from that of her male opponents; if she, too, is going to have to be better in order to be judged equal."

But Ferraro said her campaign proved that women candidates could stand pressure. "I don't think the press will be looking to see if the next female candidate will burst out crying every time she has a press conference," she said. "Perhaps the style of her campaign will be less important and the substance of her campaign will get the attention it deserves."

Chapter 9

1992 AND ALL THAT

1992 WAS BILLED BY THE NEWS MEDIA AS THE "YEAR OF THE WOMAN" IN POLITICS. Women's time had finally come. Or had it? Perhaps headlines should have said *Another* Year of the Woman, reflecting the fact that this was only the latest fanfare marking record gains by women. In fact, the media had dubbed 1969 the Year of the Woman when a record number of women were elected to the House. And it happened again in 1984 and in 1988. 1990 was proclaimed the Year of the Woman until women candidates began to look vulnerable and the Year fizzled out before election day. In reality, despite the familiar media proclamations, women politicians remained outsiders in 1992.

Redistricting, retirements, and other factors created a record eighty-six open House seats. By and large, women who won election did not have to run against incumbents. Only four of the twenty-four freshmen women in Congress defeated incumbents, two of them in the Democratic primaries in their states and two in the general election. For other women who challenged entrenched officeholders, the "Year of the Woman" proved to be an empty phrase. Despite the strong anti-incumbent sentiment in the country, many incumbents, fortified with seniority, media attention, and money, survived the challenge. As some observers later said, 1992 should not have been labeled the Year of the Woman at all but rather the Year of Opportunity.

Catherine Manegold of the *New York Times* provided a reality check a couple of weeks before the general election. "Even a wave of victories by female candidates will not give women dominance on Capitol Hill," she wrote. "Should a female candidate win in every possible race, the 103rd Congress would still be 80 percent male. More likely, many women will lose, leaving the United States still well behind most European countries in female representation." Said Gloria Steinem, "This isn't the Year of the Woman. That won't happen until we have half the U.S. Congress and every other decision-making body, a president once in a while, women leaders who are as diverse as we are." Even after a wave of primary victories for women that included Carol Moseley-Braun's upset of Al Dixon for an Illinois Senate seat and good turnouts of women voters in other early contests, Harriett Woods, president of the

National Women's Political Caucus, was reluctant to proclaim it a breakthrough year. "Sometimes you feel like Chicken Little in this business," Woods told a reporter. "We always seem right on the verge of making it, then don't quite do it."

Although Woods sounded tentative in that comment to the press, the Caucus was actually working behind the scenes to promote the notion in the media that it was going to be a good year for women candidates. It's been said that the media cannot tell people what to think but can tell them what to think *about*. And high on the media agenda in the fall of 1991 was coverage of the Senate Judiciary Committee's hearing on Anita Hill's charges of sexual harassment against Supreme Court nominee Clarence Thomas. The story "really fueled a lot of what's going on out there . . . a lot of women's discontent, a lot of women's anger," said former *Newsday* deputy Washington bureau chief Mary Leonard. *Newsday*, along with National Public Radio, had broken the story of Hill's harassment allegations.

Thomas's confirmation hearing, brought into people's living rooms by intensive television coverage, is widely credited with setting the stage for the election of so many women. Toni Bernays, author of *Women in Power*, said it had become an "event in our national psyche." Ellen Levine, editor of *Redbook*, said Anita Hill was "gang-raped by the Senate." Women in particular noticed that the committee members questioning Hill were all men and that the senators didn't seem to understand what Hill was talking about. In fact, the hearings might never have been held had it not been for the group of congresswomen who marched to the Senate and interrupted the weekly Democratic caucus lunch to demand that Hill's side of the story be heard. Barbara Boxer, who came over with six of her colleagues, says she didn't anticipate the extent of the news coverage they would get. "We didn't expect the numbers of cameras facing us," she says. "When we moved toward the Senate steps, we saw them . . . still photographers, TV cameras, tape recorders, hand mikes, boom mikes and flash bulbs." The cameras remained behind on the Senate steps but proved useful when the women were told they couldn't talk to the senators until after the caucus. "Listen, there are about one hundred cameras out there," Boxer told the staff member at the door. "They know what we came over about and they'll want to know what happened." Within minutes, the Senate majority leader met with the women representatives in a side room. Their discussions eventually resulted in hearings being scheduled to allow Anita Hill to air her charges. A year later, Boxer had become a member of the men's club herself. Barbara Mikulski and Nancy Kassebaum had been the only women in the Senate at the time of the march.

Besides prompting a record number of women to run for public office and triggering political involvement on the part of many others, the hearings also spawned a dialogue in news and analysis columns and letters to the editor over the way men and women behave toward each other. Aware that the hearings could be transformed into political capital for women, the National Women's Political Caucus took out a full-page ad in the *New York Times* with a headline asking, "What If?" What if women had sat on the all-male Senate Judiciary Committee during the confirmation hearings? "Turn your anger into action. Join us." It was a gamble. A full-page ad in the *Times* cost $50,000, which the Caucus didn't have. But it paid off big, bringing in $80,000 in contributions. Then, NWPC president Woods and an aide visited magazine editors in New York to float the idea of articles calling 1992 the political Year of the Woman.

Senator Barbara Boxer (D-California) had served five terms in the House before her 1992 election to "the old boy's club."

Several women candidates tapped into the feeling many women had that Hill was not getting a fair hearing because there were no women on the Senate committee that was questioning her. Moseley-Braun was one. "Women kept coming up to me and saying they were tired of that boys' club," she said. The extent of that sentiment can be measured by the fact that it was the first defeat for her opponent in thirty primary and general elections dating back to the Truman administration.

Meanwhile, Lynn Yeakel, running against Pennsylvania senator Arlen Specter, a member of the Judiciary Committee, ran television spots using an image of Anita Hill being questioned by fourteen skeptical white senators, as Yeakel's voice is heard asking, "Does this make you as angry as it does me?" Geraldine Ferraro, seeking the Democratic nomination in the New York Senate primary, invoked the image of Anita Hill as a way of warding off her opponents' charges. In spite of the mileage they gained from Hill, both lost their elections. But incumbency and white maleness were no longer automatic assets, and a number of women benefited from the change in outlook. Some media stereotypes of women now worked in their favor. Besides being outsiders, they were perceived to be concerned about education and family values. "We're the beneficiaries of throwing the bums out," said Jane Danowitz, executive director of the bipartisan Women's Campaign Fund, "and there are many more male bums."

Reporter Adam Clymer noted the basic outsider stereotype in a *New York Times* article about Senate races, saying, "A woman as a Senate candidate . . . symbolizes change even before she announces her platform." Actually, several of the women Senate candidates were not outsiders at all but had political experience. Barbara Boxer, for example, was a fifth-term representative who had been involved in the House banking scandal, with 143 overdrafts. Dianne Feinstein had been mayor of San Francisco and had run unsuccessfully for California governor, and Carol Moseley-Braun had held a local political position in Chicago, Cook County recorder of deeds. But the media dubbed them "outsiders" anyway and played their stories to the hilt. Journalists have always loved rags-to-riches stories and narratives patterned on the legend of David against Goliath. Almost nothing beats copy that has conflict and people overcoming enormous obstacles and winning against impossible odds. Stories about women's victories in the early primaries were often framed as underdogs toppling powerful incumbents. Repeated often enough in the media, this dramatic construction began to take on the ring of truth. Women were running for high office, and they were winning. David *can* slay Goliath. The extensive coverage had a salutary effect by suggesting that this was a year when the signs looked right for women.

When women were portrayed in the press as winners they also received more financial backing, which in turn legitimized their candidacies for the media. 1992 was the best year yet for the seven-year-old Emily's List, the group founded to support women candidates who were Democratic and pro-choice. In 1990 it had raised $1.5 million. Contributions quadrupled to $6 million in 1992, and twenty-five of the fifty-five congressional candidates the group had endorsed were elected. Membership expanded to 24,000 following the Thomas confirmation hearings. Meanwhile, a new group called WISH (Women in the Senate and House) was formed in 1992 to provide financial support to pro-choice Republican women candidates.

Women were running in greater numbers than ever before, and the numbers alone were hard for the media to ignore. One-hundred and fifty women candidates filed for seats in the U.S. House of Representatives—ninety-four Democrats, fifty-four Republicans, and two independents. Eighteen sought Senate seats and seven ran for governor. Headlines reflected the groundswell of support for women candidates—and, in turn, the headlines kept it going. *Newsweek* proclaimed "Women on the Run: With record numbers seeking public office, 1992 could be a banner year." *Business Week* declared it was "The Year of the Woman—Really." But at least one candidate was feeling as though he'd gotten run over by the media bandwagon. The *Los Angeles Times* reported that Republican Bruce Herschensohn, who was running against Barbara Boxer for one of California's Senate seats, "bristled when reporters asked him about the year of the woman in politics," saying he considered the phrase "sanctioned prejudice" against men by liberal Democratic women. It was "the year of the liberals," not women, Herschensohn said. "Can you imagine the Year of the Man?" A similar reaction was expressed by Larry Yatch, a former Pennsylvania Democratic Party chairman. Yatch accused Democratic Senate candidate Lynn Yeakel and other women candidates of saying to voters, "Here— I've got breasts—vote for me."

The stories many of these women candidates personified were irresistible to the media, which favor novelty, unusualness, and conflict. *MacLean's*, the national Canadian magazine, framed the story for its readers as "A Political Battle of the Sexes," saying many of the female candidates were running for office "to challenge macho, male-dominated politics of contemporary America." But the stories represented by various women candidates were good enough without the media having to resort to clichés. In Senate races, for example, Yeakel, a political newcomer, provided a real David vs. Goliath story for the media when she succeeded in knocking off Pennsylvania's lieutenant governor in the Democratic primary. Illinois's Carol Moseley-Braun, who "was scarcely known statewide and ran the campaign of a pauper," was another David. So was Washington's Patty Murray when she announced that she— "just a mom in tennis shoes"—would try to unseat veteran Senator Brock Adams.

Candidates for House seats also provided fodder for great stories. They included Lynn Woolsey of California, who personified a classic rags to riches, pull-yourself-up-by-the-bootstraps kind of story. After her 1968 divorce, Woolsey had turned to government assistance to help raise her three young children. Later she found work in high-tech industry, then started her own personnel business in 1980. There was Cynthia McKinney, an outspoken, single, working mother who could personify for the media the concerns people had over child care and health care and who, if elected, would be the first black woman to represent Georgia in Congress. Elizabeth Furse, an Oregon Democrat, was another woman with a background to fit any journalist's dream. Furse had been a civil rights activist who had organized a dramatic coast-to-coast train trip to promote peace and who had founded the Oregon Peace Institute.

Those whom the press built up also had a longer way to fall. Carol Moseley-Braun is a good example. After her election, newspapers and broadcasts generally celebrated the fact that Braun was the first black woman elected to the U.S. Senate. But almost immediately these congratulatory stories and editorials were followed by articles in the national press that questioned her actions. News accounts detailed activities that the *Washington Post* characterized as "a dizzying series of sometimes self-inflicted wounds, that, in the words of one of her supporters . . . has resulted in 'a tremendous squandering of goodwill and resources.'" During the two-month period between the election and her swearing-in, she was accused of mishandling sexual harassment charges

Senator Carol Moseley-Braun (D-Illinois) is the first African-American woman elected to the Senate.

against her campaign manager, who was also her boyfriend. She was criticized for the blatantly political hiring of ten patronage employees just before leaving office as Cook County recorder of deeds. Her successor promptly fired them, and Braun said she had made a mistake and she apologized. She was also chided for high living—for moving into an expensive penthouse apartment overlooking Lake Michigan and for taking a month-long vacation to Africa, returning from London to New York on the Concorde. "Carol Braun, Falling Star," was the headline over a *Chicago Tribune* editorial the day after Braun defended herself at a news conference. "Braun's recent behavior has puzzled her constituents and infuriated her supporters," said the *Tribune*, "many of whom want nothing so much as to put two firm hands on her shoulders and give her a good, hard shake." But the charges faded from the front pages after Braun got to Congress and began to make news with her activities in office.

The fact that it was the Year of the Woman didn't guarantee that every woman got extensive press coverage, good or bad. In fact, some say they found it hard to get any news coverage at all. Nydia Velazquez, the first person in her family to earn a high school diploma, challenged nine-term incumbent Stephen Solarz in the newly drawn Twelfth Congressional District in New York. She won without much media coverage. "The mainstream media, the conventional wisdom in New York, they ruled out this race," she said. "They covered this race as Stephen Solarz's race." Solarz ran a well-financed campaign and was able to flood newspapers and broadcast media with advertising, while Velazquez had no money to run an ad. "He thought he would intimidate me, that he would destroy me. But I knew that this fight was going to be fought in the street," Velazquez said, "not on TV or radio or in the newspaper. Newspapers do not vote; TV does not vote." Velazquez won the primary and seemed certain of victory until hospital records of an earlier suicide attempt were faxed anonymously to the media before the general election. Velazquez called a news conference to answer reporters' questions and allay public fears. She was subsequently elected with 77 percent of the vote.

Patty Murray's experience illustrates the advantages and disadvantages women candidates faced in dealing with the media during the Year of the Woman. After Murray won the Democratic primary, the media depicted her as the consummate political outsider—a woman seeking a place in the mostly male Senate, a relative political newcomer, and a working mother determined to bring a citizen's voice into an arena that seemed dominated by professional politicians. But the media had been slow to catch on. Although she was inundated with press coverage after she won the nomination, Murray says she found it difficult to get media attention early on. She had served in the Washington state legislature but was considered a long shot when she decided to challenge Senator Brock Adams. Then Adams bowed out of the race after the *Seattle Times* reported that several women anonymously alleged Adams had sexually molested them and one said he had raped her. But even in an open race, Murray says she had trouble getting noticed. "The mainstream media did not at first take my candidacy seriously," she says. "The campaign didn't receive heavy coverage until primary election night. Once I won the primary, the media seemed to sit up and take notice."

Murray's campaign began to attract local press attention after the national media became interested. "I think the local media figured I had to prove myself by generating interest, and they were not going to do it for me," she says. "Also, they really didn't think I could do it." Exceptions included "a few boosts I got from reporters I knew as state senator." Some editorial writers liked her, she says, even though their papers didn't endorse her. Once she began receiving media coverage, it focused mainly on her lack of experience, she says, an issue that her primary and general election opponents emphasized. In an odd twist, that message turned out to be exactly what voters wanted to hear. "They wanted an outsider—someone who didn't seem to be 'inside Washington, D.C.'" Murray also turned a potential negative into a positive by adopting the phrase "just a mom in tennis shoes" as her trademark. The phrase had once

Senator Patty Murray (D-Washington) was labeled "just a mom in tennis shoes." Voters decided that's who they wanted to represent them in the Senate.

been used against her by a Washington state senator, "in an attempt to belittle me," she says. "It became a defining campaign slogan that people still repeat to me everywhere I go. 'Just look what a mom in tennis shoes can do.'" Initially, it seemed that Murray's opponent, a man, had the right image for a U.S. senator, she says, "but increasingly during the general campaign voters rejected that image." Looking back, Murray says she's not sure what the "right" political image was in her senatorial campaign. "I think many voters might argue that I was the right image, and that's why they voted me into office," she says. "Many people identified with me being an average wife and mother, and they wanted to see if I could bring some down-to-earth, common sense to the United States Senate."

That it was a year of possibilities for women politicians was evident in the early primaries and manifested in the growth in financial support for women. But even as 1992 became widely regarded as the Year of the Woman, some in the media pointed out awkward inconsistencies in this supposedly liberated year. In a *New York Times* article headlined "Women get into Political Football—as the Ball," Catherine Manegold provided a behind-the-scenes look at how images were being carefully crafted for the wives of the Republican and Democratic presidential candidates. Women—including politicians' wives—were important in this year, but both parties were apparently having trouble figuring out what the women's appropriate image should be. The Republicans decided to tap an old message, said Manegold: "Women, God bless them, are happier at home. And those who aren't can hurt you." Barbara Bush was drafted for the self-deprecating grandma role, while Marilyn Quayle was portrayed as the mother-defender of traditional "family values."

Meanwhile, the Democrats tried to give people a little of everything. Hillary Clinton's image underwent dramatic metamorphosis. At first touted as a model new woman able to balance family and career, by early summer she was transformed into a "presumably kinder, quieter wife and mother who beams incessantly at her man," Manegold wrote. "The make-over helped quell alarm that she would crash the White House as Mr. Clinton's equal. But the attacks are still coming." At the convention, the Democrats put Hillary at center stage but restricted her to clapping and smiling, while female candidates were shown off in a "grand tableau that stretched the length of the Madison Square Garden stage." Other media observers, however, saw the Democratic National Convention in July as a marker on the trail women were blazing out of the woods. As Anthony Lewis wrote in the *New York Times*, "Women: they are the change. Their new status in society—their political power—was the message not to be missed at this convention." Even though Democratic nominee Bill Clinton wasn't considering a female running mate, the convention was being managed by two women, Barbara Mikulski and Ann Richards, and Barbara Jordan was a convention speaker. Lewis took note of the role women were playing in

1992, comparing it with 1960, when John Kennedy campaigned and women would jump to get a look at the candidate over the crowd. The press labeled them "jumpers." In 1992, women were the candidates, not the spectators—and Clinton was glad to ride their coattails.

The focus of this Year of the Woman was on campaigns and elections. But at least one national publication took a long look at how women were faring in Congress and concluded that they had not yet arrived. A *Washington Post Sunday Magazine* piece headlined "Women on the Verge of a Power Breakthrough" took note of the gains made by women in Congress but said they had not yet achieved real influence on the Hill. "In Congress, the truth is that women can preside, but they don't rule." Although women "are no longer a curiosity . . . females still find themselves clearly in the minority, still trying to be heard in a place that doesn't consider a woman's comment valid until it is repeated by a man, still straddling the line between token and true advancement."

A sub-theme of the article was how hard it was for women to balance family lives with congressional duties, and the author, David Finkel, made it sound impossible. "There exists an unavoidable tension between the roles of congresswoman and mother, and congresswoman and wife," wrote Finkel. Representative Marcy Kaptur is quoted as saying she's more likely to be able to stay in Congress because she isn't married and doesn't have children, while Representative Lynn Martin told of the conflict she felt upon coming out of a meeting with President Reagan and being asked by her child whether she would be driving the morning carpool. Barbara Kennelly said her husband had to assume responsibility for their youngest child when she came to Washington. But it is Finkel's depiction of the relationship of Louise Slaughter and her husband that sets back the notion that women can balance family and political office. Finkel portrays Slaughter as a committed, heavily scheduled member of Congress who has little time for her recently retired husband. The anecdote is featured in a pullout box: "Slaughter goes into her office followed by her chief aide, who shuts the door. Her husband takes a seat in the reception area. 'I can go in there,' he explains. 'But the best I can do for her most of the time is stay out of the way.'"

In November 1992, forty-seven women were elected or reelected to the U.S. House, a gain of nineteen seats, and four more women were elected to the Senate, bringing the total to six. (Texas Republican Kay Bailey Hutchison would come to the Senate later, via a June 1993 special election.) That fact was extraordinary, media reports proclaimed: The number of women senators would triple, and a record number of women would serve in the House. Headlines aside, the reality was that when the 103rd Congress convened, women made up only 11 percent of the House and 7 percent of the Senate. The political success of these women was news precisely because they were still so unusual. As *New York Post* columnist Amy Pagnozzi commented, the media term "Year of the Woman" didn't exactly convey the message that women were assuming control of government. "It doesn't sound like we're about to take over Congress or the Senate or the White House," she said. "What it sounds like is that they're going to give us a big, noisy parade down in Chinatown." And Pagnozzi told a conference after the Democratic National Convention, "I don't want to see us confuse speaking about change with actually making changes. . . . The story of the Year of the Woman tomorrow is going to be fish wrap, and we haven't even started yet."

Columnist Wendy Wasserstein mocked the tokenism of the Year in a *Harper's Bazaar* piece a year later: "Now that the Year of the Woman is history and we've moved on to grunge for spring, perhaps it's time to look back on the historic gains and losses. Of course, a year is a very short amount of time to mobilize an entire sex, but 365 days was all we were given." She suggested holding an all-star salute featuring Barbra Streisand singing "The Way We Were." At the end of the evening, "all the pundits who came up with the Year of the Woman motif will rest easy knowing it was a great idea whose time had come and gone."

The *Washington Post* also spoofed the media's obsession with the Year of the Woman in a national weekly edition piece by Henry Allen in January 1995: "This, say the pundits, is the Year of the White Male. We just had the Year of the Woman, but apparently it didn't take. Why haven't the supposedly vigilant media told us more about these people? Though percentages of white males are dwindling in the media (and other businesses), editors and producers could have found enough to infiltrate white male-dom. None of this happened overnight. Long before Speaker-to-be Gingrich was mailing around his motivational tapes, white males were extending their tentacles into every crevice of American life."

Another reality check in the aftermath of the Year of the Woman was provided by a *New York Times* story in May 1993 about how, despite the changes on the Hill, not much had changed at home. Marian Burros's story began this way:

> WASHINGTON—Alice Rivlin, deputy director of the office of management and budget, shops at her local Safeway, where she often runs into people who are surprised to see her there.
>
> She's just as surprised at their reaction. "How else do they think I'm going to get food?" she said as she sat in her office in the Old Executive Office Building. "Do they think I have a staff? I don't know what they think. All of us run households."
>
> In a year when more women than ever took seats in Congress and were appointed to important government posts, and when the first lady

was given the responsibility for health-care reform, very little has changed at home for women who work, even at the highest levels. . . . So much for the Year of the Woman.

Syndicated columnist Ellen Goodman wrote that the much ballyhooed Year "reminds me of the 'overnight singing sensation' discovered after twenty years of training. The breakthrough came only after a generation of women moved in a slow and grueling pace through the system." Media hype gave many people the false idea that women had finally "made it" in high-level politics. And media emphasis on gender tended to shroud a fact that was probably more important in terms of the direction the country was headed—that most of the women elected to Congress in 1992 were liberal Democrats.

The partisan makeup of the House and Senate had not changed when the 103rd Congress convened. The Democrats retained their 57-43 advantage in the Senate, while House Democrats lost just ten seats to retain a 258-176-1 edge. Nor did the upper echelon change; men still held the top leadership positions in the House and Senate. But women did increase their numbers. And women were tapped for some of the lower Senate leadership positions. Barbara Mikulski was named assistant floor leader, and one of the four vacancies on the Democratic Caucus steering committee went to Barbara Boxer, putting them in positions that would make them more valuable sources for the media.

Journalists took note of the changes, most obvious on the day the House convened for the first time. News accounts reported it was a rowdy gathering, with children and grandchildren crowding the seats along with the representatives. Some standing in the back of the chamber looked a little shaken by the noise echoing off the House floor, reported *Congressional Quarterly*, adding that in spite of the hubbub, two small boys managed to nap, leaning against their grandmother, Representative Eddie Bernice Johnson of Texas. Representative Marjorie Margolies-Mezvinsky was heard talking about how she had stuffed borrowed shoes with newspaper so that one of her eleven children would be presentable for the swearing in. Stories about the raucous behavior of small children in the grand chambers of the Capitol might have taken a stereotypical approach—assuming that because these were women representatives, they would be responsible for looking out for their children. But many articles made an effort to include descriptions of male legislators with their children.

Things were more sedate on the Senate floor, where only the senators and a few staff members were permitted. But that didn't stop those in the gallery from celebrating the arrival of the new women senators. Cheers rang out when Dianne Feinstein and Barbara Boxer escorted each other to the floor. The symbolic meaning of the women's victory was captured by news photographers as Senator Carol Moseley-Braun and two other women were sworn

Former San Francisco mayor Dianne Feinstein was elected to the U.S. Senate in 1992.

in. Moseley-Braun smiled triumphantly at the gallery, packed with women, and raised her hands in a thumbs-up salute. A few days later Feinstein and Braun made headlines again when they became the first women to be named to the Senate Judiciary Committee. Chairman Joseph Biden (D-Delaware) had promised in a television interview that there would be women on the committee, "come hell or high water." Judiciary had been one of many Senate committees lacking female members, and Feinstein had told a radio interviewer that women could bring a different outlook. If she had been sitting on the committee during the Thomas confirmation hearings, she said, "there would have been a lot of questions asked that weren't."

The 1992 elections not only brought new women's voices to Congress but in a tangible way created for the news media a heightened awareness of gender. There's a big difference between stories that include gender as an integral element and stories where a woman's gender, appearance, or supposedly "feminine" attributes are described gratuitously. The *Washington Post* ran several stories that owed their newsworthiness to gender, including articles on the informal sisterhood of black women in Congress and about continuing stereotypes faced by women candidates.

The *Post*'s Kevin Merida says he consciously tries to diversify sources in his stories so women are represented. One example is Merida's 1993 story on the disorganization and chaos that characterize the lives of many members of Congress. It opens with a quote from a man, followed by a quote from a woman, and so on. Ten years ago probably all the sources would have been male. Merida, who is African-American, says a reporter doesn't have to be black to be more attuned to underrepresented groups but that it "increases the likelihood that you'll be more sensitive to balance, to getting people included that haven't been included." One significant change he notes is that there is more diversity on the Hill than there used to be. "It's easier to find people of all different backgrounds now."

Greater numbers of women in Congress may also have helped raise the consciousness of some journalists, as this exchange between Barbara Mikulski and the press suggests: When the four new Democratic women senators came to Washington for orientation after the 1992 election, Mikulski invited them to her office. "The media wanted to know: Was I giving them a tea?" Mikulski recalls. "I said, 'No. I'm having an empowerment workshop.' I was passing along information about how to get committee assignments through the formal channels, as well as through the hidden hallways of power. This is the kind of folklore that normally only gets passed around in the men's locker room in the Senate gym."

Far more persuasive of women's influence in politics than media drum-beating about the Year of the Woman was the way the news media chronicled the stories of the women's first months in office, the ones where women ran headlong into the old-boy power structure. They didn't always win but they made great copy. Again, stories were frequently patterned on the traditional formula of David vs. Goliath or the new kid on the block taking on the bully. In July there were stories of Carol Moseley-Braun challenging conservative Republican Jesse Helms of North Carolina over the symbolic meaning of the Confederate flag. A measure to extend the patent for the Confederate flag insignia used by the United Daughters of the Confederacy had been defeated in committee, but Helms had slipped it in as an amendment to another bill. "She KO'd the body's self-designated ogre," *Washington Post* columnist Mary McGrory wrote gleefully. The Senate's "first black female member had shamed the club into realizing that it is not an old boy's club and maybe not a club at all but a body with responsibilities for protecting minorities in the country as well as in its membership."

Then there was Dianne Feinstein fighting the sexist stereotype implied in Larry Craig's comments on gun control. Feinstein had offered an amendment to the Omnibus Crime Bill that would ban sales of semiautomatic weapons, and she had explained her position on the floor. But Idaho Republican Craig disagreed with Feinstein's description of the gun used in a San Diego fast food restaurant shooting in which twenty-one people were killed. "The gentlelady from California needs to become a little bit more familiar with firearms and their deadly characteristics," Craig told Feinstein. "I am quite familiar with firearms," Feinstein responded. "I became mayor as a product of assassination. . . . I proposed gun control legislation in San Francisco. I went through a recall on the basis of it. I was trained in the shooting of a firearm when I had terrorist attacks, with a bomb at my house, when my husband was dying, when I had windows shot out. Senator, I know something about what firearms can do." Two years later Feinstein again drew on personal experience when the Senate Judiciary Committee held hearings on anti-terrorist measures.

She recalled how a bomb was left at her house while her husband was there dying of cancer, but that it was too cold to detonate, and she told how later someone shot out the windows in her house.

And there was the *Washington Post* story in August about how the "sisterhood" of the hill was trying to change the largely white, largely male Congress. Kevin Merida's story began this way:

> It was a dramatic scene on the House floor: Rep. Henry J. Hyde (R-Ill.) surrounded by angry, black female lawmakers.
>
> The women accused Hyde of using racially offensive and paternalistic language during a heated debate over federal funding of abortions for poor women. Although Hyde later apologized to one of the black lawmakers, Rep. Cardiss Collins (D-Ill.), the scene is etched in his memory.
>
> "It is intimidating to have five or six women all glaring at you," said Hyde, who is a tall, portly, white male and a leader of the anti-abortion forces. "It was like lighting a firecracker."
>
> Freshman Rep. Cynthia A. McKinney (D-Ga.) suggested Hyde should be glad he only had to withstand a verbal onslaught. "I was sizing him up," she said with a chuckle. "I figured I could take him. I know how to street fight."
>
> "We're shaking up the place. . . . If one of the godfathers says you can't do this, my next question is: Why not? And who are you to say we can't?"

In the House there was Connecticut Representative Nancy Johnson receiving an apology from her colleague, Ways and Means health care subcommittee chairman Pete Stark, over a sexist comment he had made during a public hearing after Johnson, respected as a Republican health care expert, disagreed with a provision in Stark's health plan. Stark suggested that Johnson had learned about the issue through "pillow talk" with her husband, a physician.

But all this was nothing new to Patricia Schroeder, first elected to Congress in 1972. She remembers when a committee chairman told her that "if I would use my uterus rather than my mouth I could get more of my amendments passed." Compared to that, Schroeder told the *Washington Post*, the comments made to women lawmakers in the 1990s seem like progress. "Things aren't perfect," Schroeder said, "but they're moving in the right direction."

Even in 1992, a double standard existed in the way reporters dealt with women and their campaigns. There was still a tendency to trivialize women by focusing on their appearance or by asking condescending questions. It was enough of a problem to prompt the editors of *Campaigns & Elections* to run an article advising women candidates how to avoid gender issues. The article, headlined "Beauty Pageant," described the perils of dealing with the press. Often women seem to be stuck between a rock and a hard place. Whatever they do will be criticized. For example, the article said the media love to portray emotion. But women must be careful about how much emotion they show. Tears may be interpreted by the media as a sign of weakness in a woman. But when President Bush cried over the Persian Gulf War, the media said it was good for his public image.

The article advised women politicians to be assertive in taking credit for what they have done, to stay focused in the face of questions like "How does your husband feel about your running?" and to take the emphasis off clothes, hair, height, and weight by giving the media visually appealing events to cover. Visuals can also help reinforce what a candidate wants to say, and they can send more than one message. Texas governor Ann Richards understood the value of that advice and put it into practice in political ads that showed her dressed in camouflage with a rifle, implying that she was comfortable with a gun and that she supported the right to bear arms. The underlying suggestion was that she fit right in as "one of the boys."

The news media's handling of stories in the Year of the Woman demonstrated ways in which journalists not only reflect but help create public attitudes. After the election of a record number of women to high public office, the media provided periodic reality checks on their political life. Through columns and aricles, journalists hammered home the idea that the 1992 elections were only one stage on the road toward women's full participation in government, not an idea whose time had come—and gone.

❖ *Chapter 10* ❖

THE KAMIKAZE
CAMPAIGN AND POLITICS
AS USUAL

ELIZABETH HOLTZMAN AND ANN RICHARDS WAGED ELECTION CAMPAIGNS THAT, AC-cording to media pundits, set new lows for sleaze and acrimony. After her 1992 New York Senate primary battle, Holtzman was dubbed the "town witch—the most hated Democrat in New York politics" by *New York* magazine, while Richards accepted accolades for being tough enough to take and sling back political mud in her 1990 Texas gubernatorial campaign. How did Holtzman end up in the media gutter while Richards enjoyed what the *New York Times* called the "national adoration of the press"? The most obvious answer is that the media judged them by a double standard. Holtzman was campaigning against another woman. Richards was campaigning against a man.

Holtzman was one of four candidates vying for the Democratic nomination for a New York Senate seat in 1992, and when she attacked front-runner Geraldine Ferraro it became front-page news. Journalists and observers reacted with horror or glee, depending on their point of view. Why? Because a woman had attacked another woman. The *Washington Times* called it a "cat fight," while the *New York Times* termed it a "feminist paradox." A *Washington Post* headline seemed to view it as proof that women can't get along. It read: "Political Sisterhood Sours in N.Y. Race."

At first the race was seen as evidence that times had indeed changed. In a year when more women than ever were running for elective office, the two prominent Democratic women in the race gave voters the opportunity to upset the Republican incumbent and send another woman to the Senate. But as the primary campaign heated up, some media observers expressed concern that the women weren't acting the way women were supposed to act. They were behaving more like traditional male politicians. It certainly wasn't the first time a woman candidate had run against another woman. But this was a particularly dramatic race. These were two highly visible and celebrated women.

New York Comptroller Holtzman had a reputation as a giant killer for having defeated veteran congressman Emanuel Celler in 1972 to win a seat in the U.S. House of Representatives. She resigned after four terms to run for the Senate but narrowly lost to Republican Alfonse D'Amato in 1980. The next year she was elected Brooklyn district attorney and served in that post until 1990, when she became comptroller. Ferraro was a two-term congresswoman from Queens and the 1984 Democratic vice presidential nominee.

Ferraro had considered taking on D'Amato in 1986 but decided she couldn't win. Her negative ratings were too high, a remnant of the media scrutiny she had received as a result of allegations of financial wrongdoing by her husband, John Zaccaro, in 1984. The Justice Department's investigation of Zaccaro's contributions to his wife's 1978 campaign continued in late 1985, and there were still questions about her congressional financial disclosure statements. Then, in 1988, her son, John Zaccaro Jr., was convicted of selling cocaine to an undercover agent. But Ferraro says she thought she had laid questions about campaign finances to rest when she challenged D'Amato in 1992. Her overall negative ratings stood at about 30 percent, but she had terrific name recognition, and she was convinced there would be no surprises. "If this were going to be a repeat of 1984, where we would wake up and be stunned by God knows what they were throwing at us, I wouldn't run," she told *U.S. News & World Report.* "Now, everybody knows everything that's happened to us. There's nothing there to shock." Or so she thought.

Ferraro's campaign ads played up her role as a star of the 1984 convention, a former teacher, a prosecutor, a congresswoman, and a mother. She presented herself as tough on crime—she favored the death penalty—and supportive of abortion rights. She sought to capitalize on the political sentiment that favored women as outsiders. What she didn't expect were news stories, followed by Holtzman's ads, that focused on allegations that she and her family had links to organized crime. Ferraro has repeatedly denied that she or any member of her family was involved in organized crime. "I wish I *had* organized crime connections. Nobody would have kneecaps," she says about her Senate primary opponents. Ferraro also says that during the confirmation hearings on her nomination as ambassador to the Human Rights Commission, "not one question was asked about organized crime connections because it was a joke. The only time it comes up is in politics."

Ferraro says her relationship with the media was generally good during the 1992 campaign ("I do well with the press; the press is really quite good to me") and that things turned sour only at the last, when Holtzman and a third candidate, Attorney General Robert Abrams, began making accusations and the media carried stories about their allegations. "They had to report it— there was nothing you could do about it," Ferraro says, noting that journalists obviously thought it made good copy—especially Holtzman's attacks on her. "They loved that type of thing," she says, "the fight going on between these women."

Holtzman's attack ads attracted so much media coverage that their impact was intensified. Would the ads have attracted as much attention had Holtzman not been a feminist attacking another feminist? After all, it is standard political strategy for a candidate lagging in the polls to assault the front-runner in an effort to open up the race and snag some votes. Ferraro, for instance, had attacked front-runner Abrams in the early stages of the campaign for waffling on the Persian Gulf War. But Holtzman's charges were not about mere indecisiveness. She charged that Ferraro "took $340,000 from a child pornographer." Ferraro's husband had rented warehouse space to a mob-connected pornographer for three years after she promised to have him evicted. But Ferraro said the man was out of the building by 1992 and that the matter had been fully hashed out. The child porno ad ran only once, but its ripple effect was devastating as news stories about it began cascading.

"Holtzman was hell bent on destroying me," Ferraro says. "She destroyed herself and Abrams and me—all three. This woman was so crazed. We had already gone through that; the guy was out of the building; I never even met this man." Ferraro likens Holtzman to a "kamikaze pilot" who destroyed herself in the process of taking out the target. But Holtzman says it was a legitimate question and an issue that she had long been concerned about. As a member of Congress she had introduced legislation to stem child pornography, and as Brooklyn district attorney she had worked against sexual abuse of children. "I didn't think it was an issue beyond the bounds," she says.

Holtzman was careful to delineate between Ferraro's activities and those of her family. That the issue was "delegitimized and demonized" still astonishes her. "There were people who attacked me and said it wasn't feminine. It was the outcry over 'How dare I' that made this thing so outrageous. It was an extremely clever response to take my questions and turn them into being antifeminist, so it was no longer even legitimate to ask such questions."

Holtzman's final television ad showed an unflattering still picture of Ferraro with her eyes narrowed and mouth open, next to clips of newspaper headlines about her finances. "Want to beat the sleaze and elect a woman?" says the narrator. "Liz Holtzman." Ferraro's ads tried to rebut the charges. Over footage of Anita Hill's testimony before Congress, a narrator said, "Just a year ago, a woman with courage faced lies, innuendo, and smears. Now another woman whose life has been a fight for change is being smeared." Abrams got into the act too. His last ad before the election featured harp music in the background as his face and accomplishments flashed on the screen. But when the ad focused on Ferraro's "ethics violations," the music sounded more like groaning.

Ferraro had not expected the media to figure so powerfully in her Senate race. In fact, she says, when she first decided to run in 1992 the media response was "horrendous," but she knew she was a strong campaigner. She figured she wouldn't have to rely on the media in the same way she did as a vice presidential candidate in 1984 and would be able to take her campaign directly to the people. "In local or statewide races, if they can touch you and see you, they will make decisions based on what they know about you," she says. "You can go directly to them, and the press can say you're the most vicious person" and it doesn't matter as much as it does in a national race.

Elizabeth Holtzman was a heroine of the women's movement until she attacked frontrunner Geraldine Ferraro in the 1992 New York Democratic Senate primary.

In March 1991, Ferraro trailed behind Abrams and D'Amato, and her unfavorable rating was higher than those of other potential Democratic candidates. Described by the *New York Times* as "a fierce, mercurial, engagingly physical campaigner," Ferraro set out to win the nomination. A year later she had pulled even with Abrams. Ferraro and Holtzman both had the support of women's groups such as NOW, the Women's Campaign Fund, and the National Women's Political Caucus, but only Ferraro was endorsed by Emily's List, and the early money helped put her in the lead. That troubled *The Nation*'s Katha Pollitt, who wrote that she understood the practical reasons for supporting Ferraro, who had a good shot at winning. But at the same time, she said, "the marginalizing of Holtzman testifies to a certain narrowness in this whole 'Year of the Woman' business."

The campaign was an example of genuine sleaze, wrote John Taylor in *New York* magazine, and the "most convoluted development in the gender campaigning that has been such a prominent feature of this election year." He noted that a tenet shared by feminists and liberals is that more women are needed to bring a "different and morally superior political style" to Congress. But Holtzman told the *New York Times*, "It's dangerous to sentimentalize gender. There are differences between women. You can't consign women candidates to the kitchen and say they can't ask the tough questions. Campaigns aren't necessarily polite debates."

In fact, the candidates' televised debate the week before the September primary was anything but polite. The *Washington Post*'s Helen Dewar called it "tense, riveting and a little weird." Al Sharpton arrived at the debate carrying a bucket of mud to present to his opponents, telling reporters it was "so they can sling mud while I'm discussing the issues." Holtzman and Ferraro traded icy stares as well as verbal jabs. At one point the moderator tried unsuccessfully to stop them, protesting: "Ladies, ladies! Ms. Holtzman, Ms. Ferraro!"

Abrams edged out Ferraro in the primary, and Holtzman came in last, with even fewer votes than Sharpton. D'Amato defeated Abrams in the November election and held onto his seat for another term. Holtzman said after the primary that she had no regrets about the tone of the race and that it was a mistake to set different standards of conduct for women. "I think that to apply a standard to women who run—saying that they have to be treated differently and treat others differently—it's just wrong," she told a reporter. "We have to have the same expectations of candor from all of the candidates." Holtzman told another reporter she ran a "tough and hard campaign . . . a traditional New York campaign" and said it wasn't fair to say that when a woman runs for office, she isn't entitled to try to win. "I entered this race to win."

But voters across the country came down harder on candidates they believed had failed to meet higher standards expected of women. As Democratic pollster Celinda Lake wrote in a *New York Times* op-ed piece after the election, "In the end, voters were harsher in their judgments of women than of men who fell off the pedestal." Afterward, the *Times* reported that the post-election debate among feminists was "poisonous," with *Ms.* magazine founding editor Letty Cottin Pogrebin saying she would never again support Holtzman for anything, and feminist author Betty Friedan insisting Holtzman shouldn't be blamed for Ferraro's defeat. Meanwhile, Holtzman herself appeared to have lost more than the primary. One magazine said her attack on Ferraro was the political equivalent of a suicide car bomb. "It certainly hurt Ferraro, but it destroyed Holtzman." Once routinely referred to in news reports in terms like "steely" and "feminist purist," Holtzman had evolved into the wicked witch by the time she entered the 1993 Democratic primary to retain her position as New York comptroller.

A *New York* magazine piece by Eric Pooley, headlined "Ding Dong?" opened with this question: "How did Elizabeth Holtzman get to be the town witch—the most hated Democrat in New York politics?" The answer lay partly in her 1992 "scorched earth campaign" against Ferraro and partly in her "pinched and self-righteous" demeanor, the article said. That sort of description reflects Holtzman's media reputation as a straitlaced, intensely serious, and humorless official. Actually, Holtzman has an ironic, self-deprecating sense of humor. During her years in public office she says she learned to tell what the tone of a newspaper story about her would be by looking at the photo that ran with it. The *New York Post* showed a "special degree of ingenuity" during her 1980 Senate campaign by running pictures of her with blacked-out teeth, she says. "So I figure if they haven't done that to me, I'm ahead of the game."

On top of the fallout from the 1992 campaign, Holtzman was hurt by city and federal investigations of her dealings with Fleet Bank, which had loaned her $450,000 for her 1992 media campaign. About six months later, her office chose the same banking company to market $6,000,000 worth of city bonds, which would have made Fleet hundreds of thousands of dollars in commissions. But the *Times* broke the story and the mayor nixed the deal. Holtzman said she didn't know Fleet was among the firms chosen by her office to underwrite bonds.

The *New York* article noted that Holtzman cried during a 1993 television interview after one of her opponents for the comptroller's post began running a series of television spots criticizing her job performance, her use of smear tactics against Ferraro, and her dealings with Fleet. "Some who know her actually thought the tears might be staged. (Few knew her well enough to say for sure, which is the sadness of a political life.)" New York City-based political consultant Norman Adler recalled how different the reaction had been to Holtzman's defeat in her 1980 Senate race. It was a tragedy for women and for liberal Democrats. "People wept from one end of the state to the other," he said. "She was Joan of Arc in panty hose." By the time she lost her race for comptroller, "there weren't fifty misty eyes in America. . . . She simply went from being one of the most important women in American politics to being one of the most disliked."

The Ferraro-Holtzman race prompted discussion in the national media of several important questions: Should women politicians be held to higher standards than men? Or is it sexist to suggest that women candidates should be less aggressive and campaign in a different style? Should women avoid attacking other women, especially if they're feminists? Are women politicians really "agents of change"—or are they just more of the same? Syndicated columnist Ellen Goodman said the questions about how women should run campaigns are a variation of an old and contradictory theme: Fairness and equity require that women be judged the same as men when they run for high political office, yet women are different and are expected to change politics for the better. "Our expectations . . . for women candidates are enormous. We expect them to succeed in the one existing system, and we expect them to change that system." Goodman contended that women must raise the standard of campaigning or face becoming "partners in a political system that's in full, cynical collapse." Goodman chided Holtzman for her "highly personal and often unfair attack on Ferraro," and characterized her as a spoiler.

Washington Post syndicated columnist Colman McCarthy said the two women had acted like "warped people"—like men—and he blamed their vicious campaign styles on the high cost of winning office. "In the well-hyped Year of the Woman, some women have been running for office as though they have male chromosomes. Geraldine Ferraro and Elizabeth Holtzman . . . savaged each other in old-style macho politics. Their joyless and negative campaigning against each other displayed the kind of gut-fighting that is the archetypal symbol of man-to-man hostility. The cost of winning means winning at all costs. Women politicians are ensnared by an electoral ritual that was designed by competition-driven men. . . . They were women in a man's game. They embraced the male rules of competition and abandoned sisterliness that would have enhanced their lives, in politics or out."

McCarthy said it was fair to ask that women campaign on a higher level than men, that they be sisterly even though men aren't asked to be brotherly. "How else, unless with higher standards from women, can the mess be undone that men with low standards have created? If women want to lead, let it be a new way—the higher way."

In late August, after Holtzman's first attack ad had appeared, Harriet Woods, president of the National Women's Political Caucus, took a pragmatic approach in interviews with the media. "For us, the goal is to have a woman elected senator in New York, and we would be very happy if either of them won," she told the *New York Times.* "But we will be very unhappy if they kill each other off." In September, Woods wrote a column for the *Los Angeles Times* bemoaning the nastiness of the race, noting that the press loved the conflict and saying she would be glad when it was over. She too raised the questions of whether women should set a higher standard in campaigns, particularly toward one another, and expressed concern about the impact the "mudfest" would have on voter attitudes toward women candidates in general. But Woods and some journalists saw evidence in the race that women were not only fighting each other but also fighting double standards. "Wouldn't we be cheering a woman candidate who scored some hits on a male candidate—wherever the blows landed? Why should she pull back just because her opponent shares her gender?" Responding to the contention that a feminist should not challenge or question another woman, Holtzman says it is critical to raise questions "if you want to have women who observe more than the standards of the marketplace in high positions in our country."

Woods blamed male political consultants for persuading the two women that negative commercials work, although women candidates suffer disproportionately. A woman's "harsh attacks may pull down an opponent, but she usually finds her own ratings suffering as well," Woods said. Meanwhile, Todd Purdom posed similar questions in a *New York Times* article headlined "The Feminist Paradox: Holtzman-Ferraro Battle Tests Idea of Women in Politics."

A fundamental question is this, said Purdom: Should women change politics or will politics change women? "Maybe both are in a way unacceptable," Holtzman says, "because maybe we need to allow women to do their thing. As a woman, there were boundaries for me," she says. "I couldn't ask questions, I couldn't raise questions. And in the end, the press loves to have a fight, would rather provoke a fight than discuss substantive issues." She wonders whether the same furor would have ensued if somebody else had raised the same issues.

Running an aggressive campaign doesn't always earn a woman a reputation as a witch. In 1990, Texas Treasurer Ann Richards and Attorney General Jim Mattox slugged it out in a race so tough some pundits begged them to stop. The campaign had become a series of charges and countercharges, vicious television commercials, rumor and innuendo and unrelieved bitterness. A newscaster for Houston's Channel 11 used the words "vicious" and "venomous" to describe the final days of the campaign, and the *New York Times*'s Robin Toner said it had become "a campaign without brakes, a harrowing drive to the limits of modern politics."

Mattox charged that Richards had used illegal drugs ten years before while she was a county commissioner, but he said he could not reveal who had told him. His television ads played up the theme that Richards had broken the law she had sworn to uphold. Richards, a recovering alcoholic, refused to answer reporters' questions about her alleged drug use, saying only that she had used no "mood-altering chemical" for ten years. She in turn, attacked Mattox's business dealings and ethics and questioned his integrity. Her television ads mentioned his 1985 indictment on a bribery charge but failed to note that he had been acquitted. In the final days of the campaign, Texas news organizations reported allegations by three people who said on the record that they had seen Mattox use marijuana in the late 1970s. He denied it. He in turn charged on the CBS show *Face the Nation* that Richards had been treated for cocaine addiction ten years before. She denied it. Bill

Ann Richards survived a bruising campaign to win election as governor of Texas in 1990.

Cryer, a spokesman for the Richards campaign, told reporters the "slime factor" had been so great before the primary that, "at the end of it, you just want to take a shower."

After the primary Richards told a reporter that she had had to fire back after Mattox made his charges. "The reality is that you can't fight fire with anything but a back fire because it just takes one candidate in a race to begin it." Richards won the primary and went on to face Republican entrepreneur Clayton Williams, who led in the polls at the start of the campaign but who made one gaffe after another, insulting Richards and women in general. When Richards let Williams have it in response, portraying him as a Neanderthal, it was considered a fair fight. Williams created a stir when he joked to reporters that poor weather was just like rape. "If it's inevitable, just relax and enjoy it," he was quoted as saying. Later he described how he was "serviced" by prostitutes when he was a young cowboy in West Texas. And at one point he was quoted in the press as saying about Richards that he would "head her and hoof her and drag her through the dirt." Williams also kept the drug use issue alive and joked to reporters that Richards "must be drinking again" to think she had caught up with him. At a luncheon in Dallas, he refused to shake her hand and called her a liar. But Richards took it and dished it out. She accused Williams of being involved in causing pollution, price fixing, and fraud and even alleged that drug money had been laundered through his banks.

Yet even after this mudbath, Richards had a profile that was among the highest of any politician in the country, and after a year in office her name began cropping up regularly as a vice presidential candidate. She was described in a *New York Times* Sunday magazine piece as "a national political force . . . a heroine to the women's movement and a big draw on the national fund-raising circuit." Richards's demonstrated ability to give as good as she got "only added to her legend," the article said.

Still, attacking an opponent—even if he's a man—doesn't always work out well for women. In 1986, a year that many said was marked by a new low in negative political campaigning, two women lost their races largely because of their negative campaigns. Linda Chavez opened her unsuccessful Maryland Senate campaign by charging that her opponent, U.S. Representative Barbara Mikulski, was a "San Francisco-style Democrat." Chavez was advised by Ed Rollins's consulting firm, though he didn't personally advise her. Harriet Woods, running for the Senate from Missouri, lost after running a negative campaign early on, later switching to a positive mode. But the damage had been done.

Republican Representative Lynn Martin found out that negative campaigning can backfire when she tried unsuccessfully to unseat Senator Paul Simon of Illinois in 1992. At first Simon said he felt awkward about attacking a woman. But when Martin hired media consultant Roger Ailes she lost whatever protection her gender might have afforded her. Three weeks before the election, Ailes called Simon "slimy" and a "weenie." Personal attacks must have a ring of truth in order to convince the public that they're credible, and it was hard for voters to believe Simon was slimy. Martin later apologized.

And during her 1994 bid for reelection, even Ann Richards was put in the position of defending a remark she had made. She said in a speech that she hadn't built up a record as governor only to have "some jerk" come in and criticize it. She didn't actually call her opponent, George W. Bush, a jerk, but the remark was widely publicized and caused a stir. Richards says the media were just looking for a way to get the campaign going and inflated the importance of the remark. "The media were anxious for the campaign to start—to make something seem like a contrast," she says. For Richards, that's part of a larger picture that doesn't bode well for politics. "I think we've reached a point in our politics when we don't have any fun any more and it really bothers me a lot," she told a reporter. "Everybody takes everything you say literally and they examine it with a microscope and hang it up and see how long it takes it to dry. We've wrung all of the personality out of our candidates and they've lost their verve in the process."

The political media—including paid ads and news coverage—have become too rough. Their tactics are turning off qualified candidates, both men and women. But the answer is not for journalists to ask women to stay above the fray while the news media continue their no-holds-barred coverage. Journalists must become partners in media coverage that focuses on issues, that has humor, and that discerns differences between candidates based on more than gender or appearance. Most important, it must make readers and viewers care enough to want to go to the polls.

Chapter 11

NEARING THE MILLENNIUM

WHEN HARRIETT WOODS, PRESIDENT OF THE NATIONAL WOMEN'S POLITICAL CAU-
cus, visited Louisville in April 1994 to stump for two women congressional
candidates—a Republican and a Democrat—a reporter asked her The Question: What if both women were to win the May primary and end up facing
each other in the November election? "Then we can't lose," said Woods. But
what if two men were to win their primaries and end up facing each other in
the November election? Reporters wouldn't give it a second thought. Journalists continue to make gender a primary attribute when they're covering women
politicians. Women candidates often are still perceived to be outside the norm.

Gender is still mentioned in news stories about women politicians, though
it's usually no longer enough of a news angle to hang a headline on. The
novelty of women politicians has receded as more women hold office at the
local, state, and national level. Women have challenged other women in races
for congressional seats without gender being played up as the primary news
value. But women running for Congress or governor often must field the same
outworn gender-related questions that reporters asked a century ago.

As the *Louisville Courier-Journal* reporter's question implied, women
are still considered different. In order to ensure equitable news coverage, women
still must project stereotypically masculine qualities, such as toughness and
decisiveness, and try to set themselves apart from stereotypes of women. They
can still expect reporters to ask questions about their mastery of "womanly"
arts such as cooking, sewing, and parenting, as they are being questioned about
their ability to make hard decisions. They may still be described in terms of
their relationship to a husband, father, or child. And no matter how serious
they are, they are still trivialized by media coverage focusing on how they
look or sound, what they wear, or how they style their hair. This happens in
straight news stories as well as in the lifestyle sections. The questions are
asked by both men and women journalists because both are likely to have

internalized traditional cultural norms and because they work for news organizations where the process of gathering and defining the news has not changed in fundamental ways.

Women running for office struggle with "exceptionalism—a feeling like 'I agree that Maggie Thatcher was a tough prime minister, but she was the exception,'" says Celinda Lake, a Washington-based pollster with a number of national Democratic clients. Barbara Mikulski, for example, "had a line about herself that she was a twenty-year 'overnight success,'" Lake says. "It's plugging away, plugging away, and then all of a sudden, it happens. But there's still a lot of plugging away."

Sexual stereotypes are reinforced by the media's preoccupation with image, a reflection of society's obsession with appearance. Candidates were quoted in a September 1994 *Washington Post* story as saying that women were subjected to greater scrutiny of their physical appearance than men, and that more attention was paid to a woman's age. The *Post* reported that the "image thing" was so important that Representative Helen Delich Bentley got at least one facelift to polish her candidacy for governor of Maryland. But Bentley said both men and women realize the importance of image these days. "Men are becoming more conscientious," Bentley was quoted as saying, but "I'm the best new face that Maryland has right now." Even if reporter Thomas Heath was trying to poke fun at Bentley by his choice of quotes, the story was important because it called attention to the fact that stereotypes still exist. The bias against women was vividly illustrated by the anecdote Heath used to close his story: Eleanor Carey, a Democrat running for Maryland attorney general, told about the introduction she was given recently at a Baltimore political club. The person introducing her concluded that "if you want to vote for a woman for attorney general, this would be a great one."

Another story that helped break down traditional stereotypes ran in the *Washington Post* the same day, headlined "2 Ex-Allies Claw Each Other in Bitter Run for Md. Senate." It looked as though it was going to be a classic "catfight" story—and sure enough, this was the lead: "Among the hundreds of battles raging across Maryland for 188 seats in the state legislature, none has deteriorated into a nastier catfight than the one between two former political allies vying to represent the Wheaton-Silver Spring area." But in a wonderful bit of irony the "tough, veteran politician" in the bitterly contested race turned out to be a woman; her opponent was a man. In a sense, the story blew a hole in the old stereotype of a catfight as a contest between two women.

Widespread media coverage given the Year of the Woman left a complicated situation for journalists. Is the playing field finally level? Should gender be ignored as simply an accident of birth? But if journalists ignore gender, are they failing to reflect sizable numbers of Americans who think being male or female is a significant asset or drawback to holding public office? If a candidate for public office doesn't emphasize her gender, should the media focus on it? On the other hand, if a woman plays up being a woman, should the media ignore it?

Hillary Clinton, while not an elected office holder, is a symbol of the media's confusion about how to cover politically influential women. Washington political consultant Ann Lewis says Clinton is a "national Rorschach test of how people feel about the changing roles of women and men." Quoted in *Vanity Fair*, Lewis, a former political director of the Democratic National Committee, says the First Lady gets strong personal support, especially from working women, but also provokes opposition from male "political insiders," who are angry at the way women are changing politics. "I've been taken by surprise by the depth and bitterness of the resentment. This flood of bile has come out. In the guise of insider political commentary, what you get is a kind of 50s sitcom: the lovable bumbling husband, Dagwood Clinton, who takes naps and rummages for snacks, and his competent wife, Blondie Rodham, who's making all the important decisions and the poor schnook doesn't even notice," Lewis said. "That's the oldest stereotype, that if a woman has power, it has to be at the expense of a man."

Like impeached Texas governor James Ferguson, who couldn't run again but promised voters in 1924 that they would get two for one if they elected his wife "Ma" to carry on his policies, Bill Clinton early on stoked fears that Hillary would be an unelected president. She had a harsh introduction to the media as a presidential candidate's wife. Early in the campaign she had to defend her husband on national television against charges of adultery. Later that summer her comment that she could have stayed home and baked cookies instead of pursuing a law degree and career as a lawyer made front-page news and set off a debate on women's roles that rang through the media for months. After the response to her cookie comment, Hillary Clinton's role in the campaign was scaled back and damage control instituted. She even consented to give a favorite chocolate chip cookie recipe to a woman's magazine. But the media didn't let up after the election. Her role in formulating a national health insurance plan—and opposition to her role—was seen by some news organizations as just as big a story as the plan itself. Later, the media focused on her role in Whitewater. Her ethics were questioned and a special prosecutor was appointed to investigate.

As veteran political reporter Patricia O'Brien wrote in *Working Woman* magazine, Hillary Clinton has learned that attacks can come with unexpected ferocity, as they did after a speech she gave in Austin on April 6, 1993, the day before her father died. She spoke about the politics of meaning, explaining that people need to be involved in causes larger than themselves to find true meaning in life—and that politics should also connect us to a higher meaning. The media dubbed her St. Hillary. O'Brien says the First Lady felt wounded by the response of what she called the "elite media" because she felt they mocked her values and integrity and denigrated her because they're afraid of spirituality.

Those who see Hillary Clinton as the embodiment of all the roles juggled by women in public office were concerned when the First Lady was ushered out of her prominent role in guiding the health-care reform effort and escorted to the wings for the duration of Clinton's term. Many believed she was being punished for being too active and too visible. But Hillary Clinton's trials with the press are nothing new. The media have a long history of deriding women with political power or seeking to neutralize their power by reminding mass audiences of their traditional roles.

Syndicated columnist Judy Mann observed that the United States still has trouble stomaching the idea of women as powerful people. She quoted Eleanor Roosevelt's biographer Blanche Wiesen Cook as saying, "We have yet to enter the 20th century when it comes to recognizing that women can be leaders and that women have ideas. . . . I watch media coverage every day and yet I hardly ever see a woman treated with respect or dignity. The most provocative woman in the country is Hillary Clinton, but I don't think there is a First Lady who has been treated as rudely and meanly, except for Eleanor Roosevelt. And in my opinion, it has everything to do with the fact that she is a woman, a woman with power, vision and dignity."

In a column for the *New York Times*, sociolinguist Deborah Tannen said Hillary Clinton is a prime example of the "double bind that affects all successful or accomplished women—indeed, all women who do not fit stereotypical images of femininity: women who are not clearly submissive are seen as dominating and are reviled for it. Women who do not fit the images are not taken seriously. Like Hillary Clinton, you are damned if you do and damned if you don't."

Clinton finally took a step to circumvent the filtering mechanisms of the media and help her get her message directly to a mass audience: Like Eleanor Roosevelt a half century earlier, Clinton began writing a column in the summer of 1995 that was soon syndicated to more than a hundred newspapers. She was welcomed to the "scribblers' corner" by veteran *Washington Post* columnist Mary McGrory, who advised her not to pay attention to her critics but to speak out for the little man. "Your real function is to validate the ideas of people who have nobody to speak for them, who can't get to where the action is and need someone to interpret the guff."

Maurine Beasley, who has done extensive research on women in the media and in politics, said the public loses out when the media "try to figure out how to focus on a woman who doesn't fit a conventional role. [Hillary] Clinton serves to symbolize misunderstandings between women and the media in general; old ideas about women's place in society have been eroded by changing times, but the media seem mired in 19th century mythology."

Some of those old ideas about women's proper place have crept into coverage of Texas Senator Kay Bailey Hutchison. In 1992, Hutchison, then Texas state treasurer and a rising star in the Republican Party, became a national figure when she gave the opening address at the GOP National Convention in Houston. The sudden media coverage made it seem that she was a political newcomer when actually she had won her first election, for a seat in the state legislature, in 1972. She ran for the U.S. Senate in 1993 to fill Lloyd Bentsen's unexpired term after he became treasury secretary, and she was elected by a huge majority—

Kay Bailey Hutchison had been a Texas representative and state treasurer before her election to the Senate in 1993.

almost two-thirds of the vote. But that fall she was indicted by a Texas grand jury on five counts of misusing state employees and destroying evidence in her position as state treasurer. The charges were thrown out by a federal judge, and Hutchison went on to win a full six-year Senate term in 1994.

She is described by her Senate colleagues as a savvy politician, and her Republican colleague from Kansas, Nancy Kassebaum, says Hutchison is both "shrewd and tough." One of the ways she has shown toughness is in weathering aggressive and sometimes very personal media coverage. Hutchison worked as a reporter for a Houston television station after graduating from law school in 1967, and later was press secretary to Ann Armstrong, co-chair of the Republican National Party, so she understands how the media work. "Being a reporter has helped me in dealing with the press and knowing how they think about things," she says, "but it doesn't keep you from getting cheap shots. Once that is done, once something is written, it's there for posterity. It's there for your opponent to take out of context and use against you."

Hutchison has both defenders and detractors in the press. The *Wall Street Journal*, for example, gave her the benefit of the doubt after the grand jury indictments were returned. What it looked like, said the *Journal*, was "a politically motivated fishing expedition intended to damage the new Senator, settle some scores and open the field for the Democratic Party. . . . If [the] indictment turns out to be the use of the legal process for partisan purposes, it will set another new low; but then, Texas is into setting records."

The *New Republic*, on the other end of the political spectrum, chewed

Hutchison up and spat her out, calling her "Kay Bailey Forehead," after the brainless, big-haired congressman Bob Forehead in "Washingtoon." "The possibility of petty election-fiddling is far less troubling than another aspect of the junior senator from Texas: the utter vacuousness of her views," wrote Jacob Weisberg. "In person, Hutchison seems almost an automaton, releasing a trained, expressionless smile, but concealing any spark of human warmth. Columnist Molly Ivins calls her 'The Breck Girl.' Her perfect dyed-blond hair, perfect makeup, perfect suits and perfect stockings give her an anchorwoman's sheen; think of Connie Chung crossed with Georgette Mosbacher, but icier." Other publications have called her two-dimensional, temperamental, and driven. One well-publicized story about Hutchison's reputed temper was that she allegedly struck a female staff member on the shoulder with a three-ring notebook when the staffer failed to find a campaign donor's phone number. The incident came to light during an investigation involving treasury officials.

What gall Hutchison more than political criticism are the gratuitous sexist references tucked into stories and columns, especially when they are by women. Even *Working Woman* magazine, in its 1993 issue on Women in Congress, took a shot at Hutchison, calling her "a sort of aging cheerleader," Hutchison says. Her Republican colleague Susan Molinari of New York wrote the editor chiding the magazine for its partisan attack. Hutchison says she was appalled that a women's magazine "would take a cheap shot at a woman who has just stood up against discrimination against women in the Admiral Kelso vote, and who has been standing for women for all these years. They didn't even know I had helped pass a bill for fair treatment of rape victims in Texas and equal credit rights for women."

But Hutchison also says things have changed for the better since she entered politics. Women are not being judged as much on how they wear their hair or whether their skirts are too short or too long. Ten years ago "you got criticized as a woman in ways that you would never hear criticism of a man, because there are so many options and because people were looking with curiosity at women," she says. "People were judging you on so many extraneous things besides what you were actually doing." She used to worry about how she looked but says women supporters encouraged her to wear the bright colors she favors, not to worry about presenting the "wrong" image. "Basically, the women just freed me to be what I am," she says, "and now I don't ever think any more about dressing down or dressing drab or being offensive—I just do what I would normally do at my age, dress the way I want to, wear my hair the way I do. I've had criticism of it, but mostly now I don't," she continues. ". . . Women are in so many positions now that people don't have to fear whether they'll be tough enough. We have governors, we have senators, mayors by the dozen, and we're doing fine—so there's no reason to judge them any differently. . . . We should be judged on what we do, what is our record, what are our views and what kind of a job are we doing."

A look at how the media have covered New Jersey Governor Christine Todd Whitman's election and time in office furnishes examples of coverage that's free of gender bias as well as stories shot through with vestiges of the way Jeannette Rankin was covered early in this century. When Whitman was running for governor in 1993 some of the national media attention she got stemmed from the fact that she was a woman—still a novelty—and had seemingly come out of nowhere. Whitman had served as a freeholder, the New Jersey equivalent of county commissioner, when she challenged popular Democratic Senator Bill Bradley in 1990. She was written off as the Republican Party's sacrificial lamb until election day, when she came within a few thousand votes of unseating Bradley. She had earned her stripes and demonstrated she could pull in votes. But the next year, when she challenged Governor Jim Florio, the national press still portrayed her as a woman first—and sometimes as an appendage to her husband. The *Washington Post,* for example, described her in a news article as "the preppy wife of a multimillionaire investment banker," and other news stories have described how she looked and what she wore.

After her election Whitman was barraged with questions like "How does it feel to be a woman governor?" During her first year in office, Whitman was also asked repeatedly by reporters how she balanced being a mother with being chief of state. "I don't remember a lot of stories about how [previous male governors] were balancing their lives," says press secretary Rita Manno. Those kinds of questions let up somewhat during Whitman's second year in office, but national political stories still contain references to her dress and the way she looks. Manno fields questions for her boss like "What does she cook?" and "Does she sew?" "We still get a tremendous number of requests for things like that . . . from all over." Manno says it's difficult to interject, in the middle of a discussion with the governor on policy issues, "When's the last time you sewed a button on?"

After other women governors were defeated in 1994, Whitman was the only governor in the country who happened to be a woman, and as a result she was deluged with requests for interviews and appearances on television shows. Every time a reporter or producer needs a high-level woman, "we get requests," Manno says. Will things change as more women are elected as chief executives? After her experience as Whitman's liaison to the press, Manno is skeptical. "If we had forty governors who were women we would still have coverage that looked at the Mom angle and where she bought her clothes."

National coverage of Whitman intensified in 1995 after the governor had fulfilled her campaign promise to cut taxes and was selected to give the nationally televised Republican response to President Clinton's State of the

Union speech in January. In February 1995, one hundred and twenty-one pundits and politicos, said by the *Washington Post* to be "the crème de la crème of Washington insiderism, 'The Conventional Wisdom Makers,'" chose Senate majority leader Bob Dole and running mate Whitman as the GOP's winning ticket in 1996.

Magazine journalism is generally more descriptive than newspaper reporting, though it is not always more sexist. But the *New Republic*'s February 1995 cover story is a good example of sexist

New Jersey governor Christine Todd Whitman has been mentioned as a potential vice presidential or presidential candidate.

writing passed off as sharp political reporting. Headlined "Hot Toddy," the article by John B. Judis purported to explore what it called Whitman's "closet liberalism" and to pin down how she fit into the Republican party. But there was also this description of the governor as birdlike and still under the influence of her parents: "Whitman is a tall, elegant woman with large, doleful brown eyes, a pencil-thin nose, a long birdlike neck and a small mouth that curls to one side when she laughs. She peppers her conversation with repartee and references to being a mother and having children in school. She insists on being known as 'Christie' because her parents called her that. . . . she also has an imperious quality that can be glimpsed when she is challenged. Her eyes narrow and her mouth purses, and she pulls herself up and looks hawklike down at you."

Women's magazines also wanted to profile Whitman, and she was featured in *Vogue* in August 1994 and *Town and Country* in March 1995, with a cover teaser asking: "America's First Woman President?" As might be expected, the description of the governor was far more flattering than that in the *New Republic* but was still a stereotype—a cardboard cut-out of what Hollywood imagined a woman governor might be like. The author, Patricia Beard, told readers to "imagine Katharine Hepburn at 48, cast as a governor. You know what to expect even before the movie starts: principle, gumption, follow through, outbursts of tomboyish mischief and grace under pressure. The plot: the conflict between the desire to get re-elected and the determination to do the right thing."

While the national media were abuzz with stories about Whitman as a potential president or vice president during 1995, her gender and marital status usually figured less prominently in news stories than her politics. In fact, a

New York Times article in May 1995 on Whitman's political future is a text-book example of how far some reporting on women politicians has come. It was written by a man. Headlined "Gov. Whitman Fields Vice-Presidency Question," the article by B. Drummond Ayres Jr. begins by quoting an old saying in politics, that nobody runs for vice president. "So just what was it that Gov. Christine Todd Whitman of New Jersey was doing this week for three long, hard days," Ayres asked, "as she worked the speech and news conference circuit of vote rich Southern California?"

Most of the article was devoted to Whitman's experience and prospects as a fiscally conservative, politically moderate Republican. Only twice did the story focus on Whitman's gender, and both references were integral parts of the story, not gratuitous. One reflected public interest in her gender, quoting a Republican party worker's question to Whitman: "You are a pioneer woman in the Governor's job, so would you consider doing the same for Vice President?" The second was an assessment of Whitman's chances: "And, of course, polls indicate there is still significant though not necessarily crippling opposition out in the country to a woman on a national ticket."

That kind of reporting has led some journalists to say things have changed in the way women politicians are covered. Although 1992 was dubbed the Year of the Woman, news stories about women politicians still smacked of a kind of wonderment that women were even involved in politics. "Women are now becoming a normal part of the landscape. I think there's been a real change," says Boston Globe deputy Washington Bureau chief Mary Leonard. "That's not to say men don't still run Washington and the White House, but there's not the 'Gee Whiz!' phenomenon there used to be." Leonard, who covered Geraldine Ferraro's 1984 vice presidential campaign, said there has been a "sea change" in media coverage of women politicians since then.

Los Angeles Times coverage of the 1992 California Senate elections provides a good example of the press snapping out of gender-focused coverage when gender is no longer the big question mark. Barbara Boxer and Dianne Feinstein were running for California's two seats. They weren't opposing each other, but some journalists and political observers speculated that voters would only be willing to send one woman to the Senate, not fill both seats with women. After the election, journalists seemed giddy at the fact that two women had been elected. It was a historic moment, the *Times* said. Headlines reflected this: "Women triumphed at many levels," "Opportunities, Outrage Fueled Wins by Women," "Women Made Strong Gains." Then, almost immediately after voters had answered the gender question, the coverage began to show some subtle changes. For example, a front page analysis of the relationship of the new women senators focused on "what divides the veteran—and sometimes rival—politicians [and on] what unites them." Only near the end of the lengthy story did reporter Dean Murphy touch specifically on their gender, and then only as it related to their potential ability to work together. "What political necessity does not dictate, historical legacy may," he wrote. "As the first all-female delegation to the U.S. Senate, the two women are tuned to the historic overtones of their dual presence in Washington. Neither wants their partnership to become a model of historic ridicule, aides say."

An editorial after the two women had been sworn in did take note of their gender, but in the context of Feinstein's and Illinois senator Carol Moseley-Braun's appointment to the previously all-male Judiciary Committee. The editorial quoted Judith Lichtman, president of the Women's Legal Defense Fund, that "never again will the legal rights of women be considered only by white men." In fact, after the fuss the newspaper had made about their femaleness prior to the election, it was interesting to see the *Times* urging the newly-sworn-in senators not to focus exclusively on women's issues. Noting that they had each received key committee spots, the paper said, "Feinstein and Boxer have the opportunity to fulfill their campaign promises to better serve all Americans, regardless of gender or race."

In 1994, when Feinstein sought reelection to a full six-year term against Michael Huffington, she had to contend with news stories questioning her spouse's business dealings and their employment of an illegal alien as housekeeper. In another year those kinds of stories might have suggested overzealous media scrutiny of a woman candidate. But Feinstein wasn't singled out for the coverage on the basis of gender. Huffington was hit with exactly the same kinds of stories, involving questions about his employment of an illegal housekeeper and about his wife's involvement in New Age religious groups. It was ironic that Huffington had saturated the media in the days before the November election with political ads about Feinstein's housekeeper. The ads backfired after it was disclosed that he too had illegally employed an undocumented immigrant.

Although media indulgence in gender stereotypes can diminish a woman politician's image, sometimes it can help. It is arguable that the extensive emphasis on California voters' historic opportunity to send two women to the Senate may have persuaded some voters to favor Feinstein and Boxer. In Illinois it was a different story. State Comptroller Dawn Clark Netsch was the first woman in the nation to run for governor with a female running mate, in 1994, and the first woman nominated for governor by a major party in Illinois. Yet she never appealed to voters to support her on the basis of gender and rarely spoke about the historic nature of her candidacy, generating little enthusiasm, even among women in her own party. She trailed incumbent Governor Jim Edgar throughout the campaign. "Maybe it's our fault for not having made more of it," Netsch told a reporter. "But if you beat everybody over the head with it constantly, then it sounds as if you're saying people should vote for you just because you're a woman."

In contrast, Texas governor Ann Richards welcomed being portrayed as a woman because of the general tendency of voters to perceive women as "more trustworthy, harder-working, more sincere, more understanding of 'people like me,'" she says. "If the media characterizes you as a woman first and a public official—whatever your title—second, I don't think the effect is entirely negative," she says. In a 1992 commencement speech at Smith College, Richards said, "It is not that women are better than men . . . but I hope we all accepted long ago that we are different. The most sympathetic and sensitive of our men friends, no matter how hard they try, cannot hear with a woman's ear or process information through a woman's experience."

In 1990 Richards's gubernatorial primary was one of the dirtiest races in recent political history, replete with well-reported sexist comments by her opponent, Clayton Williams. In fact, the *Washington Post* said it had become "almost a parody of the battle of the sexes." But in 1994, when the governor campaigned for reelection against George W. Bush, the race was framed by the media mainly in terms of the conflict of their political philosophies, not as a gender battle. Richards and some other female incumbents lost in 1994. Some Democratic congresswomen were challenged and ousted by other women who were Republicans. As women sought reelection, they were judged on their performance, not on expectations. "Rightfully, there is an expectation raised that women are going to bring about change, that they are going to be different, if you will," Harriett Woods told the *Washington Post* in 1994. "The plus of women's candidacies is that it touches a strong desire of voters for reform. The eventual accountability is: Have you done it, as you come for reelection?"

Former Washington, D.C., Mayor Sharon Pratt Kelly's come-from-behind victory in 1990 and defeat in 1994 demonstrated the pluses and minuses of being a woman in politics. Kelly was the first female mayor of the nation's capital, and the city teetered on the brink of financial collapse during her tenure. "She had such an amazing glow about her when she first came in, and she embodied all of the positives often associated with women candidates," Jamin Raskin, an American University law professor who observes regional politics, said before the 1994 primary in which Kelly was defeated. "She was reform, an outsider, a breath of fresh air—not beholden to interest groups and the bureaucracy. But now, there are no qualms at all about kicking the mayor around because she employs a makeup consultant or because of her husband's relations with city contractors."

Kelly's poor performance in office was enough to persuade some voters to indict all women candidates. "It's a tragedy," said State Senator Mary Boergers, who ran unsuccessfully for Maryland governor. "Some of the people who had supported Mayor Kelly ask me how I plan on running the government. They say, 'See, a woman can't handle it,'" Boergers told the *Washington Post*. "When people aren't used to somebody who looks like me in the governor's mansion, I have a greater burden to prove competence, ability and effectiveness that my male opponents don't have."

It is clear that media emphasis on gender may either benefit or hurt women politicians, depending on the circumstances and the tone of the coverage. But academic studies have shown that in both gubernatorial and congressional campaigns, women receive less issue coverage than their male counterparts. A 1994 study by political scientist Kim Kahn showed that in U.S. Senate races, not only did women received less coverage but the coverage they received was more negative—playing up the unlikelihood of their winning. Kahn said those differences in media treatment may hurt women. The lack of press attention and the scarcity of policy information hinder women from gaining recognition with voters, and the emphasis placed on the viability of women senatorial candidates—or lack of it—may color voters' opinions.

As *Congressional Quarterly*'s weekly report said in 1994, "Despite opinion polls that show non-Washington candidates and women hold a small edge with survey respondents, those candidates have been unable to overcome the financial and media advantages of their well-connected opponents." Harriett Woods was quoted as saying that gender did not cause the defeat of several women candidates. "It is because there is somebody who commands the resources of a Washington insider. An incumbent congressman on important committees who has his buddies raising money for him is able to bring resources to the race that a local candidate will have trouble matching."

Some pundits have contended that, other things being equal, gender should be a deciding factor in election contests. Women should be elected to even the balance of power, to be role models for young women, and to provide a different perspective from men. But by mid-decade a growing number of voices were calling for an end to the media's obsession with a politician's gender. *New York Times* columnist Anna Quindlen argued in 1993 that gender must not be the primary criterion for public office. In a stinging attack on Republican gubernatorial candidate Whitman the week before the November election, Quindlen found the *only* thing in Whitman's favor was her gender—and that, she said, was reason enough to vote for her male opponent. Quindlen took issue with the National Organization for Women's endorsement of Whitman. "Just like the guy who opines that he could never put the fate of the nation in the hands of a girl, NOW's support of Mrs. Whitman seemed to signal that gender is all that matters," Quindlen said. "Gender matters. But when it's the only thing that matters, we are back to square one."

In a column that ran the day before the general election, Harriett Woods chided media commentators for generalizing about gender. She said she was tired of hearing that the 1992 "Year of the Woman" was a fluke just because two women gubernatorial candidates were engaged in rough campaigns in 1993. She said one commentator had even justified his gloomy forecast for women candidates by noting that a woman headed the losing Conservative party in Canada. "This kind of gender generalization is the worst kind of offense against women candidates. Women win and lose on the same basis as men—individually—because of opportunity, because of credibility and qualifications, because of the effectiveness of their campaigns compared to those of their opponents—and sometimes because of just plain luck," Woods wrote. "We don't need to add any new myths. The women running for governor this year have earned the right to be judged on their separate merits. The same goes for all the women who have preceded or will succeed them. It's patronizing to suggest that they be evaluated primarily in relation to their gender."

But, as the *Washington Post* noted shortly before the 1993 election, the gender pendulum may have begun to swing the other way. The *Post* reported that a "macho" political climate had evolved in the year since so many women had won. Even gubernatorial victories by Mary Sue Terry in Virginia (who lost) and Christine Todd Whitman in New Jersey wouldn't change that. "Back then it was enough that women represented new domestic priorities, had a higher 'caring' quotient and were automatically 'outsiders.' Now voters have a new focus: continuing job losses, rising crime and U.S. military embarrassment overseas. All of this is generating a more macho kind of frustration politics. Support for both abortion rights and gay rights has ebbed since 1992, and public concern over Bill Clinton's relatively weak leadership seems to be increasing demand for toughness."

Toughness continued to be important throughout 1994, and several women incumbents and candidates looked vulnerable. In an October *New York Times* column headlined "Year of the Men," William Safire wrote that the year of the woman, "when some female candidates won mainly because of their gender," was having an inevitable backlash. "The moment of high-heeled shoo-ins has passed," Safire wrote. His wasn't the only voice talking backlash. A spate of stories and columns sounded that theme, such as the *Congressional Quarterly* piece saying that 1994 looked like the "Off Year" of the Woman, and the front-page *New York Times* story by Richard Berke that said the 1992 refrain—"Vote for a woman"—was no longer playing so well in 1994. Women candidates had to deal with the stereotype of not being as tough as men on crime. "In a turnabout from two years ago, it is the men who now see the benefit of playing up the sex of their opponent." The *Los Angeles Times* also waved good-bye to women's political ascendancy in a column about negative campaigning headlined "Year of Woman Gives Way to Year of Sleaze." And a *Times* column by Sherry Bebitch Jeffe on California voting patterns began:

"The anthem of the 1992 elections was 'I am woman, hear me roar!' The theme for 1994 could well be 'Why can't a woman be more like a man?'"

The cumulative effect of these kinds of media assessments was to give the impression that women couldn't cut it in tougher times and to reinforce stereotypes about women being the weaker, gentler sex. Crime was an issue in the campaigns of several women running for governor in 1994, including Ann Richards in Texas, Oklahoma state senator Bernice Shedrick, California state treasurer Kathleen Brown, and Dawn Clark Netsch, the Illinois comptroller. Netsch, trying to send an image of toughness, ran an ad showing herself playing pool. Shedrick went further, running an ad in which she staged a reenactment of a crime, kicking off her shoes when a mugger grabbed her purse, chasing him down and identifying him in a lineup. Some say a woman can't be tough on crime, she said in the ad, "But not this woman." Their male opponents stressed their differences with the women over crime. "The reason is pretty clear," wrote David Broder in mid-1994. "Voters by and large want tough action against criminals and they think the guys are less likely to flinch."

Kathleen Brown was put in the position of defending her father's and brother's records; both had been reluctant to impose the death penalty when they were governor of California. Her opponent also linked Brown with California Supreme Court Chief Justice Rose Bird, who had presided over the court when it granted every death penalty appeal. The need to prove her toughness may have prompted Brown to hire political consultant Clint Reilly to run things. Gail Sheehy describes Reilly as "the meanest, obscenity-shouting, macho street fighter among California's campaign managers . . . famously misogynistic." During Dianne Feinstein's gubernatorial race against Pete Wilson in 1990, for example, Reilly faxed reporters that he was "firing" Feinstein as his candidate because she lacked "fire in the belly." Feinstein, who was recovering from a hysterectomy, reportedly retorted, "I thought I had that removed."

In the final weeks of the campaign, Brown finally took a different tack to try to prove she understood the need to be tough on criminals. During a campaign debate, Brown disclosed that her daughter had been the victim of date rape. It wasn't the first time a candidate had revealed highly personal information about family members, but Brown's revelation about her daughter prompted criticism that it was a ploy to boost her standing, especially with female voters. Brown made the disclosure during a televised debate with incumbent governor Pete Wilson after he asked her whether she could be trusted to uphold the state's capital punishment law. She said she resented his "questioning my commitment to be tough on crime." Brown continued: "You cannot imagine what it's like to be a mother waiting at home late at night for your kids to come home, waiting for your daughter to come home in the evening and having her come home and comfort her because she has been raped." Many observers thought at first that Brown was speaking of mothers in general, not of her family's experience. Wilson called it "a moving performance," but later apologized and said he had misunderstood what she had said.

The revelation two weeks before the general election didn't make much difference. Some people praised her for standing up to Wilson and saying a woman could be tough on crime, but on the other hand people wondered if it was just a ploy and whether Brown had her twenty-five-year-old daughter's permission to expose the rape. Her disclosure "wasn't a zinger," pollster Mervin Field told the *Washington Post*. "The fact that you or someone close to you might be a victim of a crime doesn't necessarily say you are capable of combating it." Brown lost the election.

Several women who had been elected to Congress in 1992 also lost, but Representative Olympia Snowe (R-Maine) was elected to the U.S. Senate, raising the number of women in the upper chamber to eight. And some of the women who were ousted from Congress were replaced by other women, but the newcomers for the most part distanced themselves from women's issues. In 1992, the idea of change focused on the election of women, but during 1994 change meant "turn the rascals out."

Much was written about the takeover of Congress by white male Republicans. But one of the most significant consequences of the 1994 elections was the increase in the number and visibility of Republican women in Congress. Seven new Republican women were elected to the House, five of them replacing Democratic women. But none of the new GOP representatives ran on a platform of women's issues, and three of the seven have worked to pass an amendment that would deny abortion funding in cases of rape or incest. Moderate Republicans elected in the Year of the Woman, such as Nancy Johnson of Connecticut, Connie Morella of Maryland, and Susan Molinari of New York, had joined Democratic women in the 103rd Congress in voting for the Family Leave Act, the Violence Against Women Act, and bills authorizing federal funding for some abortions and the Abortion Clinic Access law, but their ability to achieve consensus had been weakened.

One positive aspect of the freshmen Republican women breaking ranks with other, more moderate representatives—what former U.S. Representative Leslie Byrne (D-Virginia) dubbed "the ladies against women"—is that it may have served to further break down the stereotype that women in Congress are concerned primarily with women's issues. "The whole sense of women as one group has been shattered in a way," said *Newsweek*'s Eleanor Clift. "You can't talk about women all caring about breast cancer and child care when you've got women cavorting with the militia." The *New Republic* took note of the phenomenon with a 1995 article by Hanna Rosin called "Invasion of the Church Ladies" that made them sound like angelic gunmolls for the religious right. All owed their start in politics to their husbands, the article said, describing them as "throwbacks to a time when women didn't run for office, a posse of Nancy Reagans unleashed."

Even if they were of a single mind, women hadn't reached a "critical mass" in Congress. Pennsylvania representative Margolies-Mezvinsky joked in 1994 that the women's caucus was smaller than the "mushroom caucus." Nancy Kassebaum doesn't believe that women will reach a critical mass in Washington until there are more women in high places, in positions of power "where they are making tough decisions involving policy and strategy." She cited Anne Wexler, assistant to former president Jimmy Carter, as a rare example of a woman in power. "Since then, no female has been assistant to the President. Except," she added wryly, "Hillary." Representative Barbara Kennelly (D-Connecticut) said women have realized "that it's still impossible to be dominant in passage of legislation—you need more than double the number [of women], especially since the number is divided among liberals and conservatives, Republicans and Democrats. We still have not reached a critical mass." But she added, "it's great not to have to search for a woman on the floor when that's who you want to talk to."

Women may not have had the numbers to constitute a critical mass in Congress, but at least there were enough of them in the Senate in the spring of 1994 to make news when they were unified in support of a bill or protesting some legislative action. The story of their opposition to allowing Admiral Frank Kelso to retire with four stars was played up on the national news and by newspapers across the country. Without Senate approval, Kelso would have left the Navy with two stars and an annual pension of almost $17,000 less. The women lost their fight—the Senate voted 54-43 to approve Kelso's retirement with four stars—but not before a bitter and sometimes emotional debate over Kelso's responsibility in the Tailhook sexual assault scandal. *Congressional Quarterly*'s weekly edition took note of the women's show of solidarity, saying, "the seven women of the Senate put their colleagues on notice April 19 that no action can be taken routinely—and without political risk—when the debate touches on sexual harassment. They did so by banding together for the first time in a floor fight." Later in the article, Barbara Boxer was quoted: "This is the first time that the seven women of the Senate have pulled together across party lines. And I want to say our unity should be noticed. It is important." Boxer addressed the Senate as five women members of the House stood behind her to show their support. Even Kelso's Senate supporters suspected ahead of time what media coverage of the session would look like. Republican Alan Simpson of Wyoming told the Associated Press that news coverage would conclude that the "bozo, baldheaded, old" senators "still don't get it."

But some women who joined in the protest of Kelso's promotion were concerned that they might be stereotyped as caring only about so-called women's issues. Patty Murray, who had rallied her sister senators after learning of the promotion and reading the Tailhook records, says the women would have preferred not to raise the issue. "The instinct within all of us was, 'We're going to be tarred with all-you-guys-ever-talk-about-is-sexual-harassment,' and none of us wanted that. We came here to fight for the economy and education and jobs and big-picture things." Kassebaum, too, believes women should try not to get labeled as being interested only in women's issues, and says it was a mistake for women from the House to march to the Senate over Kelso's retirement. It is important that women be visible in other areas such as foreign affairs and economics, she says.

Kassebaum's concern that women will limit their effectiveness if they get stereotyped in certain roles is shared by Hutchison. "You can't lump us together because we are all first and foremost representatives of our state," she says. "Experiences of women sometimes make for unanimity on issues, and sometimes it doesn't. Where it does I think we do a valuable thing." She cited women coming together on an IRA for homemakers and on women's health issues. Barbara Mikulski, who has championed women's causes such as reproductive rights, is no more comfortable than her Republican colleagues in a role as a spokeswoman only for women's rights. "I was never the senator for women," she said. "That was my point."

Anita Hill's sexual harassment charges against Supreme Court nominee Clarence Thomas had galvanized many women who watched the all-male Senate Judiciary Committee conduct televised confirmation hearings, and paved the way for public discussion of the issue. It also prompted *Washington Post* reporter Florence Graves to go to work on the story of Oregon Senator Robert Packwood's unwelcome sexual advances, which first appeared in the *Post* in November 1992. "I think it would have been difficult to get the Packwood story into the paper before the Thomas-Hill hearings," she said. "It just wasn't a story."

Journalists also began to pay more attention to what female senators had to say about the Senate's three-year investigation of sexual harassment charges against Packwood. But conflict was still a primary news value, and the media played up disagreements whenever they occurred. In 1993, for example, when the Senate was debating whether to subpoena Packwood's personal diaries, the *Washington Post* highlighted what it called Nancy Kassebaum's "rebuke" of her colleague, Washington senator Patty Murray, for urging the Senate to examine its treatment of women who complain of sexual harassment. Although several other senators took issue with Murray's remarks, the *Post* said Kassebaum's comments "took on added significance coming from the senior woman in the Senate." Kassebaum sounded resigned to the reporter's questions about her stance, saying, "Of course it's noticeable when it's a woman rebutting a female colleague." But she reminded the reporter, "We're there as senators." In fact, both Kassebaum and Murray voted on the same side of the question—to require Packwood to produce more pages from his diaries.

Women senators were again the focus of media attention during the summer of 1995 when five of them urged the Senate Ethics Committee to hold public hearings on the charges against Packwood, saying the Senate "is the people's house, not a private club." The committee ultimately held closed hearings, then unanimously recommended Packwood's expulsion for sexual and official misconduct. Syndicated columnist Ellen Goodman wrote that the Senate had recognized that Packwood's behavior was an abuse of power. She said a consensus had been reached that "sexual power-tripping isn't just a private matter or a personal peccadillo. In the hard, reluctant verdict of the committee, it's 'unethical.'"

Meanwhile, the new Republican majority indirectly influenced media treatment of women in Congress. Speaker Newt Gingrich's appointment of several women to the powerful House Rules Committee, which assigns legislation to committees and decides when bills come to the floor for consideration, automatically gave them stature as potential media sources. Susan Molinari, the GOP conference vice chair and the fifth ranking member of House leadership, for example, was frequently mentioned in Washington newspapers, often appeared on national political talk shows, and was profiled in the May 1995 *Harper's Bazaar*. In fact, she became such a prominent face in the media that the *Village Voice* dubbed her a "media darling, the favorite female face of Gingrich's army."

At the same time, the naming of Nancy Kassebaum as chair of the Senate Labor and Human Resources Committee meant she would be valued as an authoritative source, quoted in newspapers and magazines, and appear regularly on the evening news. Kassebaum was immediately thrust into the spotlight when she took over as committee chair. Republican leaders had hoped to kill off Henry Foster's nomination as Surgeon General in Kassebaum's committee after he came under fire from pro-life groups for performing abortions, although he had also been active in programs to prevent teen pregnancy. Kassebaum became a sought-after source on a highly controversial story.

In general, media coverage of Kassebaum's handling of the Foster nomination has had a tone different from those of stories appearing in the late 1970s and early 1980s, when she was a Senate newcomer. Then she frequently was referred to with labels such as "the soft-spoken" or "diminutive" Nancy Kassebaum. While she still speaks softly and her physical size hasn't changed, her stature in the Senate has, and as a result so has some of her media coverage, which now tends to portray her as a skilled mediator who tries to avoid confrontational politics. A front-page profile in the *Washington Post* , for example, didn't focus on the fact that she was a woman senator, and neither did the headline, which said, "Kassebaum's Evenhandedness Earns Respect in

Senate Debate." And yet journalists' old habits die hard. Readers were likely to come away with a picture of Kassebaum as a gentle, consensus-building, grandmotherly type ("In an age of shoot-'em dead politicians, she is from the school of grandmotherly love—more a gentle persuader than a political marksman"). Although her Kansas colleague, Robert Dole, is nearly a decade older, he was not portrayed as being from the school of grandfatherly sternness but rather depicted as a "tough-as-nails career politician with an acerbic wit and an eye for the jugular." Kassebaum is described in the next sentence as a 'demure, common-sense legislator who has what poet Maya Angelou once described as 'an equilibrium usually found only in old philosophers.'" The word "demure" would not likely have been selected for any of Kassebaum's male colleagues who, like her, work hard but shun the media limelight.

And the perennial question was still being asked in 1995: How tough is she? *Forbes* magazine said tough enough. Commenting on her criticism of inefficient federal job training and the need to turn over the welfare system to the states, the magazine asked, "Is Kassebaum tough enough to resist the inevitable pressures from the media and from the welfare constituency when they drench the country with warnings of starvation, infant mortality and the rest? Count on it." Noting that she came to the Senate from a distinguished political family, the *Forbes* article said Kassebaum is "steeped in prairie political lore. Nor is she a flaming conservative. It irks her that so many businessmen come to Washington to support job training programs when she knows full well they are just looking to soften the impact of layoffs they are making. She is well aware that hypocrisy is no monopoly of the left."

A 1995 *U.S. News & World Report* story about Kassebaum, headlined "A 'tough lady' fights a conservative tide," said Kassebaum tries to build consensus and hew a moderate course. But the old cliché about her softness crept in: "Soft edged and soft spoken, she tries to bridge gaps, not broaden them, to avoid fights, not seek them." The headline played off a comment by Maine senator William Cohen, a Republican: "It's a tough role, but she's a tough lady."

Sexist reporting, writing, and editing persists even among well-intentioned journalists—sometimes even if they're female. But several women politicians say they're more concerned about what they see as the abdication of responsible reporting. It has little to do with gender. "We have passed the 'Golden Age of Media,'" says Representative Louise Slaughter (D-New York), described in a 1992 *Washington Post* magazine article as one of the most powerful women in Congress. "I remember with great fondness when the media felt they had the obligation to tell the truth. They did research on it, and if they found out that something someone was saying about you wasn't so, they wouldn't print it. But that's all changed now. They print anything without anyone having the opportunity to say it's not so. They're obviously more interested in selling papers, [they] want to entertain, they want to make something out of nothing if they can. They're trying to out-tabloid tabloids." There are exceptions, she says. The *New York Times* and *Washington Post* stand out as generally accurate and fair newspapers. "I'm not asking anybody to give me a break," Slaughter adds. "I don't want a break. I want to read the newspaper and know that what I'm getting is a reasonable chance of it being what really happened."

Slaughter had served in the county legislature and New York Assembly before running for Congress in 1986. Local papers in her district "have relegated politics to entertainment. Often something important can't get attention." Suppose, she says, she were to discover the cure for breast cancer. In order to get some conflict into the story,

Representative Louise Slaughter (D-New York) was considered one of the most powerful women in Congress when the Democrats were in the majority.

reporters "would go and ask the Republican county chairman what he thought of it, and he would say 'I don't believe it.'" Television is no better. In fact, she says, television is "really awful. I don't have any sense that reporters have a sense of ethics." She says elimination of the fairness doctrine has been unfortunate, because it required stations to give equal time to different political views. Slaughter fears that Americans getting a steady diet of conservative talk shows may never hear the other side.

Ann Richards feels the same way, saying that the American media have become "much more like the tabloids in Great Britain." Syndicated columnist Georgie Anne Geyer has likened this kind of journalism to a malignant cancer that first started growing in 1987 with the campaign to "get" presidential hopeful Gary Hart. By the spring of 1989 the press had become prosecutor, judge, and executioner, she says. The tone of the press has become adversarial to the point of hostility. The "character" issue has dogged potential presidential and vice presidential candidates. Women may be more likely than men to suffer from overzealous media scrutiny. As Helen Thomas, chief of the UPI Washington Bureau, has said, anyone who wants to run for president must "decide at the age of five and behave accordingly."

Indeed, the hostility in news stories and in political advertising is a powerful deterrent to political involvement. Political professionals described the 1994 elections as the most bitterly negative campaign cycle in modern history. Media commentators thought so too. "In this campaign, whatever archaic or hopeful ideas the country had about the female difference were shattered," wrote syndicated columnist Ellen Goodman. "Many used to assume that women wouldn't go negative. Not anymore." Goodman said the effect of the "gruesome" 1994 campaign season could be to discourage women from becoming political candidates. According to Harriett Woods, many women see the process as "personally destructive and totally unappealing."

Is media coverage responsible for the cynicism and distrust so many people express? Are the media reflecting the mood of the country or helping to create it? A little of both. Many people say they abhor the trivia and trash that are broadcast and published about public figures, but ratings and circulation figures don't reflect the criticism.

As the media have gotten more hostile and adversarial, media representations of women have slipped. The Women, Men and Media study released in April 1994 indicated that news about women and reported by women was on the rise, but that men still got the lion's share of attention from the country's news organizations. Women were quoted or mentioned on the front pages of American newspapers more than twice as often in 1994 as in a comparable month in 1989. But men still received 75 percent of front-page references compared with 25 percent for women, up from 11 percent five years earlier. "We are still largely invisible in the media, still subject to symbolic annihilation, despite our increasing numbers in politics and the workplace," said Betty Friedan, author of the study and co-chairwoman of Women, Men and Media.

The study also found that 82 percent of positive portrayals of men were as authorities, experts, or opinion makers, while only 51 percent of portrayals of women fell into that category. Women tended to be depicted as entertainers or sports figures, the study said. Instead of getting better, media representations of women decreased slightly in 1995. Front-page female references slid to 19 percent, according to the annual Women, Men and Media survey. The average number of front-page photos with females in them also dropped substantially, from 39 to 33 percent. The average percentage of females interviewed remained at 24 percent. Furthermore, consultant Junior Bridge said the opinions, commentary, and actions of nationally known women in high positions were seldom included in key front page stories during the study. California senators Dianne Feinstein and Barbara Boxer were mentioned only four times on the front pages of the *Los Angeles Times* during the study month, for example, while Washington senator Patty Murray was missing from national political stories in the *Seattle Times* and Illinois senator Carol Moseley-Braun from similar stories in the *Chicago Tribune*.

The study's harsh findings obscure the fact that many reporters are making an effort to diversify their sources to include more women and minorities. Editors at the *Washington Post,* for example, have been talking about the need for reporters to "get a rich variety of voices into the paper." *Post* columnist Richard Harwood noted how important source selection is to getting at the truth. "There is no doubt that the media need to expand their intellectual horizons by exposing themselves to a broader mix of opinion and expertise. There is no doubt that some of this can be accomplished by broadening the range and diversity of the sources we rely on to reconstruct some sort of journalistic 'reality.'"

✧ *Chapter 12* ✧

FROM A WOMAN'S
POINT OF VIEW

LINDA WERTHEIMER, NATIONAL PUBLIC RADIO'S POLITICAL CORRESPONDENT, WAS A child when she watched Pauline Frederick's broadcasts about Soviet troops crushing the revolution in Hungary in 1956. She found herself thinking, "Look! A woman can do news!" Her surprise is understandable. Women have always been a part of American journalism, first as printers and later as reporters, editors, and occasionally as publishers, but only recently have substantial numbers of women broken into the traditionally male areas of covering politics, government, or international affairs. Women journalists have worked in a male-dominated milieu and may have experienced discrimination, so they are likely to understand what women politicians are up against. Women journalists may perceive women politicians differently from their male colleagues, be more sensitive to issues of concern to women, and be more aware of sexual bias in language. And women journalists may place topics on the news agenda that might not otherwise receive attention—just as women politicians sometimes do.

"It makes a tremendous difference at all levels" because women see and experience things differently from men, says Mary Leonard, the *Boston Globe*'s deputy Washington bureau chief. Geraldine Brooks, a former *Wall Street Journal* reporter, agrees that women journalists often take a different approach than men. She, for example, originated the idea for a 1993 *Journal* story examining why there's never been a woman president of the United States—and then successfully argued for its placement on page 1.

Women journalists are sometimes more tuned in to women politicians, former Texas governor Ann Richards says. "Women reporters pick up on body language and nuance, not just what you say but how you say it. They're much more sensitive to that." Richards says she was often more candid with women reporters because she trusted them not to reveal off-the-record information, though some male reporters also earned her trust. At least one academic study lends credence to the notion that women in general are more perceptive than men in their coverage of women politicians. A 1991 study of women candidates by political scientists Kim Kahn and Edie Goldenberg says female reporters appear to be more sensitive to a candidate's gender and that their coverage pattern may encourage positive evaluations of female candidates.

It has been said that the presence of women journalists has caused the media to scrutinize the moral behavior of politicians more closely. In the past the largely male Washington press corps often winked at moral lapses ranging from drunkenness in Congress to philandering by a president. "When women came into the pressroom, the media started covering character," said Gloria Borger, a *U.S. News & World Report* political columnist and television commentator. "For better or for worse, I don't think the character issue would be as high on the list if there weren't so many women covering politics," added Karen Tumulty of the *Los Angeles Times.* "Women define character differently."

But even if women journalists bring a different perspective to their work, it doesn't follow that they will always be more sensitive than men in their coverage of women politicians. Change has not occurred across the board. "You can find specific examples where women [journalists] make a difference," says *Newsweek*'s Eleanor Clift, "but you can't say it has affected news coverage on a broad scale. . . . I can't say as how I've seen a big change." For one thing, relatively few women direct news organizations, though their increased presence on news staffs does help shape the news. But women are just as likely as men to have internalized traditional cultural assumptions about the role of women in society or politics. Women journalists also may feel they have to prove that they are as "tough" as their male colleagues and compensate for any suspected sympathy toward female politicians by being even tougher on them. Toughness and gutsiness are rewarded in journalism with promotions and choice assignments, and peers tend to razz a reporter who writes a story perceived as fluff. Geraldine Ferraro says, for example, that many women reporters felt compelled to come down harder on her in her 1984 campaign than male reporters did. Women politicians recount times they felt they were "burned" by women journalists. When a woman columnist for the *Houston Chronicle* stereotyped Senator Kay Bailey Hutchison as a "typical Republican housewife," for example, the senator was stung both by the phrase and by the fact that the journalist was a woman. Hutchison had been a lawyer, television reporter, Texas state representative, and Texas state treasurer before her election to the U.S. Senate, and she thought the columnist's label was a ridiculous stereotype. Elizabeth Holtzman says she's been the target of stories by women reporters trying to prove they're "one of the boys," so she doesn't think it makes any difference whether journalists are male or female.

Former Vermont governor Madeleine Kunin says much depends on the individual. "Sometimes women reporters are very nervous about being considered too sympathetic to other women because of their biases and have to prove they're not," she says. Kunin remembers one woman who "earned her spurs by proving to the guys she could be as tough as any man," but Kunin says she was an exception. Generally, the endless news stories written about women's dress, hair and the "toughness" factor have sensitized women reporters, Kunin says. "Certainly there are enough women around who have been asked these questions themselves, and so they are more sensitive to that."

Senator Nancy Kassebaum isn't convinced that having more women in the media makes a difference in the way women are covered because journalists still generalize and oversimplify issues, regardless of whether they're male or female. "They still pigeonhole and lump women together," she says. Former congresswoman Bella Abzug and former Kentucky governor Martha Layne Collins both say they think women journalists should promote women's causes but say many shy away from that because they believe they have to be objective. Some women may try to avoid covering women's issues or women politicians because historically "women's news" was second-class, ghettoized in its own section of the paper, dealing with topics such as society and club notes, gardening, fashion, and care of the home and family.

Whether women journalists are different is such a sensitive topic that a 1985 University of Maryland study saying women journalists could change the nature of news caused a stir. The study found that women journalists were discriminated against in a business that was in danger of becoming a "pink collar ghetto." It also said that if women were in decision-making positions, they might make the news more "attuned to harmony and community." Yet some women professionals strongly disagreed, saying news has no gender. While there's still no consensus on how gender influences news reporting and editing, it is clear that coverage of women politicians hinges on a number of other factors as well, including the philosophy of journalists' news organizations, their position, and their awareness of their own cultural assumptions.

For most of this century, male political reporters protected their turf. Bess Furman, who first came to Washington in 1929, wrote that male reporters made sure women remained outsiders. In her autobiography, *Washington Byline,* Furman recalled covering the opening of Congress: "In the months I had spent in Washington, with a special session on, I could have easily made the acquaintance of the eight women in Congress. But the AP men on Capitol Hill kept it as holy ground, on which I was not supposed to set foot without explicit orders. And so I had to meet and interview all eight Congresswomen in one day, in addition to picking out the women notables in the galleries." *New York Herald-Tribune* editor Stanley Walker also noted the difficulties faced by women in that era: "From the first, the woman who sought to make a place for herself in newspaper work has found editors prejudiced against her. Now, this prejudice is not as great as it was, but it still exists. . . . Men are afraid of women, afraid and suspicious, for their dealings with this curious sex have taught them caution and skepticism."

In the 1930s, Washington correspondents were like sophisticated police reporters who wrote quick, lively accounts, "interpreting events in personalized, melodramatic stereotypes" in order to compete for readers, Leo Rosten wrote. "The Washington correspondent must simplify issues for a public which has neither the background nor the time to analyze what it reads. They must emphasize personalities rather than forces. They must etch those personalities into sharp stereotypes which the reader can find analogous to the ordinary types of his own experience. They must inject into politics the elements of melodrama."

Eleanor Roosevelt made a dent in that male-dominated news machine by stipulating that only women be allowed to cover her press conferences, with the result that various news organizations rushed to hire women reporters for the first time. The group of women reporters assigned to cover Mrs. Roosevelt on a regular basis tended to protect her and not to press her too hard to answer their questions. Michael Schudson tells about the time Mrs. Roosevelt leaked the news that the president had refused to sign a joint proclamation with Herbert Hoover to close the banks the day before the inauguration. The four female reporters told the First Lady that such a story could start a worldwide panic, and they refused to print it. One of them recalled many years later that "the women always covered up for Mrs. Roosevelt. All kinds of things were said [by her] that shouldn't be said in print."

Beth Campbell Short of the Associated Press, one of the women covering Mrs. Roosevelt, had reported all kinds of stories before coming to Washington—from wrestling matches to manhunts for outlaws—but said Mrs. Roosevelt's policy provided an entree for many women into political reporting. "It didn't matter if there was a story on the Hill or Mrs. Roosevelt doing something; if I was the one who was free, they sent me," she told an interviewer half a century later, "but I've thought about it lately. If the women hadn't insisted on press conferences and if she hadn't had the policy of only women covering them . . . well, that's really what gave people like me . . . our break."

Besides the reporters assigned to Mrs. Roosevelt, a few women journalists covered politics, but their presence didn't signal any sweeping change in coverage of women politicians. For the most part, women journalists who had made it onto Capitol Hill didn't want to be known for covering women's news, which had second-class status—and still does today. As Genevieve Jackson Boughner wrote in her 1937 text *Women in Journalism*, "Unfortunately, there is, and always has been, a measure of opprobrium attached to this distinctly feminine contribution—this so-called 'woman's stuff.'" The deck was stacked against them at the outset, and they had to prove themselves as capable as men. That meant that when they covered the same sort of story as male reporters, they often used a similar approach.

Ishbel Ross, who in 1936 wrote one of the first histories of women in journalism, summed up the status of women in journalism, saying that nearly twelve thousand women were working as editors, feature writers, and reporters but that "it is absurd to maintain that a woman can do everything a man can do on a paper. . . . She is denied the chummy barroom confidences of the politician, and cannot very well invade a Senator's room in Washington when he has no time to answer her questions except as he changes for dinner. . . . The fact remains that they never were thoroughly welcome in the city room and they are not quite welcome now. They are there on sufferance, although the departments could scarcely get along without them. But if the front page girls were all to disappear tomorrow, no searching party would go out looking for more, since it is the fixed conviction of nearly every newspaper executive that a man in the same spot would be exactly twice as good."

There were notable exceptions—women who carved out a place for themselves in traditionally male political coverage. Winifred Mallon, for example, had begun sending news dispatches from Washington in 1902 and was admitted to the press gallery in 1918. She wrote for the *Chicago Tribune* for twenty years and joined the *New York Times* in 1929 as a full-time member of the staff assigned to cover political stories—a breakthrough for the conservative *Times*. Doris Fleeson joined the *New York Daily News* in 1927 and was sent to the paper's Washington bureau in 1933, where she began writing a syndicated political column. Fleeson was influenced in her choice of career by William Allen White and other male journalists who seemed to her to have exciting and interesting lives. She "saw no reason why [she] should not do the same." She was also critical of the lack of women in top levels of newspaper management. *Time* listed Fleeson as one of "the best Washington newspaper reporters" in 1951, the only woman among thirteen reporters mentioned. *Washington Post* columnist Mary McGrory tells the story about the time Fleeson was told that she thought like a man. "What man?" Fleeson snapped.

Also reporting from Washington in the 1920s and 1930s was Ruth Finney, a correspondent for the Scripps-Howard papers of California and New Mexico. Finney, who had done political reporting for the *Sacramento Star*, soon discovered that the Capitol press gallery was a man's world and that the important beats were already taken. But a public utility bill was moving through Congress with little coverage, so Finney seized on that, researched the subject thoroughly, and became an expert in that area. Ishbel Ross said Finney "ranks as the leading woman political writer working in Washington . . . a recognized authority on power, oil, labor and federal budgeting."

Anne O'Hare McCormick became the first woman to join the *New York Times* editorial board in 1936 and was the first woman to win a Pulitzer Prize in journalism, in 1937. She was to be "freedom editor," publisher Arthur Hays Sulzberger told her. "It will be your job to stand up and shout whenever freedom is interfered with in any part of the world." McCormick gained a place on the *Times* staff in 1921 by submitting articles about average people she encountered during her travels abroad, which were published in the Sunday magazine. She later contributed to the editorial page, wrote a three-times-a-week column, and contributed features to the magazine section.

McCormick was said to have a "masculine mind," a judgment intended as praise for her lucidity and her objective approach to the news. But her colleagues also appreciated her femininity—used as a synonym for sensitivity. She wrote for the paper until she died in 1954, and in a tribute to her on the editorial page Bob Duffus wrote: "She was a reporter and gloried in the title. She could not understand how anyone could be satisfied with less than the personal observation on the spot. . . . In spite of all her genius for seeing, understanding and reporting, she was also a deeply feminine person and could not help being so and would not have wished not to be so."

Although she wrote mainly about international matters, McCormick was also a sharp observer of the domestic scene. In one piece she playfully gigs the Senate, saying that despite serving as a forum of perverse and long-winded oratory, the upper chamber is to be valued for serving as a truly deliberative body. She makes this observation, comparing the Senate to a men's club: "'Old boys' the Senators seem from the gallery, sometimes vain and pompous old boys, enormously pleased with themselves and their position. . . . The chamber is a debating club, and the 'old boys' are decidedly clubby. In general, their attitude toward one another is one of demonstrative affection. They are always literally patting one another on the back and the opponents in the most caustic arguments usually leave the scene of hostilities arm in arm."

McCormick urged government and business leaders to employ women because of their distinctive sensibilities and talents. Discussing her professional success and that of other women journalists of her time, she said, "We had tried hard not to act like ladies or talk as ladies are supposed to talk— meaning too much—but just to sneak toward the city desk . . . and even the publisher's office with a masculine sang-froid."

At about the same time, Dorothy Thompson was writing about politics and foreign affairs for the *New York Herald-Tribune* and the *New York Post*, authored a regular column for the *Ladies Home Journal*, and was a popular radio commentator. She became known as a passionate foe of fascism, winning the admiration of many. Winston Churchill once said that she had "won a famous name. She has shown what one valiant woman can do with the power of the pen. Freedom and humanity are grateful debtors." At the height of her career in the late 1930s, Thompson's column was syndicated to more than 130 papers and was read by millions. Thompson figured so prominently in public life that she was satirized in New Yorker cartoons and profiled in a 1939 *Time* magazine cover story. Her career was described as "phenomenally successful," and she and Eleanor Roosevelt were spoken of as "undoubtedly the most influential women in the U.S." With her syndicated column reaching an audience of more than seven million, Thompson had become for many women "the embodiment of an ideal, the typical modern American woman they think they would like to be, emancipated, articulate and successful, living in the thick of one of the most exciting periods of history and interpreting it to millions."

Although *Time* acknowledged her success, it seemed to downplay her influence by couching it only in terms of women readers who, before Thompson came along, "used to get their opinions from their husbands, who got them from Walter Lippmann." And *Time*'s portrayal of this brilliant woman included a bit of sexist description: "She is a plump, pretty woman of 45, bursting with health, energy and sex appeal. She thinks, talks and sleeps world problems and scares strange men half to death. This is too bad, because she likes men better than women, and when she takes a train, she rides in the smoking car." Thompson deliberately chose to focus on foreign affairs to avoid having to report exclusively on women, and she objected to the American habit of regarding women as "news" and assigning stories about women to women writers. Thus, she was chagrined when the *Nation* asked her to write on the "extraordinary feat" of being a female foreign newspaper correspondent. It should not be cause, she said, for "jubilation every time a woman becomes, for the first time, an iceman, a road surveyor or a senator."

As columnists, McCormick and Thompson had unlimited opportunities to write about whatever they chose and to speak freely, but their careers did not typify women in journalism in the first half of the century, most of whom were still mainly confined to working in women's sections. During the emergency war effort in World War II, women took the place of men in every industry, including journalism, but many were reassigned from the city room to their prewar places on the women's pages after the war ended. In fact, the postwar period proved to be something of a setback for women journalists. In 1949 *Mademoiselle* magazine's job editor surveyed twenty-seven daily newspapers and fifteen journalism schools and concluded, "Newspaper-bent? It's a bad year for it." Newspapers were hiring twice as many men as women, and were paying the women less. "Four years ago, before the men came back, you could have had a crack at a beginning job, even on a big-city daily, and it might have led into the metropolitan reporting most women aim for when they enter journalism. But the girls who started then and have been handling straight news now find themselves shifted to departments with a woman's angle, and when they drop out of news jobs, men replace them."

But it wasn't just that men wanted their old jobs back, though that certainly was a factor. More important was a mind-set among newspaper editors, an implicit assumption that men belonged in newsrooms, women in the women's section. The editors who responded to *Mademoiselle* magazine's survey said they hired men as reporters because "assignments take them where I wouldn't want any lady relative of mine to go at night" and because "women lack evenness of temperament, dependability, stability, quickness, range, understanding, knowledge, insight." That attitude was reflected also in a 1949 journalism textbook tellingly titled *Newsmen at Work: Reporting and Writing the News.* In those days the authors didn't have to concern themselves with inclusive language; the pronouns were all masculine. There simply weren't enough women in the news business to bother using "he or she." In the chapter on covering politics and elections, however, the authors did mention Anne O'Hare McCormick—the only woman "political interpreter" considered to have won public respect and readership.

More common in that period was to find women in the society section of the paper. Chapter 10 of *Newsmen at Work,* called "For Women Only: Society in the News," begins with a paragraph that puts women in their place: "All men are created equal, but their wives are not. Inevitable result: society pages. An unfair generalization? Perhaps, but it is the women, not the men, who read the society section. The best-read society story is read by one woman in four, one man in twenty-five." And in 1948 Vincent Jones, editorial director of the Gannett newspapers, offered this wisdom about women newspaper readers, suggesting society's view of women's interests and capabilities: "Most newspapers are edited by men—for men. Yet women are the greatest readers of both news and advertising. Why they haven't deserted us years ago is a mystery. Women's interests follow a narrow but very vital range. They are emotional, personal, practical, and of course, unpredictable. Most of our efforts to take care of them are too crude to fool that sharp-eyed breed of born shoppers."

Newspaper city rooms were still lonely places for women through the 1950s and 1960s. News magazines remained virtually closed to women, who were hired as researchers but almost never as reporters or writers. Wire services such as Associated Press and United Press International usually had at least one woman working at major bureaus, but sometimes they were given different assignments from men. Political reporting was still mainly male turf, but a few women were making headway. They included Mary McGrory, now a nationally syndicated political columnist, and Helen Thomas, now UPI's Washington bureau chief and dean of the White House press corps.

McGrory, who later won a Pulitzer Prize for commentary, started out in journalism as secretary to the book editor of the old *Boston Herald* and began writing book reviews and occasional news stories. She later moved to the

Washington Star, where she got her first break covering the Army-McCarthy hearings in 1954 and began writing a column in 1962. For years she was one of only a handful of women in the Washington press corps. And she says congressmen would gravitate to male reporters. One time the chairman of the Senate Armed Services committee, John Stennis, emerged from a closed-door session. McGrory ran over with her notebook and asked what happened. "Oh, little lady," drawled Stennis. "I don't think I want to go through all that now." Then, says McGrory, "Roger Mudd at NBC took him by the arm and they went down to an open mike." McGrory says it was difficult for women journalists to get taken seriously on the campaign trail. "They think you're related to the candidate, or that you're head of the Westchester volunteers or whatever." Women were relegated to the balcony of the National Press Club when they covered luncheon speeches—even though male lobbyists were allowed on the floor.

Male clubbiness tended to isolate female journalists, but there were some benefits to being a woman at a time when even the press corps was still chivalrous. "The fact is that being one of four women among ninety-five men traveling is by far not the worst thing that can happen to you," McGrory says. "I never carried anything. They carried my typewriter, they carried my notes, gave up their seat on the bus, the best room, and they would take you aside and tell you how glad they were that you had come, because they were getting sloppy, dirty and profane."

Helen Thomas first came to Washington in the middle of World War II, got a job as a copy girl on the old *Washington Daily News,* and had just been promoted to "cub reporter" when she was laid off. She knocked on doors until United Press hired her. She covered the Justice Department and other federal agencies during the 1950s and jokes that she wangled her way into the White House by "hanging around." After John Kennedy was elected in 1960, Thomas was sent to Palm Beach during the transition period to cover Jackie. After the inauguration, "I just kept coming [to the White House]. I was the 'man who came to dinner.'" In time she was officially assigned to the White House beat, and in more than thirty years there she has outlasted seven presidents.

During the 1950s and 1960s women journalists were regularly shut out of news events that were open to men, and Thomas remembers discrimination as the most painful part of her long career. The inequality that existed even within the Washington press corps was symbolized by women's exclusion from the National Press Club. "Little by little, we had to break that down," she says, As president of the Women's National Press Club in 1959-60 Thomas cabled a number of foreign leaders urging them to speak to the women journalists instead of at the male-only National Press Club. Segregation by gender has long since ended among Washington news organizations. Thomas was admitted to the Gridiron Club in 1975, the first woman member. The same year she became president of the White House Correspondents Association, the first woman to hold that post.

Television was emerging as a new medium in the 1950s, and in the years to come would transform American politics. But it was no more hospitable to women journalists than newspapers had been. Although stations usually had at least one woman on staff, they were hired to report the "women's angle." Pauline Frederick was an exception, becoming a full-time reporter at ABC in 1948. Frederick had written for the *Washington Star* and *U.S. News* and spent several years stringing "women's news" for the network, although she believed women should be judged not on the basis of their gender but on their ability. For twelve years she was the only woman covering hard news on network television and radio. Although Frederick covered the first televised political convention in 1948, interviewing officials and delegates, her job also included applying makeup to women guests who appeared on television.

During the 1950s Frederick's beat was the United Nations, but she anchored network radio's convention coverage in 1960. That was also the first year each of the networks sent three or four women to cover the national political conventions. One of them was CBS's Nancy Dickerson, who was promised when she became Washington correspondent that she would never have to cover women's news. In the early 1950s Dickerson had found it hard to get a job writing about politics. She turned down a position as women's editor of the old *Washington Daily News* because it "seemed foolish to try to change the world writing about politics and international affairs via the shopping and food columns." By the late 1960s and early 1970s more women were moving into the traditionally male bailiwick of reporting politics and government news, but women still had to convince their editors they could do the job.

In 1972, for example, Eleanor Randolph, then a reporter for the *St. Petersburg Times*, was told by her editor that she couldn't cover the presidential campaign "because I couldn't smoke cigars in my shorts in the back rooms with the boys." Randolph ended up going on the campaign and subsequently covered presidential campaigns for the *Los Angeles Times* and the *Washington Post*. Admittedly it wasn't always easy to be a female reporter in a mostly male environment. CBS's Connie Chung was constantly being scooped during the 1972 campaign by a fellow journalist who was getting his tips from presidential candidate George McGovern in the men's room. And although the political press corps was overwhelmingly male, at least ten women reported on the 1972 campaign, including UPI's Helen Thomas, the *Washington Post*'s Marilyn Berger, the *Washington Star*'s Mary McGrory, and the late Cassie Mackin of NBC. In his classic book about coverage of the 1972 campaign, *The Boys on the Bus*, Tim Crouse writes of the women journalists: "They had always been the outsiders. Having never been allowed to join in the cozy, clubby world of the men, they had developed an uncompromising detachment and a bold independence of thought which often put the men to shame." Sarah McClendon, in particular, a Washington reporter for the North American Newspaper Alliance and a few Texas newspapers and radio stations, had developed a toughness after years of "bullyings and petty cruelties," Crouse said. McClendon occasionally asked stupid or irrelevant questions, but also wrote some of the toughest pieces about the Nixon campaign. "But no matter what she asked [at presidential press conferences], all the male reporters laughed. Sarah McClendon was vulnerable because she was a woman in a male chauvinist profession and she did not work for a large paper."

Even though media managers were assigning women to cover politics, they were often cool to the idea that covering politics could mean covering issues of interest to women. Carol Ashkinaze's experience is one example. In 1976, after nearly ten years as a reporter for *Newsday*, the *Denver Post* and *Newsweek*, Ashkinaze wanted to be a political reporter but accepted a position as a feature columnist with the *Atlanta Constitution*. Her first column was about President Carter's 51.3 Percent Committee, formed to create a pool of women for possible political appointment. Management was skeptical. "The editor's reaction was: 'We hope you're not going to do that kind of story as a steady diet,'" she said. "But women came out of the woodwork, saying 'Please keep writing about this kind of thing.'" Later columns addressed the issues of battered women, abortion, child support, and the lack of a restroom for women legislators in the Georgia statehouse.

There was also still some resistance to women in broadcast news in the early 1970s. National Public Radio newswoman Susan Stamberg said in her case it came from station managers, not the public. She had just gone on the air as host of *All Things Considered,* the first woman to host a nightly national news program. But station mangers said a woman couldn't do the news, that people wouldn't take her seriously, she wouldn't be authoritative enough, and that her voice wouldn't carry well. "Those were the pre-satellite days, and the quality of our sound wasn't nearly as good as it is today, so voice carriage may have been a slight issue," she says. "Otherwise, the objections were simply grounded in history, precedent and probably prejudice." The program director, Bill Siemering, didn't tell her about the objections until twelve years later, figuring that if Stamberg just kept broadcasting, the "oddness" of a woman's voice would disappear and station managers would get used to it.

The old rule of thumb of one woman to a newsroom was disappearing, and more women were being hired off-camera, as producers, researchers, and production assistants. The Federal Communications Commission began requiring stations to file affirmative action plans for women in 1971 as a condition for license renewal. The next year the National Organization for Woman petitioned that WABC-TV in New York be denied a license for failing to employ women and failing to offer news and programming about women's issues. Although the Federal Communications Commission ultimately rejected the petition, the NOW action and complaints of discrimination by other feminist groups against network-owned and -operated stations resulted in increased hiring and promotion of women. Complaints of sexual discrimination were also filed by women staffers against the Associated Press, *New York Times* and *Washington Post*, as well as a number of smaller papers, resulting in increased hiring and promotion of women and minorities.

The presence of women in journalism has been important not only to provide a different perspective but also to raise significant issues, as Leslie Bennetts did in a 1979 *New York Times* story about whether women in public office are judged by a double standard. The story posed a major question for female candidates and office holders that is still relevant today, although even the *Times* editors didn't recognize its importance. It was tucked back in the Style section above an article on summer fashion: "In the aggressive field of politics, a growing number of women are troubled by what they see as a handicap: a double standard that often seems to reward men for the same qualities that are penalized in women," wrote Bennetts. "Many believe that in order to be effective, they are expected—both by the public and a male-dominated political establishment—to restrict their behavior to traditional female stereotypes." The article said women with flamboyant personalities such as Bella Abzug tended to encounter greater difficulties. Calling a man "aggressive" is a compliment, but it's not for a woman. Instead it implies pushiness. "It's all very well to say, 'speak in a soft tone of voice'—but sometimes you have to speak loud enough to be heard," Betty Friedan was quoted as saying. The article also quoted New York City Council president Carol Bellamy, who challenged stereotypical expectations for women: "I am what I am, as Popeye said. And until women know they can be who they are, act like they are and sound like they are, we're not going to make any progress."

Women continued to migrate from the ghetto of the women's pages into the city room through the 1980s. According to the *Columbia Journalism Review*, by 1982 between 30 and 40 percent of the hard news reporters at most large papers were women. Some women had worked their way into management positions such as editor, managing editor, or publisher, but only about 50 of the country's 1,700 daily papers had women publishers. More than half of the women managing editors were at papers with 25,000 circulation or less, and women accounted for only about 10 percent of all jobs at or above the level of assistant managing editor at all daily and Sunday newspapers. Most of those were in the feature departments. Still, it was a far cry from a time when there were no women copyeditors because that would have given women authority over male reporters.

"It's difficult for many people to adjust to the idea of a woman newspaper editor," Judy Clabes, editor of the *Kentucky Post*, wrote in 1984. "I suppose that's because we don't look much like what editors are supposed to look like. Which is OK with us because we've seen those other guys." Clabes, author of *New Guardians of the Press*, a book profiling women editors, described the surprised reaction she often got when callers asked to speak to the editor. When she said "This is she," she encountered silence or disbelief. Even though women were entering journalism in greater numbers and moving up the line, barriers remained. "I've seen a lot of change, but it hasn't gone far enough," said Eileen Shanahan, a former *New York Times* reporter who was one of seven women to sue the paper for sex bias in the early 1970s. By 1984 several women political reporters were assigned to cover the presidential campaign, but some major papers, the *Boston Globe* among them, had no women on the campaign. The *New York Times* and *Washington Post* each had one woman out of a presidential political staff of about a dozen each.

In television, 97 percent of local stations employed at least one woman on their news staffs by 1982, compared with 57 percent in 1972. And more women were running television newsrooms. Almost no women were news directors in 1972, but ten years later 8 percent of television news directors were women and 18 percent of radio news directors were female. By 1984 television had outdone most print news organizations in giving women campaign assignments, perhaps because of the FCC's insistence on sexual equality as part of its licensing process. But there were mixed signals for women in broadcast news. Christine Craft was fired in 1981 from her anchor slot at KMBC-TV in Kansas City and claimed in a sex discrimination suit that management had told her she was "too old, too unattractive and not deferential enough to men." She was awarded $500,000 in damages, but the jury's verdict was later overturned.

The infamous Denver Dinner in 1982 epitomized the sexism still prevalent in political journalism. As the *Wall Street Journal*'s Jane Meyer told the story, two of the nation's top political correspondents—David Broder of the *Washington Post* and Adam Clymer of the *New York Times*—arranged all-male dinners at the National Governor's Conference with reporters and political insiders, a vestige of all-male campaign coverage. National Public Radio's Linda Wertheimer tried to get invited but was turned down. So she invited a group of women and asked the restaurant to place them in full view of the Broder and Clymer tables. "We had a grand time," she said. "Everyone was smarting."

By the time the 1984 presidential campaign got under way, women could not be ignored, although they continued to be a minority on the campaign trail. Two of the three networks assigned women to cover the front-runner, Walter Mondale, and for a while all three networks had women correspondents assigned to Gary Hart's campaign—until his candidacy took off after the New Hampshire primary and the women were replaced by men. Even so, television was far better than print in terms of assigning women to national campaigns. More newspapers assigned women to national political beats in mid-summer, after Geraldine Ferraro was nominated for vice-president. Editors scurried to find women to cover the first woman vice presidential candidate, almost as though the candidate's gender made her a member of another culture or species.

By the late 1980s, women were working in television news in greater numbers. A few, such as Leslie Stahl, Diane Sawyer, and Judy Woodruff had become highly visible television reporters. Many women were co-anchoring daytime news shows and even solo anchoring news shows at local network affiliates. But if Christine Craft's situation epitomized the early 1980s, not much had changed by the end of the decade. "There is still too much of the Miss America syndrome," Jane Pauley told an interviewer. "Even with everything we've accomplished, or been allowed to accomplish, there is still the thinking that men are newsmen, and women are, I don't know, something else." Judy Woodruff talked about the "insecurity that comes with being a woman in the mostly male club that rules my profession and the political institutions I have covered." But she added that women had come far from the time in television news when a woman would never have thought of covering national politics.

By the end of the decade there were still no female solo network news anchors, a position always reserved for men. Marlene Sanders had filled in on ABC in 1964 and again in 1971, and Barbara Walters had co-anchored the news for ABC with Harry Reasoner for a brief stint beginning in 1976. But no woman had been tapped for a full-time solo anchor position on the evening network news. Some newswomen recognized the hazards of being the first to cross that threshold. Faith Daniels, who was then co-anchor of CBS *Morning News*, saw potential parallels to the media scrutiny of Geraldine Ferraro in 1984. "I would not be the first female network news anchor for all the money in the world," Daniels told an interviewer. "Never. There is no money that would compensate her for what she will go through. She will be taken apart. . . . The scrutiny that woman would be under would not be worth it. The press and public took Geraldine Ferraro apart. It would happen again."

By the "Year of the Woman" in 1992, the number of women in journalism had barely increased although news organizations had made efforts to diversify both their staffs and their coverage in terms of gender, age, and race. By 1989, women made up more than two-thirds of the students in journalism schools across the country. Yet the percentage of women in journalism rose only from 33.8 percent in 1982 to 34 percent in 1992. "The overall figure hasn't changed much, because women are getting out of journalism more quickly than men," said David Weaver, author of *U.S. Journalists at Work, 1971-1992.*

But the number of female bylines on political stories was evidence that more women were covering political campaigns in 1992 than in previous years. In 1992, women made up almost half the White House press corps, and for the first time the nation's highest ranking political reporter was a woman, Robin Toner, chief political correspondent for the *New York Times.* Increased numbers of female political reporters may have had some influence on the coverage of women's candidacies, but while more women were assigning, reporting, and editing the news in 1992, none were directing the nation's top dailies or news magazines or heading network news operations. "American journalism still views women as outsiders, suspect, 'the other' in America's newsrooms, the anomaly, exceptions to the male norm," wrote Kay Mills, author of *A Place in the News*, a history of women in journalism.

Although more women were covering politics, one study of coverage of the Democratic National Convention showed that male reporters at several large papers had nearly twice as many bylines as their female counterparts, 602 to 334. Despite gains in the number of female bylines, the study found that men were quoted in news reports twice as often as women—238 men to 92 women. When women were sought for comment, they usually were asked about so-called "women's issues." The study, sponsored by the citywide Newswomen's Caucus of New York, looked at coverage by the *New York Daily News*, the *New York Times*, *Newsday*, the *New York Post*, and the *Wall Street Journal.*

According to another study, by Women, Men and Media, the media monitoring group, even with more women reporting and editing the news, the media were still using a "Hatfields-and-McCoys approach" in covering politics, thus contributing to polarization instead of to consensus building. "The media appear to believe, rightly or wrongly, that good news doesn't sell: hence, its overemphasis on conflict and simplistic, stark drama—the infamous 'we vs. they' syndrome, the 'black and white' aspects, the horse race," wrote Junior Bridge, author of the report. The study looked at 4,000 articles from seven major newspapers and three newsmagazines during July and August 1992, when the national conventions were being held. Factors contributing to polarization included stereotypical descriptions of sources interviewed and invisibility of some segments of the population in certain contexts. Fathers were rarely mentioned in stories about families, for example, and women—often hardest hit in times of high unemployment—were mostly invisible in stories about the economy. "The media interviews, quotes and photographs mostly middle- and upper-class white men" about that subject, Bridge said. "Traffic gridlock is a good metaphor for political gridlock: we can't get anywhere because no one will give an inch," wrote syndicated columnist Judy Mann. "Combat is prized over conflict resolution, conflict over consensus. Masculinist dynamics prevail in the political dialogue and they are mirrored abundantly in the coverage of it."

Meanwhile, poor representation of women on television news prompted Nancy DeStefanis to found Women Are Good News in 1992. The San Francisco-based organization was born after DeStefanis calculated that 85 percent of the journalists on public television were white males. "Women make up 53 percent of the population and 54 percent of registered voters, said DeStefanis. "We want to see a proportional number of women commentators, reporters and experts covering politics on public television." Without pressure from voters for gender equality in public affairs programming, "they'll get a skewed, unbalanced perspective of women candidates being dismissed or treated in a diminished fashion by a male-dominated media." In contrast, a National Public Radio official said in 1995 that 52 percent of the network's employees were women, a majority of its reporters were women, and three of its most popular news shows, *Morning Edition, All Things Considered,* and *Weekend Edition,* had women in decisionmaking positions.

In 1994, the annual Women, Men and Media study found that at newspapers men continued to write the majority of front-page news stories and nearly three-quarters of the opinion pieces on the nation's op-ed pages. The number of female front-page bylines inched up from an average of 33 percent in 1994 to 34 percent in 1995. But the average percentage of stories reported by female correspondents on nightly network news shows dropped from 21 to 20 percent. Regardless of the number of women working in print journalism, the annual surveys indicate that female reporters do not include female sources in front-page stories any more often than male reporters do. In the 1995 survey, for example, "It was common to find in the January papers stories devoid of female mention, written by women, even though female commentary would have been appropriate, and female expertise existed in those areas," said Junior Bridge, who conducted the survey.

Even as the hullabaloo about the Year of the Woman was going on, newspapers were being confronted with some pretty dismal numbers about their women readers. In the 1970s more women read newspapers than men. But by the 1990s readership surveys showed women had abandoned the newspapers; they now lagged behind men, and the younger the reader, the greater the gap. Critics say one reason is that newspapers haven't made enough of an effort to reach women readers. Newspapers began scrambling in an effort to keep the women readers they still had and to attract new ones.

A 1991 survey by the Knight-Ridder Women Readers Task Force found that women are interested in many of the same issues as men, particularly health, education, social issues, and family and personal relationships. But there was a difference: the study found women wanted to know more about their children's education and how they learn, not about the politics of the school board; they wanted in-depth stories about issues, and they wanted information that was useful and easy to find. As a result, some newspapers began experimenting with women's sections, abandoned as sexist and out of date in the late 1970s and early 1980s. Unlike their "home and hearth"-focused predecessors, the new women's sections focus on female newsmakers and offer useful information for women who must balance the demands of work, home, and family. By the mid-1990s there were close to forty women's sections in the country, but there was still controversy over whether such sections represented progress or were simply modern-day ghettos for news about women.

Marty Claus, then a managing editor at the *Detroit Free Press*, attacked the idea in the Knight-Ridder report. "Please don't tell me that in a gender-obsessed world, a women's section won't emphasize the perceived and demeaning differences that women are struggling to erase," she said. "Why buy into the patriarchy [again] in newspapers? It's not right and it's not fair." On the other hand, said Scott McGehee, publisher of the *News-Sentinel* in Fort Wayne, Indiana, "When women are a significant, underserved portion of our audience with unique needs, why shouldn't they have a place in the paper to call their own?" News consultant Nancy Woodhull said special women's sections can benefit readers because reporters are specifically assigned to follow women's issues, but she said it's also important to mainstream women's news. "You have to be really careful that the result isn't ghettoizing women."

Some news organizations have redesigned their beat system, relying less on traditional coverage of politics and institutions and more on issues that readers connect with. That's what has happened at the Newhouse News Service Washington bureau run by Deborah Howell. When Howell took over the Washington bureau in 1990 she junked some traditional beats in favor of thematic areas that would affect more people. The Supreme Court beat, for example, was traded for one covering violent crime. But Howell says even traditional beats can be made relevant to all readers, including women. "You don't just cover buildings, you can cover issues," she said. "You can make traditional beats much more accessible to readers by making sure you include not all the usual white male suspects. You just enlarge your scope for what's important and what's affected."

The presence of women in journalism doesn't guarantee that news will be free of sexist reporting, editing, or headline writing. It takes a conscious effort by a journalist, male or female, to become more sensitive to gender-based stereotypes, to seek gender balance in stories, and to generate and promote stories of concern to women. "Statistics never tell the whole story," wrote Marilyn Gardner in the *Christian Science Monitor*. "But until there is somewhat comparable attention (and somewhat comparable funds) allotted to women running for office, nobody can pretend that American politics in the '90s is a gender-blind meritocracy."

❖ *Chapter 13* ❖

Ms. President?

THE PRESS WASN'T ALONE IN SHUNNING VICTORIA WOODHULL WHEN SHE RAN FOR president in 1872. Even Susan B. Anthony turned off the auditorium lights when Woodhull tried to address the National Woman Suffrage Association. Soon afterward, lacking the support of the suffrage movement, Woodhull's candidacy fell apart. Backed by the Equal Rights Party, a coalition of social-ists, feminists, Spiritualists, and communists, Woodhull advocated sexual free-dom for women and attacked marriage as an institution that enslaves women. America wasn't ready for her.

Voters wouldn't be any more eager to embrace someone like Woodhull today than they were more than a century ago. The media would probably ignore her as not being a "viable" candidate. That's understandable. But in general the media have been reluctant to treat the idea of a woman president seriously, whether she's a radical extremist or an experienced legislator. Often the media seem slower to change than the people they are said to mirror.

Surveys of the acceptability of women in public office have generally indicated that the lower the office, the more willing people would be to fill it with a woman. But the political climate has been shifting. Among the more dramatic indicators of change are responses to a Gallup question that has been regularly repeated: "If your party nominated a woman for president, would you vote for her if she qualified for the job?" In 1937, 31 percent of a national sample said they would but 65 percent said they would not. By 1952 public sentiment had tilted the other way, with a 52 to 44 percent majority saying they would vote for a woman. That proportion climbed to 66 to 29 percent in 1971 and was up to 78 to 17 percent by 1984. In 1992, a Roper poll asked Americans, "Stop me if I name an office for which you would *not* vote for a woman." A strong majority accepted the idea of a woman chief executive, but the number who said they would not vote for a woman presidential candidate or were undecided was 32 percent, up substantially from previous polls.

When only women were surveyed in the 1972 Virginia Slims American Women's opinion poll, a majority were ready to accept a woman candidate for president, and two out of three women voters said the nation would be ready to accept a woman president in fifty years or sooner. But two of five women still thought the office should be reserved for a man. And a 1990 *McCall's* survey of 7,000 women found that 78 percent believed an election should be decided on an individual basis and not because it was an important social goal to have women and minorities in office. Thirty-five percent said they would prefer voting for a woman, but 25 percent said they would rather vote for a man.

On the whole, the media has done a better job of speculating about potential women presidential candidates than of actually covering the campaigns of those who dared enter the race. In 1976, for example, after her powerful keynote speech at the Democratic National Convention, it was widely speculated in the media that Barbara Jordan could be the first black and female vice president or president, governor of Texas, speaker of the House, or member of the Supreme Court. Jeane Kirkpatrick's name kept surfacing in the media as a potential Republican candidate during the fall of 1987, months before the national political conventions. Although Kirkpatrick, former chief delegate to the United Nations, did not actively seek the presidency, her friends in the media kept the idea alive. The *San Diego Union*, for example, said Kirkpatrick would bring to the Republican race "conservative horsepower" and hundreds of eager volunteers.

Kathleen Brown was seen as a rising star in 1991 when she was elected California state treasurer, and some pundits painted her as presidential material. At the 1992 Democratic convention there was talk of her as a vice presidential nominee. But in 1994 she blew a commanding lead in the gubernatorial race against California governor Pete Wilson, and the media speculation evaporated. The name of Texas governor Ann Richards also kept cropping up in news stories as a potential presidential or vice presidential candidate in 1992, although Richards said she wasn't interested. And soon after New Jersey governor Christine Todd Whitman took office in 1993, the media began to buzz about her presidential and vice presidential prospects.

Whether Americans are ready to elect a female commander-in-chief won't be known for sure until a woman leads a major party ticket. And whether voters cast their ballots for a woman will be determined in large measure by how the media portray her candidacy. Will womanhood be presented as her primary attribute? Will she have to prove she's as tough as a man but skilled in the "womanly" arts of cooking and sewing? Will she be held responsible for the actions of her husband and children? Will she be measured by how she conforms to outmoded stereotypes of femininity? Two women have run for president in this century, and a third woman made an exploratory run. All three were experienced legislators, serious about their presidential campaigns, but that wasn't always reflected in media coverage.

Margaret Chase Smith's announcement that she was running for president raised eyebrows in 1964. As *Time* noted, "Many people shrug off the lady Senator's declaration as being something frivolously feminine. They don't know Maggie. Feminine she is, but not frivolous." In fact, it would be hard to imagine Smith as a flighty dilettante. John Kennedy's description seems more apt. Asked at his last press conference in 1963 how he would feel about having to run for reelection against Smith in 1964, he said she was "very formidable, if that is the appropriate word to use about a very fine lady. She is very formidable as a political figure." Smith had served in the House of Representatives from 1940 to 1948 and was serving her third term in the Senate when she decided to try for the presidency.

She was the first woman ever elected to both House and Senate. Her name had been mentioned frequently as a possible vice presidential candidate, and she had gotten strong support from women's groups at the 1952 GOP National Convention, but her candidacy was shelved in the interest of party harmony. So when she announced to members of the Women's National Press Club in 1964 that she would seek the Republican presidential nomination, it caused a stir. Smith said her only expenses would be for travel, that she would not buy air time for political advertisements, and that she would not campaign when the Senate was in session and voting on bills. She listed various reasons why a woman should not run for president, including the conten-

Delegates to the 1964 Republican National Convention showed their support for Maine senator Margaret Chase Smith.

tion that "no woman should ever dare to aspire to the White House—that this is a man's world and that it should be kept that way"—and then told the press women, "Because of these very impelling reasons against my running, I have decided that I shall enter the New Hampshire preferential primary and the Illinois primary. For I accept the reasons advanced against my running as challenges."

Some of the other Republicans interested in the nomination complained that the field was becoming crowded with Smith's entry before the New Hampshire primary, and they said no one would be able to emerge with a clear mandate. But Smith said she wasn't trying to sabotage any other candidate. "I am going to run my own campaign on my own record," she told *Time*. "I am running against no one. I'd like to be President. I think my experience and my record are greater than any other candidate or any other of the unannounced candidates. It's a real challenge, and that's one of the paramount things. When people keep telling you that you can't do a thing, you kind of like to try it."

Most journalists seemed to love the fact that she was in the race. They called her Maggie—a nickname she says she never minded—and they put stories about her on the front page. She had shown backbone and tenacity in Congress. She was proud of her perfect attendance record in the Senate, and she was known for her independence. As a member of the Senate Armed Services Committee, for example, she had bucked the popular course and prevented the Pentagon from promoting actor Jimmy Stewart to brigadier general in the Air Force Reserve until he had completed the required reserve training. After she denounced the 1963 nuclear test ban treaty because she thought it threatened national security, Russian premier Nikita Khrushchev said she wasn't acting the way a woman should act. "It is hard to believe how a woman, if she is not the devil in disguise of a woman, can make such a malicious, man-hating call."

A few journalists disliked the thought of Smith in the race. One of them was Ralph McGill, a syndicated columnist and former editor of the *Atlanta Constitution*, who said in his column that Smith's presidential candidacy had set the cause of women back several decades. But Smith was adamant about not running as a woman candidate. One of the reasons she chose to run was to break down barriers and to pioneer the way for other women, but in her eyes she was simply a candidate. She did not consider gender one of her qualifications or liabilities. But the media wouldn't let the public forget she was female. Even political cartoons commenting on Smith's nomination used all manner of stereotypical images to depict her. There were drawings of the "New Betsy" sewing up America's tattered flag, of Smith as a mother scolding the GOP elephant for dirtying his hands in a puddle of McCarthyism, and of Smith's hat being thrown into the ring—a flowered bonnet on a tray with fedoras and Derby hats.

During a television interview Smith was once asked how a woman president would handle other world leaders. "A woman president would probably do as well as Joan of Arc, Catherine the Great and Queen Victoria," she replied. And she made headlines in the major papers. Reporting on Smith's announcement of her candidacy, a female *New York Times* reporter led her story with what today would be considered an outrageously sexist allusion: "Sounding like a woman on the verge of saying No, Senator Margaret Chase Smith of Maine today said yes—she would run for president." The *New York Daily News* headline blared: "Maggie Smith for President." Smith came in fifth in the New Hampshire GOP primary in March, behind Henry Cabot Lodge, Barry Goldwater, Nelson Rockefeller, and Richard Nixon. But she got more votes than Pennsylvania governor William Scranton, Michigan governor George Romney, and perennial presidential candidate Harold Stassen. Her prospects for the April presidential primary in Illinois looked dim, but when the votes were counted she had racked up more than 30 percent of those cast. In the Oregon primary, as in New Hampshire, she came in fifth.

Smith says she didn't enter the presidential primaries so much to prove a woman could be considered as to show that someone didn't need to be a millionaire in order to run for public office. She was determined that gender not be made the key issue in her presidential bid. So when Senator George Aiken of Vermont nominated Smith for the presidency at the Republican National Convention in 1964, he had to do it without once mentioning the fact that she was a woman. He explained that since Smith had returned all campaign contributions, he couldn't offer the delegates a cigar or chewing gum or even a cup of coffee. Then he ticked off the attributes a president should have and demonstrated that Smith had those qualifications. "A President should have integrity. . . . My candidate stands ace-high in this respect. A president should have ability . . . if my candidate does not have ability then the forty-four universities and colleges that have awarded her degrees based solely on merit have been wrong. A president should have had wide experience in government. . . . A President should have courage . . . common sense."

Television probably reflected the woman who would be president most accurately. She was, in the Maine way, a woman of few words but proud bearing. Republican convention delegates eventually nominated Barry Goldwater as their candidate, as everyone knew they would. But before they did, millions of viewers had a chance to hear Aiken's nomination, to see the silver-haired Smith beaming, with her trademark rose pinned to her dress, and to hear the band play "Drink a toast to dear old Maine." It was a thrilling moment for many women, even though most knew she was not going to be the Republican nominee. Theodore H. White, in *The Making of the President 1964,* suggests the delight many felt at Smith's candidacy as he describes ballots being counted: "It was 528 to 122 before Ohio—and Ohio called 57 for Goldwater, 1 for

Margaret Chase Smith. In the command trailer, a girl's squeal and a voice: "How beautiful!" Oddly, that reference to Smith is the only one in White's otherwise detailed account of the 1964 campaign. Goldwater had been expected for months to win the nomination—he received 883 votes to Smith's 27 on the first ballot—but Smith later observed, "I didn't win the nomination, but I don't think I lost—instead I think I made a gain for women for the future."

On January 25, 1972, Shirley Chisholm made her announcement in the elementary school auditorium of Brooklyn's biggest Baptist church. It was packed with television cameras and lights, reporters, and about five hundred supporters. Chisholm, a two-term congresswoman, told the audience of mostly black women that she wanted "to repudiate the ridiculous notion that the American people will not vote for a qualified candidate simply because he is not white or because she is not a male." Chisholm declared: "I stand before you today as a candidate for the Democratic nomination for the Presidency of the United States. I am not the candidate of black America, although I am black and proud. I am not the candidate of the women's movement of this country, although I am a woman, and I am equally proud of that. I am not the candidate of any political bosses or special interests. . . . I am the candidate of the people."

But as soon as Chisholm entered the race, skepticism was expressed in the media. The *New York Times*, for example, said she had three strikes against her—her sex, her race, and the fact that she "did not appear to have overwhelming support among women, blacks or youths." *Washington Post* feature writer Myra MacPherson later wrote that Chisholm had been "kissed off as a member of the lunatic fringe . . . and both voters and other politicians narrowly viewed her only as a woman's or black candidate." But members of the congressional Black Caucus gave her a standing ovation at a repeat of the announcement ceremony in Washington later that day, when she told them, "I'm the only one among you who has the balls to run for president." MacPherson described her as "cocky, self-assured and messianically driven."

Chisholm told a number of women's groups that she knew she would encounter anti-black and anti-feminist sentiments during her campaign. "What surprised me was the much greater virulence of the sex discrimination." She said that while many still harbored racist emotions, paternalism had largely disappeared. "But I was constantly bombarded by both men and women exclaiming that I should return to teaching, a woman's vocation, and leave politics to the men."

It was not the first time Chisholm had confronted the system. When she was a rookie member of Congress in 1968, representing an inner-city New York district, she protested her assignment to the House Agriculture subcommittees on Forestry, and Rural Development and Family Farms. Chisholm received nationwide coverage for attacking the seniority system in general and for her assignments in particular. "All the gentlemen know about Brooklyn is that a tree grew there" became her well known one-liner. She was reassigned to the Veterans' Affairs Committee.

Chisholm surprised many people when she announced she would run for president. Other candidates were already actively campaigning, and Maine senator Edmund Muskie was considered the front-runner. Muskie won the Iowa caucuses the same day Chisholm announced her candidacy, but the eventual Democratic nominee, George McGovern, was said to be closing the gap. Chisholm's decision to seek the Democratic nomination put many women in a difficult position. Should they support a man who had a good record on women's issues

Representative Shirley Chisholm (D-New York) wanted to jar the nation into considering a woman and an African-American for president when she campaigned for the Democratic nomination in 1972.

and who had a chance of winning, or should they support a woman whose candidacy had extraordinary symbolic value but who had little chance of victory? Chisholm got lots of encouragement but few endorsements. Gloria Steinem, for example, made a televised statement to the effect that "I'm for Shirley Chisholm, but I think George McGovern is the best of the male candidates."

And Chisholm got a lukewarm response from her congressional colleague Bella Abzug, who observed in her journal that Chisholm "likes to do the unexpected." Abzug, along with Steinem and Betty Friedan, had been instrumental in founding the National Women's Political Caucus, and Abzug was worried about prematurely committing to a candidate. "As far as the Caucus is concerned, most women who've spoken out feel that if we were to launch a candidate at this point—even for pressure purposes—it would largely be a diversion of our energies." The Caucus wanted to organize statewide caucuses, secure representation of women at the conventions, and encourage women to run for local, state, and congressional offices. "This is the building up from the grass-roots approach," said Abzug, "setting reasonable goals and objectives which, once attained, will inspire more women to join us. Shirley understands this, but she's always operated as an individual to a large extent."

Without the organized backing of women's groups and as the "candidate of the people," Chisholm did not have the financial or organizational support that would indicate to the media that she was a "serious" candidate. The question that haunted her throughout her campaign was whether she was really serious about running. She knew what the question meant: "You would have to be crazy to think a black woman has any chance to be president." She was portrayed in some news accounts as entering the race as a stalking horse—to split the vote and benefit another candidate. Other stories said she had announced in order to be able to pressure other Democratic presidential contenders to name blacks to agency or cabinet posts. Chisholm said the speculation was to be expected from political reporting, "a field in which the writers who sound most authoritative are those who have no idea about what is really going on." What galled her most was that it "typified the basic misconception about my candidacy, that it had some other objective than winning the nomination for president. It was another way of expressing the judgment 'she must know she can't win, so obviously she isn't serious.'"

Chisholm's road to the convention was rocky. She had only three full-time staff people working with her, along with part-time and volunteer help, and no press secretary. Her advance publicity consisted mostly of telephone calls and notices posted on church bulletin boards. By her own account, she received only $95,000 in contributions, most of them for less than ten dollars. Her campaign cost close to $300,000. Money problems plagued her candidacy. There wasn't ever enough of it, and there were allegations of mismanagement. The General Accounting Office said her husband, Conrad, who wasn't listed as a campaign official, was actually in charge of all revenues and spending. Chisholm's campaign committee submitted a final report claiming a $6,000 deficit, while the GAO found an $18,000 surplus and was unable to document her reports of campaign spending. Eventually, however, the Justice Department absolved her of wrongdoing.

One result of her lack of campaign funds and her skeleton staff was that the media tended to dismiss her as a fringe candidate and she had to push for equal treatment from the media. Chisholm credits Liz Carpenter, former press secretary to Lady Bird Johnson, with opening media doors for her in Washington. Carpenter encouraged reporters to listen to what Chisholm had to say and to cover her campaign. She also called Ben Bradlee, then managing editor of the *Washington Post*, and suggested that *Post* editors hold a background session with Chisholm just as they had with the front-runners, Ed Muskie and Vice President Hubert Humphrey. Carpenter also lent her name to Washington fundraising events for Chisholm.

But media coverage on a par with any of the "serious" candidates was one of the hardest things for Chisholm to secure. In fact, she had to file a protest with the Federal Communications Commission to get equal air time with other candidates. When Humphrey challenged North Dakota senator George McGovern to a series of television debates prior to the California primary, the three networks donated their weekly half-hour public affairs interview programs—*Meet the Press, Face the Nation,* and *Issues and Answers*—to the two candidates and stretched each program to an hour to accommodate the debates. Chisholm thought she was entitled to time as well. So the Media Service Project in Washington filed a protest with the FCC on Chisholm's behalf, citing the equal opportunity section of the Federal Communications Act. At first the networks successfully claimed the programs were regular interview shows and thereby exempt from the FCC requirement. But a court of appeals ordered ABC and CBS to provide her with a half-hour of air time. NBC had already scheduled her on one half-hour of its morning program, *Today.*

Chisholm was often discouraged about her media coverage, but the lack of coverage was sometimes the fault of her own campaign staff. The campaign was notorious for spotty scheduling, last-minute changes, and no-shows by the candidate. Reporters covering political campaigns become accustomed to delays in the campaign schedule, but in Chisholm's case they would sometimes have to wait until it became clear she wasn't going to arrive at all. She acknowledges that her campaign did not inspire confidence among the press and tells about the time her trip to St. Petersburg, Florida, was rescheduled five times and finally canceled—but no one thought to tell the *St. Petersburg Times* reporter, who went out and waited for her. "It was not a good way to treat one of the state's leading newspapers," she observed. In the same vein, one of her staff called the radio stations to tell them about a press conference at the Vizcaya Gardens in Miami. The only problem was that it actually was being held at the Vizcaya Restaurant. No one from the media came. Some of the best press of her whole campaign wasn't "scheduled" news at all. It was coverage of her visit to Alabama governor George Wallace in the hospital after he was shot. She says she didn't tell anybody in the media she was going.

Chisholm acknowledged that her campaign limped "from crisis to crisis in state after state" and she couldn't have achieved national recognition without media coverage. Her appearances on national television gave her candidacy a certain legitimacy. She says her campaign was an illustration of what Marshall McLuhan meant by "the medium is the message." "The mere fact that a black woman chose to run for President, seriously, not expecting to win but sincerely trying to, is what it was all about. 'It can be done.' That was what I was trying to say, by doing it."

Reflecting on the campaign later, Chisholm wondered how far she might have gotten with money and organized support, "if we had done it right," but said she hoped she had made it a little easier for a woman or dark-skinned person to run for president in the future. "I started out as a freak candidate, a kind of political sideshow. But I wound up in the main tent," she said. "Although I did not come very close to the nomination, I came closer than several of the white candidates who, at the outset, were given a fair chance to make it all the way."

Pat Schroeder made it official in September 1987 that she would *not* seek the Democratic presidential nomination. Then she cried. Those two facts were reported as equally significant in many newspapers, and in some media reports the crying upstaged the campaign news. Schroeder's announcement came at an open-air rally in Denver after she had spent four months exploring the possibility of running, visiting twenty-nine states, giving speeches, being grilled by editorial boards, and being written about by various columnists. She says she hadn't considered getting into the race until Democratic front-runner Gary Hart was knocked out of the competition by media coverage of his womanizing. After people started calling and urging her to get in the race, she decided to test the waters. "I wanted to see if a woman could really be president of the United States."

Although she was a member of Congress with fifteen years of experience, inevitably she was seen as a symbol of all women. "Like it or not, my potential candidacy for the highest elective office in our country was going to be a hook for America watchers, political analysts and newspaper columnists to appraise the progress of women in this country." Her stock response? "America is man enough to back a woman." Schroeder said she was frequently asked, "Why are you running as a woman?" Her answer: "Do I have an option?" There wasn't any option as far as the media were concerned. It had only been three years since Geraldine Ferraro's run for vice president, and reporters often compared the two women. "If Ms. Ferraro was very careful about her attire, Mrs. Schroeder is freewheeling," wrote the *New York Times*'s Maureen Dowd. "One recent day in Iowa, the Harvard law school graduate and deputy House whip wore layers of beads, a long chiffon scarf and a blouse elaborately trimmed with lace; she sported violet eyeliner and lavender eyeshadow and she Scotch-taped a pink carnation from her hotel breakfast tray onto the lapel of her purple Anne Klein blazer."

By the end of her campaign swing around the country, Schroeder says she was sure she was right not to seek the nomination. But when she told supporters, they groaned, shouted "No," and began to chant "Run, Pat, Run." "When I heard the audience groan, I began to cry," she said. "I knew I had underestimated how much I wanted to pursue the presidency. I went on with my speech but . . . it was my tears, not my words, that got the headlines." Columns and letters appeared in newspapers and news magazines for weeks afterward, supporting and criticizing her—including some from critics who said they wouldn't want someone who cries to have her finger on the nuclear "button." Schroeder responded in an op-ed piece in the *Washington Post* that she wouldn't want someone in the presidency with a finger on the button who *didn't* cry.

The *New York Times* was one of the few papers that didn't mention tears, although the story did describe Schroeder as "choking up with emotion" at several points during her speech. But after television clearly showed Schroeder crying, the *Times* came back with a story the next day headlined "Are Female Tears Saltier Than Male Tears?" The lead was "She cried." The story reported on the range of reactions to Schroeder's tears,

Representative Pat Schroeder (D-Colorado) made an exploratory run for the presidency in 1987.

from surprise to embarrassment to acceptance that people cry at emotion-charged moments. Schroeder explained her tears by saying she hadn't planned to be emotional. "We have a president [Reagan] who can plan to be emotional, and that seems to be OK. I prefer people who are human and who are real. I am not an actress. Sure I got up to give the speech, and when the groans came from the crowd, that I was not prepared for. It hits you like a truck."

After the news had broken earlier in the year that she would take a "look at the race," Schroeder rose steadily in the polls over the summer, although by early August a Harris Poll showed that fewer than 30 percent of people knew her name. Yet some columnists were saying she might have a chance. By mid-September, two weeks before she stopped campaigning, a *Time* magazine poll placed her third in name recognition and first in trust. But Schroeder lacked an organized network of campaign workers. She would go wherever volunteers called and offered to organize for her. Similarly she lacked money. She raised about one million dollars, enough to qualify for federal matching funds, but nothing close to the three and a half million she estimated it would take to enter every presidential primary. She had decided that she would not go into debt to finance her campaign, but looking back she sounds a little wistful about the lost opportunity. "Partly I regret that I would not risk enough," she says. "Any male candidate would have borrowed the money and not thought another thing about it."

Ultimately, what caused Schroeder to withdraw had less to do with organization and campaign funds than it did with the delegate selection process. She hadn't thought it out fully and didn't realize that her inability to win delegates would hamstring her. In her *Washington Post* op-ed piece, Schroeder expressed her frustration with the process, saying that the early primaries bore voters and demean candidates. She said the worst part is that some candidates are forced out of the race before people have an opportunity to cast a primary vote in their own state.

Schroeder's was a very public bid for office, in sharp contrast with the behind-the-scenes explorations being carried on by potential candidates such as New York governor Mario Cuomo or New Jersey senator Bill Bradley. She did it that way because the insiders wouldn't take a woman seriously, said Kathy Bonk, a communications consultant. "It was a big risk. She probably didn't realize how high risk it was until she got out there." And Schroeder said that while progress was being made toward accepting the idea of a woman president, women still didn't "look presidential" to many voters. "My laugh, my signature [she draws a smiley face beside her name], my mannerisms, were seen as too feminine. I was told that in politics boyish charm is fine but girlish charm is out of place. I was told that the first woman president would be a tough character, 'weaned on a pickle'—in other words, just like a man. I hope they're wrong."

Support for a presidential run by Texas governor Ann Richards had come from many quarters in the media, following her hard-won victory in 1990, but the talk faded when she was defeated for reelection by George W. Bush in 1994. Two years before, she had been riding the crest of an Ann for President movement that began in January with a speech—carried live on C-SPAN—to about two hundred congressional Democrats and their staffers, and culminated in her masterminding the Democratic National Convention in July. Actually, Richards had first captured people's attention outside Texas in 1988 with her well-publicized quip about George Bush at the Democratic National Convention that year. "Poor George," she had said. "He can't help it. He was born with a silver foot in his mouth."

Syndicated *New York Times* columnist Anna Quindlen commented in April 1992 that it wouldn't be Richards's competence that would keep her from being considered as a national candidate—it would be her chromosomes. "You've got to wonder, approaching a new century, when America will begin to take seriously the idea of being led by a woman," Quindlen wrote. "The concept heretofore has always been presented as a cross between a futuristic fantasy and a sitcom premise. Cue the laugh track."

Barbara Jordan, in her 1992 keynote address to the Democratic National Convention, spoke of the change represented by the women running for office. "We are challenging the councils of political power because they have been dominated by white, male policy-makers, and that's wrong," Jordan said in her widely reported speech. "That horizon of gender equity is limitless, and what we see today is simply a dress rehearsal for the day and time we meet in convention to nominate Madam President."

After the success of women candidates in the 1992 November election, various media voices began to reflect the idea that women could now contemplate running for president—thereby helping to make the idea sound reasonable. Ellen Malcolm, president of Emily's List, for example, was quoted in an Associated Press story as saying that women's gains in the House had made it possible for women to run for higher office—including the presidency. "I think the next time we have a conversation about who is going to be the Democratic nominee, we are going to hear a lot about women in the mix as the candidate instead of Vice President," said Malcolm. And National Women's Caucus president Harriett Woods was quoted in the story as saying the election proved that "there is no office that women cannot attain in this country." The *New York Times* and hundreds of other papers across the country ran the story, adding weight to the notion that women could now aspire to be president. But by 1995, Woods was sounding a more cautious note. She told a Minneapolis gathering that women had lost ground in the 1994 elections and hit a political plateau nationally. An aggressive strategy was needed to target seats and recruit candidates. "We have to take a different approach. It isn't going to 'just happen.' We've supported women candidates, but we haven't taken the lead in creating women candidates."

The media has typically covered women presidential candidates pretty much as they do other "minor" candidates, except that in the case of women candidates the novelty of having a woman in the race was often the primary focus of stories. A vicious circle is at work for all such candidates, including women. Unless candidates get name recognition and standing in the polls, they are not likely to receive extensive media coverage. But at the same time, unless they get media coverage, they won't be recognized and their polls will be weak. Even the League of Women Voters, which has sponsored televised debates among presidential candidates, takes into account "recognition by the national media." Buying television time is not an option because candidates usually don't have the money to do that until after they have recognition.

Kansas senator Bob Dole experienced that problem in 1980 when he was a candidate for the Republican presidential nomination. "I just wasn't covered. Maybe the press decided I wasn't a serious candidate," he said. "We never could get the networks to take a hard look at what we'd done in the Senate or at the issues. They just wanted to know how much money you've raised and do you have momentum. Our little debates were all of the coverage that some of us got. There has to be some way to have some balance so responsible candidates can have an equal chance." Ross Perot had an equal shot at the presidency in 1992 primarily because he could afford it.

As the twentieth century draws to a close, no official standards exist for selecting candidates for presidential debates. Yet the debates are not open to every candidate. "The amount of space in a newspaper is finite; our attention span [for television news] is finite," said Stephen Hess, a senior fellow at the Brookings Institution. "Should we really be exposed to everything?" The decision is left to the media, whose judgment may be inconsistent—and sometimes just plain wrong. It is up to the media to help create a climate in which it is possible to take seriously the idea of being led by a woman. The *Wall Street Journal* did just that by putting this question at the top of page 1 in 1993: "*Ms. President*: Other Nations Elect Women to Lead Them. So Why Doesn't U.S.?" The story said it was odd that so many other nations had chosen women leaders, while the prospect of an American woman president still seemed remote. Reporter Geraldine Brooks, who thought up the idea for the story, says it was unusual for the male-dominated *Journal* to run it on page 1 and attributed its play to the fact that a woman, Jane Berentsen, was editing the front page. "She pressed for it in the face of tremendous skepticism," says Brooks.

The story quoted Lynn Martin, former congresswoman and secretary of labor in the Bush administration, as saying that the public is closer to embracing a woman presidential candidate than political insiders think: "The people are so far ahead of the press and the politicians, it will take your breath away." Martin was described by the *Journal* as the only woman seriously considering a presidential race. Since then, the media buzz has mainly been about New Jersey governor Christine Todd Whitman. Her 1993 win, in a year that some pundits had said was the "Year of the UnWoman," drew national media attention. After one year in office, Whitman was the only remaining woman governor in the country, a moderate Republican who had delivered on her campaign promises to cut taxes. After she gave the GOP response to President Clinton's State of the Union address in early 1995, the buzz picked up in the national press that Whitman could be president one day, and somebody's running mate in the near term. Whitman didn't say anything to encourage this media speculation. She didn't have to. Apart from her administrative effectiveness, Whitman has another quality that makes her special. As *Newsweek*'s Eleanor Clift observed, Whitman is neither a member of the old boys' club nor does she come across as being too female. "Her tomboy appeal wins over men and women."

By fall 1995, long after most would-be presidential contenders had announced their intentions, Whitman endorsed Bob Dole. The New Jersey primary wouldn't be held until June 1996, but the questions kept coming. "It's getting irritating. You hear the same questions over and over," says Whitman's press secretary, Rita Manno. "We say 'no' to most of the interview requests we get—inevitably they're about her vice presidential aspirations. . . . There's not much she can say at this point." News media seem to feed on each other's reports, and the governor has no control over what is published or aired, Manno says. "One says it and another picks it up. . . . She's in the spotlight all the time."

Every time Whitman made an appearance out of state, it rekindled media speculation that she was interested in a higher position. They jumped to conclusions, Manno says. "If she accepts an invitation to attend a high profile event, then we get stories that she's going because she's interested in being someone's running mate," but if she doesn't go, it hurts New Jersey. "The choices are to hide and don't do anything or to accept and do the best job you can." Whitman decided "not to hide in the closet" because she realizes that "whatever she decides to do will be looked at in whatever way they want," says Manno, adding, "It will all play itself out when the media latches on to someone else."

Ann Richards says she "really kind of felt for" Whitman when the media started promoting her. "They want to include the name of a woman because women will scream if they don't—so they include her on the list when she hasn't even had the opportunity to prove herself yet." People will see the stories and say "who does she think she is?" Richards says. "Sometimes journalists inflate our role because they need some balance—women out there who are leaders. They make you look more important than you really are," Richards adds. "In the game of politics—and this is true of men and women—speculation about what you're going to do next starts before you even do what you've just been elected to do. That begins on election night." Speaking from personal experience, Richards says women get mentioned in stories for higher office when they have "no interest, no intention or hopes of being there."

The news media influence voters' decisions through the facts they select and the way they present information. Balanced, equitable coverage of women politicians at all levels will come only when journalists realize, as Eleanor Clift put it, that the gender of a woman politician is the least remarkable thing about her.

❖ NOTES ❖

Chapter 1
GOING FORWARD, WALKING BACKWARD

1   "The press was as kind . . . . than it knew how." From a speech by Susan B. Anthony, in Lynn Sherr, *Failure Is Impossible: Susan B. Anthony in Her Own Words* (New York: Times Books/Random House, 1995), 203.

2   It began to feel . . . knew about." Interview with Representative Marjorie Margolies-Mezvinsky, June 21, 1994.

2   "How am I . . . answer that?" Interview with Rita Manno, press secretary to New Jersey Governor Christine Todd Whitman, May 18, 1995.

2   she doesn't have time . . . labels. Interview with James Mazzarella, press secretary to Representative Susan Molinari, Sept. 7, 1995.

2   "Strangers in the Senate." From the title of Senator Barbara Boxer's book, *Strangers in the Senate* (Washington, D.C.: National Press Books, 1994).

3   news stories reflect the values . . . white males. For further discussion of how the media construct a version of reality, see Edward Jay Epstein, *News From Nowhere* (New York: Vintage, 1974); Herbert Gans, *Deciding What's News* (New York: Pantheon, 1979); Michael Schudson, *Discovering the News* (New York: Basic Books, 1978); and Gaye Tuchman, *Making News: A Study in the Construction of Reality* (New York: Free Press, 1978).

3   journalists "do not try . . . obtruded itself." Walter Lippmann, *Public Opinion* (New York: Macmillan, 1945), 338, 341.

3   "The daily persuasions . . . our own." Schudson, *Discovering the News,* 194.

3   women are more interested in compromise and collaboration. See Carol Gilligan, *In a Different Voice* (Cambridge: Harvard Univ. Press, 1982).

4   television news in particular . . . the news story. Epstein, *News from Nowhere,* 261

4   a continuing problem . . . that's changing. Interview with Senator Nancy Kassebaum, June 20, 1994.

4   "If it's not controversial . . . attention." George J. Mitchell, "The Media May Devour Democracy," *Los Angeles Times,* March 13, 1994, M2.

4   "Women are at . . . each other." In "Women in Words and Pictures," *Nieman Reports,* Summer 1989, 59.

5   Katherine Langley . . . blue-black hair." Hope Chamberlin, *A Minority of Members: Women in the U.S. Congress* (New York: Praeger, 1973), 62.

5   The *Chicago Tribune* . . . Equal Rights Amendment." Ibid., 303, 306.

5   by wearing a gray flannel . . . you have children." Susan and Martin Tolchin, *Clout—Womanpower and Politics* (New York: Coward, McCann & Geoghegan, 1974), 96.

5   a typical story . . . Barbara Mikulski." Quoted in Bella Abzug, *Gender Gap* (Boston: Houghton Mifflin, 1984), 169.

6   "I told people . . . follow a goal." Ruth Mandel, *In the Running: The New Woman Candidate* (New York: Ticknor & Fields, 1981), 36.

6   During the campaign . . . stages of baldness. Abzug, *Gender Gap,* 169.

6   Ann Richards . . . light." *New York Times Magazine,* Feb. 7, 1993, 25.

6   a woman in public . . . in the public eye." Interview with Ann Richards, May 31, 1995.

6   "It's how I started . . . my life." Interview with Ann Richards.

7   In the 1992 Colorado Senate . . . investment banker. *Christian Science Monitor,* Aug. 17, 1992, 7.

7   Mary Sue Terry . . . wife and children. *Women's Political Times,* Winter 1993-94, 8.

7   Barbara Mikulski . . . husband anyway." Quoted in *McCall's,* Aug. 1994, 105.

8   "Is there something . . . affect the family." Peggy Lamson, *Few Are Chosen: American Women in Political Life Today* (Boston: Houghton Mifflin, 1968), xii.

8   "There is . . . invisible and elusive." Ibid., xxv.

8   A study of . . . nightly news. Unabridged Communications press release, 1992.

8   Unless the media . . . problem for media." "In the Media, A Woman's Place," *Media Studies Journal,* Winter/Spring 1993, 62.

9   As ABC Capitol Hill . . . never ends." At *Times-Mirror* forum on "The Press and Congress," Washington, D.C., Sept. 26, 1986.

9   Stephen Hess . . . newsworthy. Stephen Hess, *The Washington Reporters* (Washington, D.C.: Brookings, 1981), 15.

9   Covering Congress . . . legislative aides. David Broder, *Behind the Front Page* (New York: Simon & Schuster, 1987), 209-16.

10   Humor columnist Russell Baker . . . Capitol Hill." Quoted in Lewis W. Wolfson, *The Untapped Power of the Press: Explaining Government to the People* (Westport: Praeger, 1985), 36.

10   "We have come . . . their existence." "Bandwagons, Women and Cultural Mythology," *Media Studies Journal,* Winter/Spring 1993, 2.

10   A study published . . . taken for granted." S. Robert Lichter, Stanley Rothman, and Linda S. Lichter, *The Media Elite* (Bethesda, Md.: Adler & Adler, 1986), 297.

10   "Perceptions of reality . . . are distorted." Jeane J. Kirkpatrick, *Political Woman* (New York: Basic Books, 1974), 106.

11   The power of journalists . . . particular dimension." David Halberstam, *The Powers That Be* (New York: Knopf, 1979), 182.

11   Newspapers and political parties . . . party ties by 1930. Richard Davis, *The Press and American Politics: The New Mediator* (New York: Longman, 1992), 77.

11   New papers . . . convictions." Ibid., 78.

11   As Margaret Mead . . . less a woman." Quoted in *Media Studies Journal,* Winter/Spring 1993, 41.

11   *New York Times* . . . explained." Anne O'Hare McCormick, *The World at Home,* ed. Marion Turner Sheehan (New York: Knopf, 1956), v.

12   "Everywhere the radio . . . friends." *Woman's Journal,* Dec. 28, 1928, 9.

12   Radio had led to . . . "about it." *New York Times,* Aug. 12, 1928, 1.

12   "I featured overmuch . . . at all." Quoted in Gaye Tuchman, ed., *Hearth and Home: Images of Women in the Mass Media* (New York: Oxford Univ. Press, 1978), 191.

12   "The most significant . . . don't see it." "In the Media, a Woman's Place," 63.

13   the 1956 *Life* . . . housekeeping ability. See "After 36 Years of Suffrage, U.S. women are a force from grass roots to the Senate," *Life,* Dec. 24, 1956, 49.

13   Kennedy wrote . . . kept her wits." *McCall's,* Jan. 1958, 36-37.

13   An exclusive round-table interview. See *McCall's,* Aug. 1994, 102-5, 128-30.

13   *Glamour* . . . Let's Not Lose Now." *Glamour,* Nov. 1994, 81, 82.

14   More than twenty million . . . each month. Davis, *The Press and American Politics,* 164.

14   Nearly all American . . . as newspapers. Austin Ranney, *Channels of Power: The Impact of Television on American Politics* (New York: Basic Books, 1983), 13-14.

15   The interpretation . . . by words." Neil Postman and Steve Powers, *How to Watch TV News* (New York: Penguin, 1992), 164.

15   Geraldine Ferraro . . . size six!" Martin A. Lee and Norman Solomon, *Unreliable Sources: A Guide to Detecting Bias in News Media* (New York: Lyle Stuart Book, Carol Publishing Group, 1990), 229.

15   "Always try to . . . authoritative." Sue Slipman, *Helping Ourselves to Power: A Handbook for Women on the Skills of Public Life* (Oxford: Pergamon Press, 1986), 92.

15   "Aggressive courting . . . I wish I could." Interview with Nancy Kassebaum.

16   Television has . . . government functions." Ranney, *Channels of Power,* 123.

16   "Journalism is . . . subsequent decisions." Stephan Lesher, *Media Unbound: The Impact of Television Journalism on the Public* (Boston: Houghton Mifflin, 1982), 7.

16   "You cannot get a message out . . . four seconds." Interview with Louise Slaughter, Sept. 26, 1994.

16   "The 30-second soundbite . . . issues as well." Interview with Kay Bailey Hutchison, June 21, 1994.

16   California Senator Dianne Feinstein . . . C-SPAN cameras. *Washington Post,* May 16, 1993.

16   C-SPAN "has helped . . . well informed." Interview with Kay Bailey Hutchison.

17   people used . . . politics." Interview with Nancy Kassebaum.

17   National news . . . therefore I am." Quoted in Burdett Loomis, *The New American Politician* (New York: Basic Books, 1988), 106.

17   Journalists covering Washington . . . the world." William Rivers, *The Other Government* (New York: Universe Books, 1982), 10.

17   Nearly half . . . press coverage. In Davis, *The Press and American Politics,* 31.

17   News is . . . kills you." Interview with Nancy Kassebaum.

17   Marjorie Margolies-Mezvinsky . . . about something." Interview with Marjories Margolies-Mezvinsky.

18   The answer . . . be a woman." Interview with Rita Manno.

Chapter 2

THE FIRST AND ONLY

19   Even the *New York Times* . . . before the election. Hannah Josephson, *Jeannette Rankin, First Lady in Congress* (Indianapolis: Bobbs-Merrill, 1974), 55.

19   Montana newspapers . . . her campaign. Josephson, *Jeannette Rankin,* 54-55.

19   As Rankin's brother . . . to Rankin. Kevin S. Giles, *Flight of the Dove: The Story of Jeannette Rankin* (Beaverton, Ore.: Touchstone Press, 1980), 72.

20   Advertisers wanted . . . her teeth. Giles, *Flight of the Dove,* 76.

20   Montana's new member . . . red-haired Republican." *New York Times,* Nov. 9, 1916, A1.

21 "Miss Rankin . . . excellent cook." Ibid., Nov. 11, 1916.
21 Rankin's hair . . . keep her busy." Ibid., Nov. 12, 1916.
22 "She was sewing . . . needlework. Ibid.
22 "There are . . . was a joke." *Helena* (Montana) *Independent,* Nov. 12, 1916, 1.
23 "Breathes there . . . and gaiters." Giles, *Flight of the Dove,* 77.
23 "There is . . . wide experience." Ibid., 79.
23 "I have so . . . at least." Ibid., 82.
23 A *New York Times* . . . her dress. *New York Times,* April 2, 1916.
24 "In spite of . . . of purpose." Quoted in Chamberlin, *A Minority of Members,* 8.
24 The *New York* . . . and sobbed." *New York Times,* April 6, 1917, 4.
24 "drawing from . . . straight reasoning." Ibid., April 7, 1917, editorial page.
25 only Rankin's . . . lead story. *New York Times,* April 6, 1917, 4.
25 "I expect . . . the ropes." Giles, *Flight of the Dove,* 101.
25 "Tell him . . . hell!" Ibid., 107.
25 Rankin promoted . . . community feeding." "What We Women Should Do," *Ladies Home Journal,* Aug. 17, 1917.
26 "They own . . . I was here." In Giles, *Flight of the Dove,* 114.
26 "Symbol of martyrdom . . . war and violence. Ibid., 185.
26 Most of us . . . by men." *McCall's,* Jan. 1958, 37.
27 people turned . . . to say tonight." Chamberlin, *A Minority of Members,* 39.
27 "One never . . . prevailing mode." Ibid., 40.
28 The *Times* saw . . . propaganda." *New York Times,* Aug. 11, 1921, 1.
28 "banged the gavel . . . voice." *New York Times,* June 21, 1921, 1
28 The anti-Felton . . . Wife?" Chamberlin, *A Minority of Members,* 28.
29 "Over fifty . . . the whites." Ibid., 31
29 "romantic . . . unstinted usefulness." Ibid., 36.
30 "Curiously . . . own right." Kirkpatrick, *Political Woman,* 218-19.
31 "Congress treats . . . to her.' In Chamberlin, *A Minority of Members,* 50.
31 "On the floor . . . to tread." Ibid., 59.
31 "new type . . . energies." *New York Times,* Aug. 12, 1928, 1.
31 "A man enters . . . office concerned." *Ladies Home Journal,* May 1928, 8.
32 "The opposition . . . man's job." Eleanor Roosevelt and Lorena Hickok, *Ladies of Courage* (New York: Putnam's, 1954), 113.
32 "practically forced . . . party managers." *New York Times,* Nov. 6, 1924.
33 "I ask you . . . help her? Roosevelt and Hickok, *Ladies of Courage,* 116.
33 "The advice of . . . out of place." In *New York Times,* Nov. 8, 1924.
33 "'governess' . . . woman-hater." Ibid., editorial page.
34 "She fell victim . . . resist it." Roosevelt and Hickok, *Ladies of Courage,* 117-18.
34 In 1924 . . . outcome." *Woman's Journal,* Dec. 28, 1928, 8.
34 Publicity bureaus . . . the country. Ibid., 9.
35 "Mary Norton had . . . impossibility." Roosevelt and Hickok, *Ladies of Courage,* 165.
35 "Huey's echo . . . its problems." Chamberlin, *A Minority of Members,* 94.
35 "diminutive . . . Louisiana yield?" Ibid., 119.
37 "notable for their . . . made the congresswoman." *Woman's Journal,* Dec. 28, 1928, 18.
37 unwise to . . . has been overcome." *Woman's Journal,* Jan. 1931, 22.

Chapter 3

THE "GLAMOUR GIRLS" OF CONGRESS

38 "Connecticut's gift . . . Congress. *New York Daily News,* Feb. 3, 1944.
38 "Whether she . . . ever since." Roosevelt and Hickok, *Ladies of Courage,* 235.
38 "attention was . . . . Mrs. Luce.'" Helen Gahagan Douglas, *A Full Life* (Garden City, N.Y.: Doubleday, 1982), 196.
39 Even the *New York* . . . fencing.'" *New York Times,* July 16, 1944.
39 "For reporters . . . as I could." Douglas, *A Full Life,* 198.
39 "I told Mrs. Douglas . . . had said." Stephen Shadegg, *Clare Boothe Luce* (New York: Simon & Schuster, 1970), 123.
40 Douglas and Luce . . . to pieces." Roosevelt and Hickok, *Ladies of Courage,* 54.
40 Columnist Drew Pearson . . . 'glamour girl' honors." Shadegg, *Clare Boothe Luce,* 190.
40 "pretty enough to . . . her colleagues." In Chamberlin, *A Minority of Members,* 160.
40 Luce likened . . . her country." Shadegg, *Clare Boothe Luce,* 120-21.
40 "a confrontation . . . ships of state." Marion Sanders, *Dorothy Thompson: A Legend in Her Time* (Boston: Houghton Mifflin, 1973), 268.
40 Columnist Walter Winchell . . . gentlemen present." In Shadegg, *Clare Boothe Luce,* 122.
40 Luce said she . . . another woman. Ibid., 123.
41 "Women who . . . important committees." *New York Times,* Nov. 12, 1944.
41 "For a breathless . . . life." In Shadegg, *Clare Boothe Luce,* 158-59.
42 "The boys at *Time* . . . his wife." Wilfred Sheed, *Clare Boothe Luce* (New York: Dutton, 1982), 91.
42 "It is . . . won respect. Roosevelt, *Ladies of Courage,* 231.
42 Only after Luce . . . flattering article about her. The article is accompanied by a note acknowledging that the editors had fumbled Luce's story, "because they were too fearful of being damned if they told it or damned if they didn't." *Time,* Aug. 26, 1946, 19-20.
42 "She is bound . . . attack on us." In Shadegg, *Clare Boothe Luce,* 162.
42 "Time Inc. . . . dreamed up." Sheed, *Clare Boothe Luce,* 78.
43 She told reporters . . . "Never explain." Shadegg, *Clare Boothe Luce,* 164.
43 "No doubt . . . those days." Sheed, *Clare Boothe Luce,* 9.
43 Her rebuke of FDR . . . the broadsword." Shadegg, 175-76.
43 seventeen newspapers . . . two weeks." Ibid., 177.
43 When reporters asked . . . to Talk." Ibid., 202.
44 a public opinion poll . . . really functioning?" Ibid., 177.
44 "the only American . . . into it." *New Haven Journal-Courier,* Oct. 20, 1944, quoted in James Baughman, *Henry R. Luce and the Rise of the American News Media* (Boston: Twayne, 1987), 141.
44 She had told . . . millions. Ibid
44 she was attacked . . . Washington hall. Shadegg, *Clare Boothe Luce,* 197-98.
45 Luce, said Roosevelt, . . . least interesting." Roosevelt and Hickok, *Ladies of Courage,* 230.
45 Roosevelt said her male . . . another play." Ibid., 232.
45 Gold calls Luce . . . her resignation. Vic Gold, *I Don't Need You When I'm Right* (New York: William Morrow, 1975), 99-102.
46 "I had . . . take it." Douglas, *A Full Life,* 161.

46 It was wartime . . . of Scotland. Roosevelt and Hickok, *Ladies of Courage*, 54.
46 "The ten most . . . world." Ibid., 47.
46 She was . . . background. Ibid., 54.
47 Douglas says she . . . thunderous. Douglas, *A Full Life*, 215, 222.
47 "It was my job . . . rent controls. Ibid., 252.
47 "Has read as if . . . about himself." *Newsweek*, June 5, 1950, 25.
48 "It made me feel . . . keep up with it." Douglas, *A Full Life*, 317.
48 "Even Richard . . . my sex." Ibid., 329.
48 California voters . . . "my reputation." Ibid., 319.
48 Few in Congress . . . social economics. Ibid., 324.
49 Columnist Drew Pearson . . . out of the Senate." Ibid., 327-28.
49 *Times* political reporter . . . real accountability. Halberstam, *The Powers That Be*, 262-63.
49 "Her service . . . innuendo." *Los Angeles Times*, 1 July 1980, editorial page.

Chapter 4
A ROSE BY ANY OTHER NAME

51 She became friends . . . reelection time. Margaret Chase Smith, *Declaration of Conscience* (New York: Doubleday, 1972). 3.
51 Craig "has . . . from Maine." *Colliers*, July 29, 1950, 44.
52 The Women's National . . . in 1948. Roosevelt and Hickok, *Ladies of Courage*, 179.
52 Former CBS . . . of their own. Nancy Dickerson, *Among Those Present: A Reporter's View of Twenty-five Years in Washington* (New York: Random House, 1976), 16.
52 McCarthy gave his . . . anticommunist mood. For a detailed account, see Edwin Bayley, *Joe McCarthy and the Press* (Madison: Univ. of Wisconsin Press, 1981).
52 Smith says . . . same party. Smith, *Declaration of Conscience*, 9.
52 Initially Smith . . . accusations. Ibid., 8.
53 she called Walter Lippmann . . . helped her decide. Ibid., 10.
53 "Mr. President . . . advisedly." Ibid., 13-17.
54 "What many . . . man-sized will." *Newsweek*, June 12, 1950, 24-25.
54 Maine's earnest . . . Smith. *Time*, June 12, 1950, 19.
54 The *Washington Star* . . . American life." Ibid.
54 And political guru . . . were Quixotic." Smith, *Declaration of Conscience*, 19.
54 "Maine's charming . . . big speech . . . " *Colliers*, July 29, 1950, 20.
54 "McCarthy...got . . . His Lady." *Time*, Feb. 5, 1951.
54 expressing disdain . . . "Joe's boy." Smith, *Declaration of Conscience*, 56.
54 She basically ignored . . . the election. Peggy Lamson, *Few Are Chosen: American Women in Political Life Today* (Boston: Houghton Mifflin, 1968), 22.
55 "I was always . . . somewhere else." Interview with Margaret Chase Smith, July 10, 1994.
55 Margaret Chase . . . Senate. *Washington Post*, Jan. 24, 1990, op-ed page.
55 "Well, they were . . . unfair. Interview with Margaret Chase Smith.
55 the resulting debate . . . covered at all. Chamberlin, *A Minority of Members*, 147.
55 Smith figured Roosevelt . . . her talk more." Smith, *Declaration of Conscience*, 208.
56 Doris Fleeson . . . backside either." Lamson, *Few Are Chosen*, 7.
56 Smith had told a reporter . . . rebuild entirely." Chamberlin, *A Minority of Members*, 351.
56 "I never thought . . . not their sex." Interview with Margaret Chase Smith.

57 "I was not . . . put a handle on it." Ibid.
57 Harper's magazine . . . for office?'" Chamberlin, *A Minority of Members,* 257-58.
57 In the closing . . . TV performer. Marion Sanders, *Lady and the Vote,* 90.
58 "The diminutive . . . battles. *Wall Street Journal,* Dec. 3, 1969, 1.
58 "In my judgment . . . about women." Quoted in Fern Ingersoll, *Women in Washington,* 196.
58 "A feminine voice . . . "surviving spouse." Chamberlin, *A Minority of Members,* 263.
59 "Word was then. . . . *Wilkes-Barre Record.* Sanders, *Lady and the Vote,* 91.
59 "Friendly reporters . . . and applejack." Ibid., 154-55.
59 "This is subversive . . . of coffee." Ibid., 153.
60 The magazine described . . . Andy." *Time,* May 19, 1958, 17-18.
60 "Many in Washington . . . for protection." Quoted in Chamberlin, *A Minority of Members,* 265.
60 "To link their . . . reputation for centuries. Sanders, *Lady and the Vote,* 9.
61 One example was this . . . reason: women." Chamberlin, *A Minority of Members,* 248.
61 Margaret Chase . . . and grandmothers." Sanders, *Lady and the Vote,* 153.
61 One afternoon . . . in politics." Roosevelt and Hickok, *Ladies of Courage,* 177.
62 "Are lady lawmakers . . . fading interest. Chamberlin, *A Minority of Members,* 301.

Chapter 5
THE PUSH FOR EQUAL RIGHTS

63 "We are still novelty acts." Quoted in Mandel, *In the Running,* 61.
64 "Because you are a woman . . . male candidate." Full text of remarks in Tolchin and Tolchin, *Clout,* 259ff.
64 A woman running . . . male identifications." Kirkpatrick, *Political Woman,* 99.
64 "That image . . . ability or intelligence." Susanne Paizis, *Getting Her Elected: A Political Woman's Handbook* (Sacramento: Creative Editions, 1977), 85.
64 Kirkpatrick says . . . in a woman." Kirkpatrick, *Political Woman,* 101.
64 Mink was arguing . . . "Hormones in the White House." The story is retold in Chamberlin, *A Minority of Members,* 313-14.
65 "It is absolutely indefensible . . . represent our interest." *New York Times,* March 25, 1971.
65 "It doesn't bother me . . . I *made* today." Quoted in Myra MacPherson, *The Power Lovers* (New York: Putnam, 1975), 341.
65 Jack Anderson . . . about inequality. "The Washington Merry-Go-Round," *Washington Post,* Sept. 7, 1966, B11.
65 *Time,* for example . . . still loves me.'" Quoted in *Time,* Aug. 24, 1970.
66 U.S. News . . . modest in dress." *U.S. News & World Report,* Aug. 24, 1970, 30.
66 "On the issue . . . explosions." Mandel, *In the Running,* 233.
66 Mandel illustrates . . . twenty thousand votes. Ibid., 233-34.
66 Guidelines issued . . . in the same style. Reprinted in Toni Delacorte, *How to Get Free Press* (San Francisco: Harbor, 1981), 109-11.
67 When Connecticut Representative . . . Congress in 1970. MacPherson, *The Power Lovers,* 342.
67 When Ann Richards . . . of a housewife. Tolchin and Tolchin, *Clout,* 190.
68 In 1977 . . . at any given time." "A Change in Style," *Nieman Reports,* Summer 1979, 24.
68 The front-page story . . . Didn't you notice?'" *New York Times,* April 24, 1974, A1.

69 Determined to get . . . of the trip. MacPherson, *The Power Lovers,* 350.

69 Before that . . . not much use as a token." Barbara Jordan and Shelby Hearon, *Barbara Jordan: A Self-Portrait* (Garden City, N.Y.: Doubleday, 1979), 192.

70 The *Wall Street Journal* . . . in a lifetime." *Wall Street Journal,* Feb. 5, 1975, A1.

70 Meg Greenfield . . . political blah." James Haskins, *Barbara Jordan* (New York: Dial, 1977), 186.

70 In fact, she . . . try to help it." Ibid., 19.

70 The *New York Times* . . . their offspring." *New York Times,* July 13, 1976.

70 The *Washington Star* . . . national superstar." Jordan and Hearon, *Barbara Jordan,* 233.

71 "During my uphill . . . a congressperson." Ibid., 236-37.

71 Jordan said she . . . but not now." Ibid., 246.

71 Celler commented . . . exist." Peggy Lamson, *In the Vanguard: Six American Women in Public Life* (Boston: Houghton Mifflin, 1979), 79.

72 "The newspaper . . . planned it better." Ibid., 79.

72 "Otherwise . . . at subway entrances. Interview with Elizabeth Holtzman, July 21, 1995.

72 "They didn't see . . . cigar-smoking machine." Lamson, *In the Vanguard,* 71

72 Newspaper columnist Jimmy Breslin . . . see some people." In Ibid., 79-80.

72 After the election . . . anymore." Interview with Elizabeth Holtzman.

73 Standards of acceptable behavior . . . one of the big problems." Ibid.

73 Holtzman had been . . . destructive and distortive." Ibid.

74 "Some women candidates . . . even to be noticed." Quoted in MacPherson, *The Power Lovers,* 324.

74 By 1976, gender . . . campaign efforts." Susan J. Carroll, *Women as Candidates in American Politics* (Bloomington: Indiana Univ. Press, 1983), 62.

74 "In a way . . . her umbrella." Quoted in Rosemary Breslin and Joshua Hammer, *Gerry! A Woman Making History* (New York: Pinnacle Books, 1984), 134.

74 "I think he . . . very costly." Ibid.

74 Commenting on her . . . inexperience as assets." *New York Times,* Nov. 13, 1978, op-ed page.

74 The *London Daily Mail* . . . his cook." *Christian Science Monitor,* Jan. 9, 1979, B1.

75 *Christian Science* . . . unassuming manner." Ibid.

76 She was often attacked . . . development. *Time,* Dec. 12, 1977, 26.

76 "Ray feuds . . . baiting her." Ibid., 31.

76 Ray, in turn . . . extremist environmentalists." *Wall Street Journal,* Dec. 6, 1977, 14.

76 One of her . . . mediocre and incompetent." Ester Stineman, *American Political Women* (Littleton, Colo.: Libraries Unlimited, 1980) 130.

77 "I was appointed . . . all right with me." Ibid.

77 The *Wall Street Journal* . . . close-cropped hair." *Wall Street Journal,* Dec. 6, 1977, 1.

77 *Time* described her . . . Peter Pan." *Time,* Dec. 12, 1977, 27.

77 But *Newsweek* got it . . . chain saw for Christmas." *Newsweek,* April 11, 1977, 45.

77 *U.S. News* . . . let-them-eat-cake expression." *U.S. News & World Report,* Oct. 10, 1977, 45.

77 Her press secretary . . . with a smile." *Wall Street Journal,* Dec. 6, 1977, 14.

77 naming a litter . . . to love pigs." *Mother Jones,* Jan. 1979, 11.

77 Ray expressed her . . . Pacific Northwest." The story is told in Norman Isaacs, *Untended Gates* (New York: Columbia Univ. Press, 1988), 58-59.

Chapter 6
BATTLING BELLA

79   "I've been described . . . very serious woman." Bella Abzug, *Bella!* (New York: Saturday Review Press, 1972), 3.

79   Looking back . . . for change." Interview with Bella Abzug, May 2, 1995.

79   Club members . . . seal on it. Abzug, *Bella!* 211.

80   Some of the women . . . one dimensional." Interview with Bella Abzug.

80   Norman Mailer . . . grooves in wood." In Abzug, *Bella!* 49.

80   "Say it softly . . . in drag." *National Review,* March 14, 1975, 290.

81   former president . . . terrifying to him." *Washington Post,* Sept. 12, 1995, A3.

81   "Republicans should work . . . hot pants." Quoted in Abzug, *Bella!* 49.

81   "I swear I . . . all their lives?" Ibid., 169-70.

81   "They got part of it . . . comment, I would." Interview with Bella Abzug.

82   The *New York Times* . . . black members." *New York Times,* March 29, 1972, op-ed page.

82   "Many of her . . . behind-the-scenes work." Tolchin and Tolchin, *Clout,* 162.

82   "You haven't got . . . doing things." Interview with Bella Abzug.

82   *New York Times* Sunday . . . of the House. Abzug, *Bella!* 282.

82   As she tells it . . . where she lived. Bryna J. Fireside, *Is There a Woman in the House . . . or Senate?* (Morton Grove, Ill.: Albert Whitman, 1994), 61.

82   Abzug herself . . . volunteer workers. Bella Abzug, *Gender Gap* (Boston: Houghton Mifflin, 1984), 157.

82   She started wearing . . . hats, she says. Interview with Bella Abzug.

83   such a sighting . . . Abzug's head. *New York Times,* June 6, 1972, A29.

83   One of her hats . . . Caucus. *New York Times,* Oct. 21, 1972.

83   Her style . . . 'dynamic.' Abzug, *Gender Gap,* 171.

84   "What the Associated Press . . . Fishbait Miller." Abzug, *Bella!* 29.

84   She "responded . . . words now and then." Ibid.

84   She says the stories . . . personal lives. Interview with Bella Abzug.

84   The same sort of thing . . . I look like." Abzug, *Bella!* 72.

85   "I speak for . . . her candidacy. *New York Times,* March 22, 1972.

85   "I act as . . . to change." *New York Times,* April 29, 1972, A29.

85   Ryan believed . . . a woman." Quoted in Tolchin and Tolchin, *Clout,* 171.

85   She was criticized . . . newspapers. See *Ms.,* Feb. 1973, 76.

85   "Bella Abzug forces . . . born a man." *New York Times,* April 21, 1972, op-ed page.

86   Elizabeth Harris wrote . . . doing that themselves." *New York Times,* June 6, 1972, 40.

86   Writing in the . . . a woman." *New York Times,* July 19, 1972, 43.

86   Reaction to . . . the pie." *New York Times,* July 20, 1972, 29.

87   She said the press . . . threatened by me." Tolchin and Tolchin, *Clout,* 161.

87   Ruth Mandel . . . other women candidates." Mandel, *In the Running,* 47.

88   She "came across . . . press portrayal." Ibid.

88   "You're always sensitive . . . one-dimensional." Interview with Bella Abzug.

Chapter 7
ARE WE THERE YET?

89   "A lot of people . . . 88 percent men. Quoted in Breslin and Hammer, *Gerry!* 124.

90 Female candidates have . . . candidates differently." Leonie Huddy and Nayda Terkildsen, "The Consequences of Gender Stereotypes for Women Candidates at Different Levels and Types of Office." *Political Research Quarterly* 46 (Spring 1993): 520.

90 "Miss Holtzman was dining . . . her appeal, too." *New York Times* Magazine, June 22, 1980, 18.

91 "What counts . . . campaign you run.'" Ibid., 18.

91 "As though that . . . independent woman." Interview with Elizabeth Holtzman.

91 "Do not cry . . . seems to remember." Quoted in Jerry Roberts, *Dianne Feinstein: Never Let them See You Cry* (New York: HarperCollinsWest, 1994) 4.

91 "I have nine . . . Peter Rabbit." In Breslin and Hammer, *Gerry!* 130.

91 *Newsweek* suggested . . . ever faced." *Los Angeles Times,* Dec. 5, 1984, 1.

92 "A party worker . . . into the ring.'" *Media Report to Women,* May-June 1983, 13.

92 On July 1 . . . resultant furor." Ibid.

92 "Register's reputation . . . 'holy crusade?'" *Wall Street Journal,* Aug. 18, 1982, editorial page.

92 The *Kansas City Star* . . . "waist deep" in "hypocrisy." In *Media Report to Women,* May-June 1983, 13.

92 "Despite record-breaking . . . support my opponent." Ibid.

92 "The issue is dead . . . Mikulski." Quoted in Breslin and Hammer, *Gerry!* 133.

93 A 1983 study of . . . objective reporting." Peter Clarke and Susan H. Evans, *Covering Campaigns: Journalism in Congressional Elections* (Stanford: Stanford Univ. Press, 1983), 84.

93 The first critical . . . in the media." Timothy E. Cook, *Making Laws and Making News: Media Strategies in the U.S. House of Representatives* (Washington: Brookings, 1989), 117.

94 In 1988 . . . at all levels." Lois Lovelace Duke, ed., *Women in Politics: Outsiders or Insiders?* (Englewood Cliffs, N.J.: Prentice-Hall, 1993), 133.

94 Women must decide . . . are accepted. See Barbara Trafton, *Women Winning: How to Run for Public Office* (Boston: Harvard Common Press, 1984), 9, 82.

94 "Those of us . . . mirror at all." Quoted in *Professional Communicator,* Winter 1990, 11.

95 Mann's comments . . . as experts. Ibid.

95 At newspapers . . . photos of women. October 1990 study of *Time, Newsweek* and *U.S. News & World Report* by Women in Communications Inc.

95 A survey of four . . . 'testing the waters' campaign." *Media Report to Women,* March/April 1988, 7.

95 "I would watch . . . They're out front." Quoted in *New York Times,* Dec. 20, 1992.

96 That's the conclusion . . . own property." Quoted in *Media Report to Women,* March/April 1984, 8.

96 a study by . . . written by women. Kim Kahn and Edie Goldenberg, "Women Candidates in the News: An Examination of Gender Differences in U.S. Senate Campaign Coverage" *Public Opinion Quarterly,* Summer 1991, 180-99.

97 "So much of it . . . innuendo." Interview with Martha Layne Collins, June 29, 1995.

97 "I was 'that icy blonde.'" Interview with Martha Layne Collins.

97 "Kentucky's first . . . can't think." *Time,* June 4, 1984, 28.

97 "When a man . . . to me." Interview with Martha Layne Collins.

98 "It seemed . . . that way." Interview with Larry Hayes, June 27, 1995.

98 Collins describes herself . . . talking about." Interview with Martha Layne Collins.

98 "If Larry Hayes . . . as governor." Interview with Larry Hayes.

99 In Collins's experience . . . not a good time . . . ." Interview with Martha Layne Collins.

99 Hayes said . . . put things together." Interview with Larry Hayes.

99 "There was mutual . . . coalition?" Interview with Martha Layne Collins.
100 "once you step . . . totally vulnerable." Interview with Madeleine Kunin, July 6, 1995.
100 "Very few people . . . managerial ability." Madeleine Kunin, *Living a Political Life* (New York: Knopf, 1994), 279.
100 Women face gender assumptions . . . too emotional." Interview with Madeleine Kunin, July 6, 1995.
101 In a newspaper . . . Role in Her Defeat." Kunin, *Living a Political Life,* 280-81.
101 she learned . . . .each other out. Ibid., 278.
101 Kunin says dealing . . . didn't think so." Interview with Madeleine Kunin.
102 "I did not search . . . myself." Kunin, *Living a Political Life,* 320.
102 "It's an ideal situation . . . always on stage. Interview with Madeleine Kunin.
102 "Sometimes . . . to the soundbite." Ibid.
103 "If women would run . . . might be instituted." *Los Angeles Times,* Nov. 10, 1990, B7.
103 "Progress is much . . . regardless of sex." William Safire, *New York Times,* Dec. 20, 1990, op-ed page.
103 "This may be . . . for mankind." *Newsweek,* Oct. 29, 1990, 35.
103 "In the national . . . we women lose." Quoted in *The Quill,* March 1992, 17.

Chapter 8
ALMOST A BRIDESMAID

105 "I hadn't been . . . ourselves in." Geraldine Ferraro and Linda Bird Francke, *Ferraro: My Story* (New York: Bantam, 1985), 157-58.
105 "They say it . . . started with me." Interview with Geraldine Ferraro, March 30, 1995.
105 attacks on Ferraro . . . tip of the iceberg. Interview with Eleanor Lewis, March 28, 1995.
106 "We have been . . . competence." Quoted in Susan Stamberg, *Talk* (New York: Turtle Bay Books/Random House, 1993), 200.
106 India Edwards . . . ticket nationally. Ibid., 202.
106 In 1972 . . . with commercials. The story is told in "The Ticket That Might have Been . . . Vice President Farenthold," *Ms.,* Jan. 1973, 74.
106 "to convince . . . for the public." Ferraro and Francke, *Ferraro,* 73.
106 "It was important . . . recognition. Interview with Geraldine Ferraro.
106 "They loved . . . real woman." Ferraro and Francke, *Ferraro,* 73.
107 "I happened . . . interview her." Quoted in Stamberg, *Talk,* 202.
107 "All of a sudden . . . that threshold." Quoted in Roberts, *Dianne Feinstein,* 215.
108 *Time's* June 4 . . . Perhaps." *Time,* June 4, 1984, 28.
108 Polls indicated . . . it's about time." Dennis Gilbert, *Compendium of Public Opinion* (New York: Facts on File, 1988), 401-3.
109 Published leaks . . . can you get?" Ferraro and Francke, *Ferraro,* 102.
109 "It was an astonishing . . . jumped on it." Ibid., 249.
109 "Are you strong . . . protect this country." Ibid., 273.
110 Ferraro grew impatient . . . pull the trigger." Interview with Francis O'Brien, March 28 1995.
110 she also acknowledges . . . dumb questions." Interview with Geraldine Ferraro.
110 She was asked . . . her husband's identity." Interview with Francis O'Brien.
110 On July 8, . . . did want it." Ferraro and Francke, *Ferraro,* 104.
110 "GERRY, WILL YOU . . . 'I will.'" *Washington Journalism Review,* Nov. 1984, 25.

111 "Keep your hands . . . nuclear freeze." Quoted in Lee Michael Katz, *My Name Is Geraldine Ferraro* (New York: New American Library, 1984), 211.

111 Ferraro was described . . . mother of three. *Washington Journalism Review*, Nov. 1984, 26.

111 "were infused . . . wonder." and "She gets upset . . . of it." Ibid., 27.

111 The *New York Post* . . . almost unbearable." Ferraro and Francke, *Ferraro*, 23.

111 Capitol Hill police . . . bedlam." Ibid., 141.

112 "my candidacy . . . to myself." Ibid., 156.

112 Ferraro says she stopped . . . of the press. Interview with Geraldine Ferraro.

113 *Time* said she . . . far more pernicious." *Los Angeles Times*, Dec. 6, 1984, 28.

113 But the *New York Post* . . . ON THE GRILL." *Washington Journalism Review*, Nov. 1984, 29.

113 The *Atlanta Constitution* . . . dreary business." Ibid.

114 "because you take . . . persecuting her." *Los Angeles Times*, Dec. 6, 1984, 28.

114 "Writing a story . . . smear." Quoted in ibid., 30.

114 "The stoning of . . . woman." Quoted in Ferraro and Francke, *Ferraro*, 234-35.

114 "Where there was a legitimate . . . legitimacy and credibility. *Los Angeles Times*, Dec. 6, 1984, 30.

114 O'Brien, her former . . . survive." Interview with Francis O'Brien.

115 law enforcement agencies . . . the White House. Philip Seib, *Who's In Charge? How the Media Shape News and Politicians Win Voters* (Dallas: Taylor, 1987), 77.

115 Ferraro says . . . of the charge." Interview with Geraldine Ferraro.

115 Reporters interviewed . . . new to cover. *Washington Journalism Review*, Nov. 1984, 16ff.

116 After a media roller . . . just a symbol." Ibid., 29.

116 When she traveled . . . kissed her. Ferraro and Francke, *Ferraro*, 113.

116 "Reporters were totally . . . himself. Interview with Francis O'Brien.

116 "I instantly stepped . . . take the heat." Geraldine Ferraro, *Changing History* (Wakefield, R.I.: Moyer Bell, 1993), 174.

117 "I suppose if God . . . Feinstein?" Ferraro and Francke, *Ferraro*, 81.

117 More women . . . women. *New York Times*, Nov. 3, 1994.

117 That would be . . . equation. Quoted in *Ms.*, Dec. 1984, 125.

117 To some extent . . . them as people." *Washington Post*, July 30, 1984, A4.

117 "I don't know any woman . . . male counterpart." *Ms.*, Dec. 1984, 125.

117 Ferraro might agree . . . by being objective." Interview with Geraldine Ferraro.

118 "This was their . . . you can be." Interview with Francis O'Brien.

118 "Only then will . . . judged equal." Ferraro and Francke, *Ferraro*, 322.

118 "I don't think the press . . . attention it deserves." Ibid.

Chapter 9

1992 AND ALL THAT

119 "Even a wave . . . female representation." *New York Times*, Oct. 21, 1992.

119 "This isn't the . . . as we are." *Ms.*, Jan./Feb. 1993, 28.

120 "Sometimes you feel . . . quite do it." *New York Times*, March 23, 1992, A14.

120 The story "really fueled . . . women's anger." Interview with Mary Leonard.

120 Toni Bernays . . . gang-raped by the Senate." *Los Angeles Times*, Oct. 20, 1991.

120 "We didn't expect . . . in a side room. Barbara Boxer, *Strangers in the Senate* (Washington, D.C.: National Press Books, 1994), 32.

120 Aware that the hearings . . . Year of the Woman. *Kansas City Star,* June 28, 1993, A12.

121 "We're the beneficiaries . . . male bums." *MacLean's,* Sept. 14, 1992, 32.

122 "A woman as . . . her platform." *New York Times,* Sept. 20, 1992, E3.

122 "The Year of the Woman—Really." *Business Week,* Oct. 26, 1992, 106.

122 The *Los Angeles Times* . . . Year of the Man?" *Los Angeles Times,* June 4, 1992.

123 Yatch accused . . . vote for me." *MacLean's,* Sept. 14, 1992, 32.

123 "was scarcely known . . . of a pauper." *New York Times,* April 30, 1992, A22.

123 "a dizzying series . . . and resources." *Washington Post,* Jan. 5, 1993.

123 During the two-month . . . hard shake." Quoted in Ibid.

124 "The mainstream media . . . Solarz's race" and "He thought . . . does not vote." Marjorie Margolies-Mezvinsky, *A Woman's Place . . . The Freshmen Women Who Changed the Face of Congress* (New York: Crown Publishing, 1994), 144.

125 Although she was . . . to the United States Senate." [This covers several paragraphs of quotation.] Personal communication from Patty Murray, Oct. 6, 1994.

126 "Women, God bless . . . Madison Square Garden stage." *New York Times,* Aug. 23, 1992, E1.

126 "Women: they are . . . their coattails. *New York Times,* July 17, 1992, op-ed page.

127 "In Congress . . . true advancement." *Washington Post Sunday Magazine,* May 10, 1992, 28.

127 "There exists an unavoidable . . . came to Washington. Ibid., 28.

127 "Slaughter goes . . . out of the way." Ibid., 32.

128 "It doesn't sound . . . started yet." Quoted in *Editor & Publisher,* Aug. 1, 1992, 11, 34.

128 "Now that . . . come and gone." "Backlash Blues," *Harper's Bazaar,* May 1993, 77-78.

128 "This, say the pundits . . . American life." *Washington Post National Weekly Edition,* Jan. 6, 1995, 3.

128 "Alice Rivlin . . . of the Woman." *New York Times,* May 31, 1993, 1.

129 "Reminds me of . . . the system." *Washington Post,* Nov. 7, 1992, op-ed page.

129 Some standing . . . the swearing in. *Congressional Quarterly Weekly Edition,* Jan. 9, 1993, 60.

130 "there would have . . . that weren't." Ibid., 64.

130 a reporter doesn't . . . different backgrounds now." Interview with Kevin Merida, April 1995.

131 "The media . . . Senate gym." Quoted in *Ms.* (Jan./Feb. 1995), 87.

131 "She KO'd . . . its membership." *Washington Post,* July 27, 1993, op-ed page.

131 "The gentlelady . . . firearms can do." Quoted in Roberts, *Dianne Feinstein,* 4.

131 Two years later . . . in her house. C-SPAN coverage of Senate Judiciary Committee hearings, April 1995.

132 "It was a dramatic . . . say we can't?" *Washington Post,* Aug. 2, 1993, 1.

132 Connecticut representative . . . a physician. *Washington Post,* March 30, 1994.

132 "if I would use . . . right direction." Ibid., A12.

132 The article . . . one message. *Campaigns & Elections,* Jan. 1992, 41-42.

Chapter 10
THE KAMIKAZE CAMPAIGN AND POLITICS AS USUAL

135 But Ferraro says . . . D'Amato in 1992. Interview with Geraldine Ferraro.
135 "If this were . . . to shock." *U.S. News & World Report,* Sept. 14, 1992, 35.
135 "I wish I . . . in politics." Interview with Geraldine Ferraro.
135 Ferraro says . . . "these women." Ibid.
136 "Holtzman was . . . the target." Ibid.
136 But Holtzman . . . the bounds." Interview with Elizabeth Holtzman.
136 Holtzman was . . . such questions." Ibid.
137 Ferraro had not . . . national race." Interview with Geraldine Ferraro.
137 "A fierce . . . campaigner." *New York Times Magazine,* 22 March 1992.
137 "the marginalizing . . . Woman' business." *The Nation,* Aug. 17/24, 1992, 160.
137 The campaign . . . to Congress. *New York,* Sept. 14, 1992, 28.
137 But Holtzman . . . polite debates." *New York Times,* Aug. 30, 1992.
138 "tense, riveting . . . Ms. Ferraro!" *Washington Post,* Sept. 13, 1992.
138 I think . . . "the candidates." Quoted in *New York Times,* Sept. 16, 1992.
138 Holtzman told . . . "to win." *New York Times,* Sept. 17, 1992.
138 "In the end . . . the pedestal." *New York Times,* Nov. 7, 1992, op-ed page.
138 the post-election . . . Ferraro's defeat. *New York Times,* Sept. 17, 1992.
138 "It certainly . . . destroyed Holtzman." *Gentleman's Quarterly,* Feb. 1994, 96.
138 How did . . . "self-righteous demeanor." *New York,* Sept. 20, 1993.
139 She says she . . . the game." Interview with Elizabeth Holtzman.
139 Holtzman was hurt . . . underwrite bonds. *New York,* Sept. 20, 1993, 16.
139 Holtzman cried . . . political life.)" Ibid.
139 "People wept . . . disliked." Quoted in *Gentleman's Quarterly,* 96.
139 Syndicated columnist . . . a spoiler. *Washington Post,* Sept. 19, 1992, op-ed page.
140 *Washington Post* . . . the higher way." *National Catholic Reporter,* Oct. 9, 1992.
140 "For us . . . other off." Quoted in *New York Times,* Aug. 30, 1992.
140 In September . . . "shares her gender?" *Los Angeles Times,* Sept. 14, 1992.
140 Holtzman says . . . "our country." Interview with Elizabeth Holtzman.
140 "harsh attacks . . . suffering as well." *Los Angeles Times,* Aug. 30, 1992.
141 A fundamental . . . change women? *New York Times,* Aug. 30, 1992, 33.
141 "Maybe both are . . . same issues. Interview with Elizabeth Holtzman.
141 A newscaster . . . modern politics." *New York Times,* April 9, 1990.
142 The "slime . . . a shower." Quoted in *New York Times,* May 6, 1990.
142 "The reality . . . begin it." Ibid.
142 "A national political . . . her legend." *New York Times Magazine,* Feb. 7, 1993.
143 Richards says . . . like a contrast." Interview with Ann Richards.
143 I think . . . the process." *New York Times,* Nov. 2, 1994.

Chapter 11
NEARING THE MILLENNIUM

144 What if . . . we can't lose." *Louisville Courier-Journal,* April 18, 1994, B1.
145 Women running . . . plugging away." *Washington Post,* March 24, 1994, 10.
145 Candidates were . . . great one." *Washington Post,* Sept. 9. 1994, B1, 4.

145 Another story that . . . two women. Ibid., B1, 4.

146 "national Rorschach . . . of a man." "Pinning Down Hillary," *Vanity Fair,* June 1994, 154.

146 Hillary Clinton has learned . . . of spirituality. "Reality Bites," *Working Woman,* June 1994, 82.

147 Syndicated columnist . . . vision and dignity." *Washington Post,* March 14, 1994.

147 "double bind . . . you don't." "The Real Hillary Factor," *New York Times,* Oct. 12, 1992, op-ed page.

147 "Your real function . . . the guff." *Bangor Daily News,* June 30, 1995, op-ed page.

147 Maurine Beasley . . . mythology." *Media Studies Journal,* Winter/Spring 1993, 242.

148 "shrewd and tough." Interview with Nancy Kassebaum.

148 "Being a reporter . . . against you." Interview with Kay Bailey Hutchison.

148 "a politically . . . records." *Wall Street Journal,* Oct. 1, 1993, editorial page.

149 "The possibility . . . but icier." *New Republic,* Oct. 18, 1993, 12.

149 Even *Working* . . . for women. Interview with Kay Bailey Hutchison.

149 But Hutchison . . . are we doing." Ibid.

150 "The preppy . . . banker." *Washington Post,* Oct. 31, 1993, C1.

150 After her election . . . their lives." Interview with Rita Manno.

150 "What does . . . her clothes." Ibid.

151 In February 1995 . . . in 1996. *Washington Post,* Feb. 15, 1995, A17.

151 "Whitman is . . . down at you." *New Republic,* Feb. 1995, cover story.

151 "Imagine Katherine . . . right thing." *Town & Country,* March 1995, 102.

152 Headlined "Gov. Whitman . . . national ticket." *New York Times,* April 30, 1995, A16.

152 "Women are . . . since then. Interview with Mary Leonard.

152 "What divides . . . aides say." *Los Angeles Times,* Nov. 8, 1992.

153 An editorial . . . gender or race." *Los Angeles Times,* Jan. 10, 1993, editorial page.

153 "Maybe it's . . . a woman." *New York Times* Oct. 3, 1994.

154 "more trustworthy . . . negative.' Interview with Ann Richards.

154 "It is . . . woman's experience." From Ann Richards's remarks at Smith College, May 17, 1992.

154 "Almost a parody . . . sexes." *Washington Post,* June 10, 1990.

154 "Rightfully . . . re-election?" *Washington Post,* March 24, 1994, A1.

154 "She had such . . . city contractors." Ibid., A9.

154 "It's a tragedy . . . don't have." Ibid., A1, 9.

155 A 1994 study . . . voters' opinions. Kim Fridkin Kahn, "The Distorted Mirror: Press Coverage of Women Candidates for Statewide Office." *Journal of Politics,* Feb. 1994, 154.

155 "Despite opinion . . . opponents." *Congressional Quarterly Weekly Edition,* Aug. 6, 1994, 2274.

155 "It is because . . . trouble matching." Ibid.

155 In a stinging . . . square one." *New York Times,* Oct. 24, 1993, 15.

156 "This kind of . . . their gender." *USA TODAY,* Nov. 1, 1993, opinion page.

156 "Back then . . . for toughness." *Washington Post,* Oct. 31, 1993.

156 In an October . . . shoo-ins has past." *New York Times,* Oct. 6, 1994, A29.

156 1994 looked . . . "Off Year" of the Woman. *Congressional Quarterly Weekly Edition,* Oct. 15, 1994, 2972.

156 The 1992 refrain . . . their opponent." *New York Times,* Oct. 3, 1994, A1.

157 "The anthem . . . like a man?" *Los Angeles Times,* Oct. 9, 1994, M6.

157 "The reason . . . to flinch." David Broder column, *Lexington Herald-Leader,* June 12, 1994, op-ed page.

157 "The meanest . . . that removed." *Vanity Fair,* June 1994, 67.
157 Brown made the disclosure . . . combating it." See *Washington Post,* Oct. 20, 1995, A28.
158 "ladies against women." Quoted by Eleanor Clift in an interview, June 2, 1995.
158 The whole sense . . . the militia." Interview with Eleanor Clift.
158 The *New Republic* . . . Reagans unleashed." *New Republic,* April 24, 1995, 20-27.
159 women's caucus . . . "mushroom caucus." Interview with Marjorie Margolies-Mezvinsky.
159 Nancy Kassebaum . . . "Hillary." Interview with Nancy Kassebaum.
159 "That it's still . . . to talk to." Quoted in *Glamour,* Jan. 1994, 20, 176.
159 "The seven women . . . don't get it." *Congressional Quarterly Weekly Edition,* April 23, 1994, 1014.
160 Women would have . . . big-picture things." Quoted in *Ms.,* Jan./Feb. 1995, 88.
160 Kassebaum, too . . . and economics. Interview with Nancy Kassebaum.
160 "You can't lump . . . health issues. Interview with Kay Bailey Hutchison.
160 "I was never . . . my point." Quoted in *Ms.,* Jan./Feb. 1995, 87.
160 "I think it . . . a story." Quoted in Ellen Goodman column, *Lexington Herald-Leader,* Sept. 9, 1995, op-ed page.
160 "Took on added . . . as senators." *Washington Post,* Nov. 3, 1993, A1.
161 "sexual power-tripping . . . 'unethical.'" Ellen Goodman column, Sept. 9, 1995.
161 "A media darling . . . army." *Village Voice,* May 30, 1995, 16.
161 A front-page profile . . . media limelight. *Washington Post,* May 14, 1995, A1.
162 *Forbes* magazine . . . the left." *Forbes,* Feb. 13, 1995.
162 A 1995 *U.S. News* . . . tough lady." *U.S. News & World Report,* June 1995, 28.
162 "We have passed . . . other side." Interview with Louise Slaughter.
163 "much more . . . Great Britain. Interview with Ann Richards.
163 Syndicated columnist . . . executioner. *The Quill,* Sept. 1992, 12-13.
163 Anyone wanting . . . behave accordingly." Joe Creason lecture., Univ. of Kentucky, April 1993. See also "Trust Politicians, Not the Press," *New York Times,* Dec. 15, 1993, A27; and "Voters' Hostility Is Shaping the Business of Congress," *Congressional Quarterly Weekly Edition,* April 2, 1994, 785.
164 Political professionals . . . modern history. *Washington Post,* Oct. 11, 1994. See also *New York Times,* Nov. 13, 1994, sec. 1, 1; and *Advertising Age,* Oct. 31, 1994, 40.
164 "In this campaign . . . totally unappealing." *Los Angeles Times,* Nov. 10, 1994, op-ed page.
164 The Women, Men . . . sports figures. *New York Times,* April 13, 1994, A10.
164 instead of . . . *Chicago Tribune.* Women, Men and Media press release, 1995.
165 Editors at . . . journalistic 'reality.'" *Washington Post,* Jan.7, 1995, op-ed page.

Chapter 12
FROM A WOMAN'S POINT OF VIEW

166 "Look! A woman can do news!" Quoted in Susan Stamberg, *Talk* (New York: Turtle Bay Books/Random House, 1993), 181.
166 "It makes . . . all levels." Interview with Mary Leonard.
166 Women journalists . . . page 1. Interview with Geraldine Brooks.
166 Women reporters . . . her trust. Interview with Ann Richards.
167 A 1991 study . . . female candidates. Kim Kahn and Edie Goldenberg, *Public Opinion Quarterly,* Summer 1991, 194-95.

167 "When women . . . covering character." *U.S. News & World Report,* Aug. 7, 1995, 34.
167 "For better . . . character differently." *Vogue,* Aug. 1992, 164.
167 "You can find . . . big change." Interview with Eleanor Clift.
167 many women . . . reporters did. Interview with Geraldine Ferraro.
167 When a woman . . . stereotype. Interview with Kay Bailey Hutchison.
167 She's been . . . or female. Interview with Elizabeth Holtzman.
168 "Sometimes women . . . sensitive to that." Interview with Madeleine Kunin.
168 "They still . . . together." Interview with Nancy Kassebaum.
168 women journalists . . . be objective. Interviews with Bella Abzug and Martha Layne Collins.
168 The study found . . . no gender. Maurine H. Beasley and Sheila J. Gibbons, *Taking Their Place: A Documentary History of Women and Journalism* (Washington, D.C.: American Univ. Press, 1993), 30. See also Maurine H. Beasley and Kathryn T. Theus, *The New Majority: A Look at What the Preponderance of Women in Journalism Education Means to the Schools and to the Professions* (Lanham, Md.: Univ. Press of America, 1988).
168 "In the months . . . galleries." Bess Furman, *Washington Byline* (New York: Knopf, 1949), 36.
169 "From the first . . . skepticism." Ross, *Ladies of the Press* (New York: Arno Press, 1936), xi.
169 Washington correspondents . . . for readers. Leo Rosten, *The Washington Correspondents* (New York: Harcourt Brace, 1937), 269.
169 "The Washington . . . melodrama." Ibid., 257.
169 Mrs. Roosevelt leaked . . . in print." "Inventing the Interview," *American Heritage,* Oct. 1994, 49.
169 "It didn't matter . . . our break." Quoted in Kay Mills, *A Place in the News* (New York: Dodd, Mead, 1988), 44-45.
169 "Unfortunately, . . . 'woman's stuff.'" Genevieve Jackson Boughner, *Women in Journalism* (New York: D. Appleton-Century, 1937), viii.
170 "it is absurd . . . as good." Ross, *Ladies of the Press,* 2-13.
170 Winifred Mallon . . . conservative *Times.* Ibid., 344.
170 "saw no . . . the same." Marion Marzolf, *Up From the Footnote* (New York: Hastings House, 1977), 57.
170 One of "the best . . . reporters." *Time,* July 9, 1951, 55.
170 Finney "ranks . . . budgeting." Ross, *Ladies of the Press,* 340.
171 "It will be . . . the world." McCormick, *The World at Home,* x.
171 "She was a reporter . . . not to be so." Ibid., xii.
171 she playfully gigs . . . arm in arm." Ibid., 18.
171 "We had . . . sang-froid." In *Dictionary of Literary Biography,* 29:197.
171 "Won a famous . . . grateful debtors." Sanders, *Dorothy Thompson,* 274.
172 Her career . . . to millions." *Time,* June 12, 1939, 47-49.
172 "used to get . . . smoking car." Ibid.
172 It should not . . . a senator." Marzolf, *Up from the Footnote,* 55.
172 "Newspaper-bent? . . . knowledge, insight." Ibid., 75-76.
173 "All men . . . twenty-five." Lawrence R. Campbell, *Newsmen at Work* (Boston: Houghton Mifflin, 1949), 140.
173 "Most newspapers . . . born shoppers." Vincent Jones, "Women's Interests in the Press," in George Bird and Frederic Merwin, *The Press and Society* (New York: Prentice-Hall, 1951).

173   "McGrory . . . "and profane." Interview with Mary McGrory for Maria Braden, *She Said What?* (Lexington: Univ. Press of Kentucky, 1993), 25-30.

174   Helen Thomas . . . hold that post. Interview with Helen Thomas for "Thank You, Mr. President," *Kentucky Living,* Feb. 1991, 20-24.

175   Nancy Dickerson . . . "food columns." Nancy Dickerson, *Among Those Present,* 20.

175   Eleanor Randolph . . . the men's room. *Wall Street Journal,* June 6, 1984, 1.

175   "They had always . . . large paper." Tim Crouse, *The Boys on the Bus* (New York: Random house, 1973), 210.

176   Carol Ashkinaze's . . . Georgia statehouse. *Columbia Journalism Review,* March/April 1984, 26.

176   National Public Radio . . . used to it. Stamberg, *Talk,* 185-86.

176   The next year . . . women and minorities. For an expanded discussion, see Maurine H. Beasley and Sheila J. Gibbons, *Taking Their Place,* 235-65.

177   "In the aggressive . . . progress." *New York Times,* Feb. 2, 1979, B13.

177   By 1982 . . . features departments. *Columbia Journalism Review,* March/April 1984, 25.

177   "It's difficult . . . or disbelief. Judith Clabes, "Women Ready for New Role in Leadership." *Press Woman,* Jan. 1984, 1.

178   "I've seen . . . far enough." *Columbia Journalism Review,* March/April 1984, 25.

178   By 1984 . . . dozen each. *Wall Street Journal,* June 6, 1984, 1.

178   In television . . . were female. *Columbia Journalism Review,* March/April 1984, 26.

178   "We had . . . smarting." The scene described in this and the next paragraph is from the *Wall Street Journal,* June 6, 1984, 1.

179   "There is still . . . something else." Daniel Paisner, *The Imperfect Mirror: Inside Stories of Television Newswomen* (New York: William Morrow, 1989), 251.

179   "insecurity . . . politics. Judy Woodruff, *This is Judy Woodruff at the White House* (New York: Adddison-Wesley, 1982), xiv.

179   "I would not . . . again." Paisner, *Imperfect Mirror,* 258.

179   By 1989, women . . . the country. Marion Marzolf, "Deciding What's 'Women's News,'" *Media Studies Journal,* Winter/Spring 1993, 43.

179   the percentage . . . than men. Quoted in Sheryl Oring and Pete Danko, "Kissing the Newsroom Goodbye," in *American Journalism Review,* June 1995, 35.

180   women made up . . . *New York Times.* "The Girls on the Bus," *Vogue,* Aug. 1992, 158.

180   "American journalism . . . male norm." Kay Mills, "The Media and the Year of the Woman," *Media Studies Journal,* Winter/Spring 1993, 20.

180   One study . . . "women's issues." *Editor & Publisher,* Aug. 1, 1992, 11.

180   A National . . . decisionmaking positions. *New York Times,* May 24, 1995, A16.

180   Another study . . . Bridge said. Quoted in Judy Mann column, "Fighting Words," *Washington Post,* Oct. 7, 1992.

180   "Traffic gridlock . . . of it." Ibid.

181   "Women make . . . male-dominated media." *Psychology Today,* July/Aug. 1992, 12.

181   In 1994 . . . op-ed pages. Women, Men and Media press release on 1994 study.

181   The number of female . . . 20 percent. Women, Men and Media press release on 1995 study.

181   "It was common . . . those areas." Quoted in press release on 1995 study.

181   A 1991 . . . ghettoizing women." *American Journalism Review,* July/Aug. 1993, 40.

182   "You don't . . . what's affected." Ibid., 42.

182   "Statistics never . . . gender-blind meritocracy." *Christian Science Monitor,* July 20, 1995, 13.

Chapter 13
Ms. President?

183 Even Susan B. Anthony . . . enslaves women. The story of Woodhull's presidential candidacy is told in *Ms.* (Sept. 1972) 84-89.

183 "If your party . . . by 1984. Gallup opinion index, cited in Gilbert, *Compendium of Public Opinion,* 403-4.

183 In 1992, a Roper poll . . . . 32 percent. Information from Roper Starch Worldwide Inc., Oct. 24, 1995.

184 A 1990 McCall's survey . . . vote for a man. Shawn Brennan and Julie Winklepleck, *Resourceful Woman* (Detroit: Visible Ink Press, 1994), 466.

185 "Many people . . . not frivolous." *Time,* Feb. 7, 1964, 23.

185 "Very formidable . . . political figure." Quoted in Margaret Chase Smith, *Declaration of Conscience* (New York: Doubleday, 1972), 361.

185 She listed . . . challenges." Ibid., 371.

186 "I am going . . . to try it." *Time,* Feb. 7, 1964, 23.

186 They called . . . minded. Interview with Margaret Chase Smith.

186 "It is hard . . . man-hating call." *Time,* Feb. 7, 1964, 23.

186 Smith's presidential . . . several decades. Smith, *Declaration of Conscience,* 378.

186 There were drawings . . . Derby hats. Political cartoons and other Smith memorabilia are on display in the Margaret Chase Smith Library in Skowhegan, Maine.

187 "A woman president . . . Queen Victoria." Fireside, *Is There a Woman in the House . . . or Senate?* 40.

187 "Sounding like . . . for president." *New York Times,* Jan. 28, 1964, A1.

187 "Maggie . . . for President." *New York Daily News,* Jan. 28, 1964, 1.

187 "A President . . . common sense." Quoted in Lamson, *Few Are Chosen,* 29.

187 "It was 528 to 122 . . . "How beautiful!" Theodore H. White, *The Making of the President 1964* (New York: Atheneum, 1965), 204.

188 I didn't win . . . the future." Framed quote on display at Smith Library.

188 "to repudiate . . . not male." *New York Times,* Jan. 26, 1972, A1.

188 "I stand . . . of the people." Shirley Chisholm, *The Good Fight* (New York: Harper & Row, 1973), 71.

188 She had three . . . blacks or youths." *New York Times,* Jan. 26, 1972, A1.

188 "kissed off . . . messianically driven." Myra MacPherson, *The Power Lovers* (New York: Putnam, 1975), 333.

188 "What surprised me . . . to the men." From her speech on economic justice, in Chisholm, *The Good Fight,* Appendix.

189 "I'm for Shirley . . . male candidates." In Chisholm, *The Good Fight,* 76.

189 "This is the . . . large extent." Abzug, *Bella!,* 219-20.

190 "You would have to be crazy . . . isn't serious." Chisholm, *The Good Fight,* 86.

190 She had only . . . $300,000. Ibid., 45.

190 The General Accounting Office . . . wrongdoing. Tolchin and Tolchin, *Clout,* 236.

190 Chisholm credits Liz Carpenter . . . for Chisholm. Chisholm, *The Good Fight,* 75.

191 she had to file . . . morning program, *Today.* Ibid., 80.

191 She acknowledges . . . leading newspapers." Ibid., 64.

191 Her campaign limped . . . after state." Ibid., 57.

191 She says her campaign . . . all the way. Ibid., 160-61.

192 "I wanted to see . . . United States." Quoted in *Ms.,* Feb. 1988, 47.

192 "Like it or not . . . back a woman." Pat Schroeder, *Champion of the Great American Family* (New York: Random House, 1989), 4.

192 "If Ms. Ferraro . . . Anne Klein blazer." *New York Times,* Aug. 23, 1987.

192 "When I heard . . . the headlines." Schroeder, *Champion of the Great American Family,* 8.

193 Schroeder responded . . . who *didn't* cry. *Washington Post,* Oct. 4, 1987, C7.

193 the story did . . . her speech. *New York Times,* Sept. 29, 1987.

193 But after television . . . like a truck." *New York Times,* Sept. 30, 1987.

193 After the news . . . first in trust. *Ms.,* Feb. 1988, 50.

193 "Partly I regret . . . about it." Ibid., 50.

194 the early primaries . . . own state. *Washington Post,* Oct. 4, 1987, C7.

194 "It was a big . . . out there." Quoted in *Ms.,* Feb. 1988, 51.

194 "My laugh . . . they're wrong," Schroeder, *Champion of the Great American Family,* 7.

194 "You've got to wonder . . . laugh track." *New York Times,* April 19, 1992, op-ed page.

195 "We are challenging . . . Madam President." Quoted in *Congressional Quarterly Weekly Edition,* July 18, 1992, 2118.

195 Ellen Malcolm . . . in this country." *New York Times,* Dec. 20, 1992.

195 She told a Minneapolis . . . women candidates." *Minneapolis Star Tribune,* June 8, 1995, B1.

195 Even the League . . . national media." "Who Decides Who's Serious," *Washington Journalism Review,* June 1992, 31.

195 "I just wasn't . . . equal chance." "Candidates and their Gurus Criticize Coverage" *Washington Journalism Review,* Sept. 1980, 31.

196 "The amount of . . . to everything?" *Washington Journalism Review,* June 1992, 31.

196 *"Ms. President* . . . seemed remote. *Wall Street Journal,* Dec. 14, 1993, 1.

196 Reporter Geraldine Brooks . . . skepticism." Interview with Geraldine Brooks.

196 "The people are . . . breath away." Quoted in *Wall Street Journal,* Dec. 14, 1993, 1.

196 "Year of the UnWoman." *Washington Post,* Oct. 31, 1993, C1.

196 Whitman is neither . . . men and women." Interview with Eleanor Clift.

196 "It's getting . . . all the time." Interview with Rita Manno.

197 They jumped to . . . someone else." Ibid.

197 she "really . . . being there." Interview with Ann Richards.

197 The gender of . . . least remarkable thing about her." Interview with Eleanor Clift.

SELECTED
BIBLIOGRAPHY

Note: Information from magazine and newspaper articles and from interviews the author conducted with incumbent and former governors and members of Congress is cited in the Notes.

Abzug, Bella. *Bella!* New York: Saturday Review Press, 1972.

———. *Gender Gap.* Boston: Houghton Mifflin, 1984.

Aron, Michael. *Governor's Race: A TV Reporter's Chronicle of the 1993 Florio/ Whitman Campaign.* New Brunswick: Rutgers Univ. Press, 1994.

Baughman, James L. *Henry R. Luce and the Rise of the American News Media.* Boston: Twayne, 1987.

Bayley, Edwin R. *Joe McCarthy and the Press.* Madison: Univ. of Wisconsin Press, 1981.

Beasley, Maurine H. *Eleanor Roosevelt and the Media.* Urbana: Univ. of Illinois Press, 1987.

———, and Gibbons, Sheila J. *Taking Their Place: A Documentary History of Women and Journalism.* Washington, D.C.: American Univ. Press, 1993.

———, and Theus, Kathryn T. *The New Majority: A Look at What the Preponderance of Women in Journalism Education Means to the Schools and the Professions.* Lanham, Md.: Univ. Press of America, 1988.

Bird, George, and Merwin, Frederic. *The Press and Society.* New York: Prentice-Hall, 1951.

Boggs, Lindy. *Washington Through a Purple Veil.* New York: Harcourt, Brace, 1994.

Boughner, Genevieve Jackson. *Women in Journalism.* New York: D. Appleton, 1926.

Boxer, Barbara. *Strangers in the Senate*. Washington, D.C.: National Press Books, 1994.

Bozell, L. Brent, and Baker, Brent H. *And That's the Way It Is(n't): A Reference Guide to Media Bias*. Alexandria: Media Research Center, 1990.

Braden, Maria. *She Said What? Interviews with Women Newspaper Columnists*. Lexington: Univ. Press of Kentucky, 1993.

Brennan, Shawn, and Winklepleck, Julie. *Resourceful Woman*. Detroit: Visible Ink Press, 1994.

Breslin, Rosemary, and Hammer, Joshua. *Gerry! A Woman Making History*. New York: Pinnacle Books, 1984.

Broder, David. *Behind the Front Page*. New York: Simon & Schuster, 1987.

Campbell, Laurence, and Wolseley, Roland. *Newsmen at Work: Reporting and Writing the News*. Boston: Houghton Mifflin, 1949.

Cantor, Dorothy, and Bernay, Toni. *Women in Power: The Secrets of Leadership*. Boston: Houghton Mifflin, 1992.

Carroll, Susan J. *Women as Candidates in American Politics*. Bloomington: Indiana Univ. Press, 1983.

Chamberlin, Hope. *A Minority of Members: Women in the U.S. Congress*. New York: Praeger, 1973.

Chisholm, Shirley. *The Good Fight*. New York: Harper & Row, 1973.

Clarke, Peter, and Evans, Susan H. *Covering Campaigns: Journalism in Congressional Elections*. Stanford: Stanford Univ. Press, 1983.

Conway, Jill; Bourque, Susan; and Scott, Joan, eds. *Learning About Women: Gender, Politics and Power*. Ann Arbor: Univ. of Michigan Press, 1989.

Cook, Elizabeth Adell; Thomas, Sue; and Wilcox, Clyde, eds. *The Year of the Woman: Myths and Realities*. Boulder: Westview Press, 1994.

Cook, Timothy E. *Making Laws and Making News: Media Strategies in the U.S. House of Representatives*. Washington: Brookings, 1989.

Creedon, Pamela J., ed. *Women in Mass Communication*. 2nd ed. Newbury Park, Calif.: Sage, 1993.

Crouse, Timothy. *The Boys on the Bus*. New York: Random House, 1973.

Davis, Richard. *The Press and American Politics: The New Mediator*. New York: Longman, 1992.

Delacorte, Toni. *How to Get Free Press*. San Francisco: Harbor, 1981.

Dickerson, Nancy. *Among Those Present: A Reporter's View of Twenty-five Years in Washington*. New York: Random House, 1976.

Donovan, Robert J., and Scherer, Ray. *Unsilent Revolution: Television News and American Public Life*. Cambridge: Cambridge Univ. Press, 1992.

Douglas, Helen Gahagan. *A Full Life*. Garden City, N.Y.: Doubleday, 1982.

Douth, George. *Leaders in Profile: The United States Senate*. New York: Sperr & Douth, 1972.

Duke, Lois Lovelace, ed. *Women in Politics: Outsiders or Insiders?* Englewood Cliffs, N.J.: Prentice-Hall, 1993.

Epstein, Edward Jay. *News from Nowhere*. New York: Vintage, 1974.

Faludi, Susan. *Backlash: The Undeclared War against American Women*. New York: Anchor Books, Doubleday, 1991.

Ferraro, Geraldine. *Changing History*. Wakefield, R.I.: Moyer Bell, 1993.

———, and Francke, Linda Bird. *Ferraro: My Story*. New York: Bantam, 1985.

Fireside, Bryna J. *Is There a Woman in the House...or Senate?* Morton Grove, Ill.: Albert Whitman, 1994.

Furman, Bess. *Washington Byline: The Personal History of a Newspaperwoman*. New York: Knopf, 1949.

Gans, Herbert. *Deciding What's News: A Study of CBS Evening News, NBC Nightly News, Newsweek and Time*. New York: Pantheon, 1979.

Gilbert, Dennis A. *Compendium of American Public Opinion*. New York: Facts on File, 1988.

Giles, Kevin S. *Flight of the Dove: The Story of Jeannette Rankin*. Beaverton, Ore.: Touchstone, 1980.

Gilligan, Carol. *In a Different Voice*. Cambridge: Harvard Univ. Press, 1982.

Gold, Vic. *I Don't Need You When I'm Right*. New York: William Morrow, 1975.

Halberstam, David. *The Powers That Be*. New York: Knopf, 1979.

Halcomb, Ruth. *Women Making It!* New York: Atheneum, 1979.

Haskins, James. *Barbara Jordan*. New York: Dial, 1977.

Hess, Stephen. *Live from Capitol Hill! Studies of Congress and the Media*. Washington, D.C.: Brookings Institution, 1991.

———. *The Washington Reporters*. Washington, D.C.: Brookings, 1981.

Isaacs, Norman. *Untended Gates*. New York: Columbia Univ. Press, 1988.

Josephson, Hannah. *Jeannette Rankin, First Lady in Congress*. Indianapolis: Bobbs-Merrill, 1974.

Jordan, Barbara, and Hearon, Shelby. *Barbara Jordan: A Self-Portrait*. Garden City, N.Y.: Doubleday, 1979.

Katz, Lee Michael. *My Name Is Geraldine Ferraro*. New York: New American Library, 1984.

Kessler, Lauren. *The Dissident Press*. Beverly Hills, Calif.: Sage, 1984.

Kirkpatrick, Jeane J. *Political Woman*. New York: Basic Books, 1974.

Kunin, Madeleine. *Living a Political Life*. New York: Knopf, 1994.

Lamson, Peggy. *Few Are Chosen: American Women in Political Life Today*. Boston: Houghton Mifflin, 1968.

———. *In the Vanguard: Six American Women in Public Life*. Boston: Houghton Mifflin, 1979.

Lee, Martin A., and Solomon, Norman. *Unreliable Sources: A Guide to Detecting Bias in News Media*. New York: Lyle Stuart Book, Carol Publishing Group, 1990.

Lesher, Stephan. *Media Unbound: The Impact of Television Journalism on the Public*. Boston: Houghton Mifflin, 1982.

Lichter, S. Robert; Rothman, Stanley; and Lichter, Linda S., *The Media Elite*. Bethesda, Md.: Adler & Adler, 1986.

Lippmann, Walter. *Public Opinion*. New York: Macmillan, 1945.

Loomis, Burdett. *The New American Politician*. New York: Basic Books, 1988.

MacPherson, Myra. *The Power Lovers*. New York: Putnam, 1975.

Mandel, Ruth. *In the Running: The New Woman Candidate*. New York: Ticknor & Fields, 1981.

Margolies-Mezvinsky, Marjorie. *A Woman's Place...The Freshmen Women Who Changed the Face of Congress*. New York: Crown, 1994.

Marzolf, Marion. *Up from the Footnote*. New York: Hastings House, 1977.

McCormick, Anne O'Hare. *The World at Home*. Marion Turner Sheehan, ed. New York: Knopf,1956.

McCracken, Ellen. *Decoding Women's Magazines*. New York: St. Martin's, 1993.

Media Studies Journal. New York: Freedom Forum Media Studies Center, Winter/Spring 1993.

Mills, Kay. *A Place in the News*. New York: Dodd, Mead, 1988.

Miraldi, Robert. *Muckraking and Objectivity: Journalism's Colliding Traditions*. Westport, Conn.: Greenwood, 1990.

Nimmo, Dan, and Combs, James E. *Mediated Political Realities*. New York: Longman, 1983.

Office of the Historian. *Women in Congress, 1917-1990*. Washington, D.C.: U.S. Government Printing Office, 1991.

Paisner, Daniel. *The Imperfect Mirror: Inside Stories of Television Newswomen*. New York: William Morrow, 1989.

Paizis, Suzanne. *Getting Her Elected: A Political Woman's Handbook*. Sacramento: Creative Editions, 1977.

Paletz, David, and Entman, Robert. *Media. Power. Politics*. New York: Free Press, 1981

Postman, Neil, and Powers, Steve. *How to Watch TV News*. New York: Penguin, 1992.

Rakow, Lana F., ed. *Women Making Meaning: New Feminist Directions in Communication*. New York: Routledge, 1992.

Ranney, Austin. *Channels of Power: The Impact of Television on American Politics*. New York: Basic Books, 1983.

Rivers, William. *The Other Government*. New York, Universe Books, 1982.

Roberts, Jerry. *Dianne Feinstein: Never Let Them See You Cry*. New York: HarperCollinsWest, 1994.

Robertson, Nan. *The Girls in the Balcony*. New York: Random House, 1992.

Roosevelt, Eleanor, and Hickok, Lorena. *Ladies of Courage*. New York: Putnam's, 1954.

Ross, Ishbel. *Ladies of the Press*. New York: Arno Press, 1936.

Rosten, Leo. *The Washington Correspondents*. New York: Harcourt Brace, 1937.

Sabato, Larry J. *Feeding Frenzy: How Attack Journalism Has Transformed American Politics*. New York: Free Press, 1991.

Sanders, Marion K. *Dorothy Thompson: A Legend in Her Time*. Boston: Houghton Mifflin, 1973

———. *The Lady and the Vote*. Westport, Conn.: Greenwood, 1955.

Sanders, Marlene. *Waiting for Prime Time*. New York: Harper & Row, 1988.

Schilpp, Madelon, and Murphy, Sharon. *Great Women of the Press*. Carbondale: Southern Illinois Univ. Press, 1983.

Schroeder, Pat. *Champion of the Great American Family*. New York: Random House, 1989

Schudson, Michael. *Discovering the News: A Social History of American Newspapers*. New York: Basic Books, 1978.

———. *The Power of News*. Cambridge: Harvard Univ. Press, 1995.

Seib, Philip. *Who's in Charge? How the Media Shape News and Politicians Win Voters*. Dallas: Taylor, 1987.

Shadegg, Stephen. *Clare Boothe Luce*. New York: Simon & Schuster, 1970.

Sheed, Wilfred. *Clare Boothe Luce*. New York: Dutton, 1982.

Sherr, Lynn. *Failure Is Impossible; Susan B. Anthony in Her Own Words*. New York: Times Books, Random House, 1995.

Slipman, Sue. *Helping Ourselves to Power: A Handbook for Women on the Skills of Public Life*. Oxford: Pergamon Press, 1986.

Smith, Hedrick. *The Power Game: How Washington Works*. New York: Ballantine, 1988.

Smith, Margaret Chase. *Declaration of Conscience*. New York: Doubleday, 1972.

Stamberg, Susan. *Talk*. New York: Turtle Bay Books/Random House, 1993.

Stineman, Ester. *American Political Women: Contemporary and Historical Profiles*. Littleton, Colo.: Libraries Unlimited, 1980.

Tinker, Irene, ed. *Women in Washington: Advocates for Public Policy*. Beverly Hills: Sage, 1983.

Tolchin, Susan, and Tolchin, Martin. *Clout—Womanpower and Politics*. New York: Coward, McCann & Geoghegan, 1974.

Trafton, Barbara M. *Women Winning: How to Run for Public Office*. Boston: Harvard Common Press, 1984.

Tuchman, Gaye. *Making News: A Study in the Construction of Reality*. New York: Free Press, 1978.

————, ed. *Hearth and Home: Images of Women in the Mass Media*. New York: Oxford Univ. Press, 1978.

Weinberg, Steve. *Trade Secrets of Washington Journalists*. Washington, D.C.: Acropolis, 1981.

White, Theodore H. *The Making of the President, 1964*. New York: Atheneum, 1965.

Wolfson, Lewis W. *The Untapped Power of the Press, Explaining Government to the People*. Westport: Praeger, 1985.

Witt, Linda. *Running As a Woman: Gender and Power in American Politics*. New York: Free Press, 1993.

Woodruff, Judy. *This Is Judy Woodruff at the White House*. New York: Addison-Wesley, 1982.

INDEX